FREEDOM AND AMERICAN SOCIETY

Volume II

Freedom and Economic Order

FREEDOM AND AMERICAN SOCIETY

Volume II

Freedom and Economic Order

Linda C. Raeder

⚜

Sanctuary Cove Publishing
Palm Beach and Richmond

Library of Congress Cataloguing-in-Publication Data

Raeder, Linda C.
   Freedom and Economic Order / Linda C. Raeder.
   Includes bibliographical references.
   ISBN 13-978-1544890906

Typeface: Garamond Pro

In loving memory of my father,
Howard M. Maxwell

CONTENTS

ACKNOWLEDGEMENTS

I am indebted above all to the many students at Palm Beach Atlantic University who participated in my courses in political philosophy and political economy over the past sixteen years. This work would not appear in its present form without the knowledge and understanding I have gained through my experience teaching undergraduates at PBA, and especially those enrolled in my "Freedom and American Society" and "Roots of American Order" courses. I would like to thank all those students who shared their perspectives and insights over the years and provided indispensable feedback to the ideas presented in this work.

I am further indebted to the PBA administration, particularly President Bill Fleming and Dr. Ken Mahanes, both of whom have provided unwavering support and encouragement for my scholarship and teaching. My colleagues in the Politics Department, Dr. Francisco Plaza and Dr. James Todd, have also earned my deepest gratitude, not only for their graciousness and collegiality but also the maturity and penetrating insight that mark their scholarship and teaching.

Thank you as always to my mother, Evelyn Pokorny Maxwell, for her steadfast love, support, and strength, and my dear animal companions, Max, Sophie, Callie, and the Muscovies, who make day-to-day existence a continual joy.

FREEDOM AND ECONOMIC ORDER

SIX

ECONOMICS: THE KNOWLEDGE PROBLEM

Economic control is not merely control of a sector of human life which can be separated from the rest; it is the control of the means for all our ends.

—F.A. Hayek

Freedom—the ability to act in a voluntary manner, free from subjection to arbitrary coercion by other persons—is a generalized quality of human action. Individuals want to be free in a myriad of daily situations, whether relating to home, work, school, church, business, or pleasure. Human action is always purposive and oriented toward fulfillment of value, and people want to be free to fulfill their own purposes and values. The central tenet of traditional American political philosophy is that individuals have a right to such freedom. They are morally entitled to pursue their own goals and values and should not be forced to fulfill those imposed by others. Such a conviction—freedom is morally and intrinsically right and arbitrary coercion morally and intrinsically wrong—saturated American consciousness from the outset.

Human action has many dimensions and forms of expression. Human goals and values are diverse and fluid, ranging from desire for a new cell phone to desire to feed hungry children. In a free or pluralistic society human beings are regarded as individuals with unique purposes and values; no two individuals are any more identical than two snowflakes. Whatever an individual's personal values and ends, moreover, the nature of earthly existence requires their fulfillment through a particular kind of means, namely, acquisition and utilization of material goods or services. A person who wants a new phone must obtain a material object called a phone. A person who wants to feed the starving children of Calcutta must obtain a material object called food. A person who wants to propagate religious beliefs through publication must obtain material

1

goods such as paper upon which to write, pen and ink, and so on. A person who wants to engage in cyber-theft must have a computer and other requisite technical equipment.

All human goals and values, however high or low, moral or immoral, however spiritual or materialistic, altruistic or selfish, require for their realization physical or material entities of one kind or another. Human beings live neither on clouds nor within their minds but rather on earth, and within that *kind* of world the expression of values and fulfillment of goals are inseparable from matter—tangible goods or services. The necessary relation between human ends and material means leads directly to the topic presently under consideration—the relation between traditional American order and the economic arrangements of society. The science of economics is concerned precisely with the problem of how human beings acquire the material means requisite to fulfillment of their values and realization of their purposes. The present inquiry will explore the implications of that science for fulfillment of characteristically American political values—constitutional or limited government in general and freedom and justice in particular.

To introduce the discipline of economics is to enter a realm where angels may fear to tread. The "dismal science," in the well-known phrase of Thomas Carlyle, typically evokes a wide range of emotional response, from passionate interest through contempt to sheer and utter boredom. Economics is commonly associated in the popular mind with money, wealth, business, perhaps even greed and selfishness. High-minded idealists may consider economic concerns vulgar and contemptible, beneath their consideration. Economics is also a difficult and complex subject that can appear forbidding if not explained in clear terms that honor common sense. All too often professional and academic economists employ dense technical jargon that renders economic theory all but incomprehensible to those without formal training in the discipline. Understanding the basic laws of economics, however, does not require extensive formal training. The best economic theory is simply the rational and systematic articulation of the manner in which human beings actually behave in pursuing their goals. Every person, with the possible exception of infants and babies, is intimately familiar with the subject matter of economics; every person knows how to behave economically and does so, moreover, on a daily basis. Economic theory simply describes or raises to consciousness practices that are familiar to everyone, and its basic principles can be conveyed to any literate person with a desire to learn.

The Economic Problem

Economic considerations are inescapable for human beings, mandated by the very nature of the world they inhabit. Contrary to popular belief, economics is not essentially concerned with money, business, or profit. Economic concerns relate not to material wealth but rather the fundamental fact of life from which all economic behavior and all economic reasoning flows, namely, the central fact of *scarcity*. All human beings are confronted by the immovable fact that the material goods and services required to sustain and enhance their existence simply do not exist by nature in quantities sufficient to fulfill all such needs and desires merely for the taking. Houses and electricity and cell phones, milk and shoes and clothing, do not "grow on trees." The seven billion human beings presently alive on earth cannot simply pluck from the bounty of nature all the orange juice, automobiles, paper, ice cream, and surgical skills they need or would like to possess. Material goods and services are intrinsically *scarce*, a fact that no human effort or desire, no personal or political will, can eradicate.

The fact of *scarcity* is the starting point for all discussion of economic arrangements in society. Every human society, however primitive or complex, must deal with the fact of irremediably limited resources. From this central fact follows the second inescapable fact of economic reality, namely, the necessity for *choice*. Resources are by nature scarce or limited, a fact that immediately confronts human beings with two unavoidable choices, the economic choices relating to so-called production and distribution. The first inevitable choice confronted by every society known to man involves production—*what* is to be produced, and *how*. Production decisions involve several related considerations. First, someone must decide which specific goods and services are to be produced with the limited resources of nature; and, second, someone must also decide how they are to be produced, that is, which inputs are to be employed in their production. Once such production decisions have been made, every society confronts the second inevitable choice, relating to the problem of distribution: *Who* is to receive the goods and services initially chosen for production, that is, how are they to be "distributed" among the populace? Obviously production necessarily precedes distribution; nothing can be distributed unless it has first been produced.

Every society, then, confronts what we shall term the "economic problem": how to determine the best possible manner in which to employ the irremediably limited resources of this earth. "Best" in this regard means, among other things, the most efficient or least wasteful employment of scarce resources. Resources are limited but human needs and wants are not. For that reason, it is wrong to waste scarce resources which could rather be used to satisfy the ever-pressing needs of the human community. The best use of limited resources thus involves two related criteria. First, production must proceed in the least costly manner; and second, it must be directed toward fulfillment of actual human needs and wants. To employ scarce resources in the production of unneeded or unwanted items is to waste precious resources that could have been used to fulfill real wants and needs. Such is wrong from any point of view, rational or moral.

We previously noted that the discipline of economics is not fundamentally concerned with money or material wealth but rather the problem of scarcity. Similarly, the economic problem is not fundamentally a physical or material problem but rather a problem of (immaterial) knowledge. Mere physical, material, or quantifiable data, however comprehensive or intricate, are insufficient to determine the best use of resources as described. Rational economic decisions can only be made by persons possessing accurate knowledge of what to produce and how to produce it, as well as accurate knowledge of the persons who should receive the produced goods. More particularly, economic decision-makers must know which specific resources are available for production, the most efficient means of using them, and also which specific goods and services are actually needed or wanted by their fellow men. If some person or persons should actually possess all such knowledge, the economic problem confronting humankind would be solved once and for all. We could simply assign such persons the task of rationally allocating the scarce resources of this earth toward their best possible uses.

Such, however, is not, and never can be, within the realm of possibility. Every human being, no matter how stellar the genius, is confronted with an "irremediable ignorance" that arises from inherent limits of the

4

human mind.[1] The knowledge requisite to sound economic choices in the face of scarcity is neither a gift of nature nor available as a whole to any individual mind or group of minds. No human being does or can know the precise status of resource availability throughout a society, let alone the world. No one does or can know the least wasteful methods of production of the innumerable goods and services produced in any society beyond the most primitive. Nor does or can anyone know the precise needs and wants of the millions upon millions of individuals who constitute American society, let alone the billions of individuals who inhabit the contemporary world, or which of them should receive the fruits of production. Despite such constitutional ignorance on the part of all human beings without exception, decisions of production and distribution must nevertheless be made if the human race is not to perish. The solution to the economic problem—achieving the best use of scarce resources—thus involves finding a means of acquiring the knowledge requisite to rational economic decision-making in the face of the intrinsic and unalterable ignorance of every human being. Economic theory deals precisely with the solution to the economic problem so conceived.

To recapitulate the argument to this point: human beings are confronted by the fundamental fact of scarcity. As a result, they are forced to make certain choices. First, they must decide what is to be produced among the myriad of possibilities, and, second, which factors of production or inputs are to be utilized in the production of the chosen goods. Finally, a decision must be reached regarding the distribution of the produced goods; there must exist some way of deciding "who is to receive what." All such decisions require appropriate knowledge in three specific areas: first, the actual resources available for production; second, the most efficient method of producing the goods chosen for production; and, third, the goods and services actually needed or desired by other human beings. The economic problem, at bottom, is clearly a problem of knowledge. Its solution involves acquiring the means whereby the knowledge requisite to rational economic choice in the face

---

[1] F. A. Hayek, *Law, Legislation and Liberty,* in 3 volumes, *Rules and Order,* Vol. 1 (Chicago: University of Chicago Press, 1978), 12. Hereinafter cited as *Rules and Order.*

of both scarcity and the inherent limits of the human mind can be obtained.

In the modern era, there are essentially two proposed solutions to the economic problem so conceived, which may loosely be classified as "capitalism" and "socialism." We shall not discuss earlier forms of economic organization, such as feudalism, which are not of direct relevance to the present study, the relation of traditional American social and political order to economic order. In recent centuries, the great contest has been between free-market capitalism and the planned economy of socialism, and the analysis will be confined to these two forms of economic arrangement. It should also be noted that the terms capitalism and socialism refer to the *economic* organization of a society, not its political form. While capitalism is generally and historically associated with liberal democracy and limited government, capitalism is also compatible with various forms of nondemocratic limited government, for instance, constitutional monarchy. While socialism and other kinds of planned economy are historically associated with illiberal government, whether fascist, communist, or some variant thereof, it too refers to the economic organization of a society and not its political form. Various attempts have been made to combine socialist economic planning with limited or democratic government, and we will examine the viability of such approaches over the long run.

The primary distinction between the two rival schools of economic thought, as we shall see, concerns the *locus* of economic decision-making, that is, *who* is to be charged with making the decisions forced upon human beings by the fact of scarcity. Capitalism and socialism assign to different actors the responsibility for deciding *what* is to be produced, and *how*, and determining *who* is to receive the fruits of production. Capitalism assigns such responsibility to individual members of society at large; socialism, by contrast, assigns it to a select group of politically determined officials, experts or "planners." We have characterized the economic problem as essentially a problem of knowledge. The high level of material prosperity characteristic of modern capitalist economic arrangements will be seen to arise from capitalism's significant success in solving the knowledge problem in the face of scarcity and irremediable human ignorance. The uniformly less impressive material performance of modern socialized or planned economies, on the other hand, will be seen to result from the inherent inability of such economic organization to solve the same problem. *Who is to decide?* That is the question, and its answer will prove decisive.

Capitalism: The Price System

The term capitalism is widely applied to the economic system that emerged in the West over the course of centuries, a system also referred to as the free-enterprise system, free market, market system, process, or order, and, perhaps most precisely, the price system. The nature of capitalism and its contribution to human wellbeing is not universally understood or appreciated, even within traditionally capitalist societies such as the United States. Failure to appreciate the market order is perhaps related to the human propensity to take things for granted. Participants in a developed capitalist economy may easily assume that the bounty and plenty that surrounds them is somehow a fact of nature like the sun and seasons, an aspect of life itself. Their main concern usually involves the ability to afford the goods and services they desire, whether they personally possess sufficient resources to acquire them. Few persons pause to wonder how the desired goods and services came into being in the first place, why they exist at all, available for the taking to anyone with the requisite means of purchase. Persons who were born into less-developed societies, travel extensively, or study history, on the other hand, well understand that the prosperity and abundance characteristic of contemporary American society is among the rarest experiences in human history. The lives of most people who have lived and continue to live on this earth are characterized not by plenty but rather want and privation, poverty and unsatisfied need. It has often been noted that the poorest person in contemporary American society enjoys a higher level of material wellbeing than enjoyed by most kings and royalty of previous historical eras. Prosperity and abundance are the exception to human experience, not the rule.

The question, then, is how the United States and other developed societies came to achieve such a high level of material wellbeing. Certain possibilities can be eliminated out of hand. Prosperity did not arise because the American people are smarter than other peoples; intelligence is rather evenly distributed throughout the world. It did not arise because Americans work harder than other people. Consider the millions upon millions of people who must labor for the greater part of each day merely to provide the barest subsistence for their children, as is not uncommon in less-developed societies. Nor did abundance arise because the United States has greater natural resources than other countries; natural resources, like intelligence, are widely distributed throughout the world. The reason for the exceptional prosperity that characterizes the American experience is the fact that throughout most of its history the United States embraced the free market as its preferred economic system. Capitalism, the market process, and the presence of the necessary conditions of its operation, account for American prosperity and plenty.

The classic definition of capitalism is an economic system characterized by "private ownership of the means of production." While such a definition is accurate, it provides little insight into the nature of capitalism or the actual manner in which the market process solves the economic problem. As previously noted, the essential difference between capitalism and socialism concerns the locus of economic decision-making within the two systems, that is, *who* decides what is to be produced, how to produce it, and who is to receive the fruits of production. In a market economy, all such choices are made by private individuals or groups of private individuals voluntarily associated in pursuit of a common objective (business firms and the other voluntary associations that constitute civil society, the private sector). Individuals in a society ordered by market exchange are able to make such choices because a market order, as the textbook definition indicates, presupposes the right to private property.

A "property right" in an economic context is best understood as a "decision right." The existence of defined property rights in a market-based society means that private individuals—those who own various resources—are morally and legally entitled to decide how such resources are to be employed. Private property, as we have seen, is regarded as a natural and universal right in American society, which means that every person is entitled to make relevant economic decisions with respect to his personal possessions and, moreover, typically does so on a daily basis. In a market economy, every private individual, and not governmental or public authority, decides how his personal property is to be employed in acts of both production and consumption. Private individuals decide *what* is to be produced, and *how*, and they also decide *who* is to receive or consume the goods and services so produced. In other words, the essence of a market economy is the radical *decentralization* of decision

8

processes, and such, as we shall see, is the chief reason for the unrivaled material prosperity of capitalist economic arrangements. As said, the economic problem, in the end, is a knowledge problem. The success of capitalism can be attributed to the fact that a market order formalizes or institutionalizes the decentralization of decision processes, which allows in turn for the emergence and utilization of the knowledge upon which the solution of the economic problem ultimately depends.

Kinds of Knowledge in Society

The economic achievements of modern Western civilization, then, do not reflect superior knowledge *per se*. Such success must rather be attributed to the historical development and eventual embrace of a method of coordinating human activity that encourages greater generation and utilization of knowledge than any other method yet discovered, namely, the institutionalized market process known as capitalism. No human mind or group of minds could consciously assimilate or coordinate the vast knowledge and information that daily enters the social process via the market mechanism. Human knowledge, as we shall see, is an extraordinarily complex entity. A recognition of such complexity is crucial to grasping the complexity of the economic problem confronting modern society as well as the means of its solution.

Accordingly, an elaboration of the divergent manners in which capitalism and socialism attempt to solve the economic problem, discussed in following chapters, requires a preliminary exploration of certain epistemological issues in some depth. Such is essential background not only for understanding the ordering principle of the market but also the reasons for its demonstrated superiority over socialized economic organization.[2] As we shall see, the success of capitalism stems from its ability to bypass the difficulties raised by both the inherent complexity of human knowledge and inherent limits of the human mind. Socialism and other forms of planned economy, by

---

[2] Consider, for instance, relevant statistical comparisons of West and East Germany, South and North Korea, and Taiwan and China for the period 1960-1988. "Communism, Capitalism, and Economic Development: Implications for U.S. Economic Assistance," Backgrounder No. 41 (Heritage Foundation: Washington DC, Dec. 8, 1989).

contrast, are constitutionally unable to overcome the obstacles posed by such epistemological constraints. For that reason, socialized economic organization is ultimately incapable of solving the economic problem, that is, achieving an efficient allocation of scarce resources toward fulfillment of actual human needs and desires.

Human knowledge comprises distinct kinds or categories, all of which are relevant to solution of the economic problem. It includes not only *explicit* knowledge, consciously systematized theories and data ("knowledge that"), but also the *tacit* or inarticulate "know-how" embodied in culturally acquired habits of thought and practice, disposition and custom. The former kind of knowledge, explicit and systematized knowledge, can generally be articulated and deliberately or consciously communicated from one person to another and is of course crucial to rational human action. Tacit or implicit knowledge is equally crucial to human action but, unlike explicit knowledge, is not generally susceptible of deliberate interpersonal communication. A further type of knowledge, one that is of special economic relevance, involves the fleeting knowledge of local circumstances, knowledge relating to particular time and place, the utilization of which is essential to the functioning of a complex social order constrained by the fact of scarcity. Both tacit and fleeting knowledge, in contrast to the systematized knowledge communicated by books, lectures, and similar vehicles of communication, are held within and *only within* the minds of individuals and, again, generally in a form that is not consciously transmissible to other persons. Such kinds of knowledge, in the formal language of economic theory, are said to be *essentially dispersed.*

The first kind of relevant knowledge, as said, is technical knowledge, expertise, "knowledge that" such and such is true, knowledge that may be embodied in and conveyed by textbooks, college courses, and other forms of explicit communication. Technical knowledge or expertise, as said, is transmissible to other persons. Scholars and scientists can study the laws of physics or biology and transmit that knowledge to other interested persons through education. They can study engineering techniques or foreign languages or auto mechanics and pass that knowledge on to others through books or personal instruction. Such technical knowledge, however, is only one dimension of the totality of knowledge possessed by individuals and that must be incorporated into the social process if scarce resources are to be allocated to their best possible use. The economic problem is decidedly *not* a simple problem of expertise or technique. The most brilliant engineers in the world cannot determine, for instance, whether it is economically desirable to build a bridge in a certain location. They can explain *how* to build the bridge but not establish whether such would be a rational use of scarce resources, a very different matter. Perhaps people in the community do not want or need a bridge; perhaps they would prefer that scarce resources be instead used to produce bread or clothing or cell phones. An engineer as engineer has no way of knowing such crucial facts. His expertise is technical and not economic, that is, concerned with rational choices in the face of scarcity, with efficiently employing scarce resources to produce goods and services that people actually want or need. Once an economic decision to build a bridge has been made, the special kind of expertise of the engineer is of course essential, but such technical knowledge is distinct and separate from the question of desirability from an economic point of view.

The second kind of knowledge essential to solving the economic problem is the aforementioned concrete and local knowledge of time, place, and circumstance. Such knowledge and information, unlike technical knowledge, is not readily transmissible by means of books, lectures, courses, and the like. It is different in kind from technique or expertise—conscious and explicit knowledge that can be systematized or centralized and made available to anyone with an interest in learning. As mentioned, the second kind of knowledge is rather essentially dispersed or decentralized knowledge, that is, held within the minds of individual members of society and in no other form. Such knowledge cannot be assembled or collected, consolidated in a universal data base that anyone might consult. Nor can it be organized and transmitted through formal channels of education or communication. This is because knowledge of time, place, and circumstance is not only essentially dispersed but also fleeting and, moreover, often tacit or implicit rather than conscious or explicit. The tacit knowledge possessed by every individual is not usually recognized until some circumstance or other raises it to consciousness. The individual is generally unaware that he actually possesses such knowledge unless and until some trigger in his immediate environment calls it to mind. For that reason—the fact that the individual himself is not consciously aware of possessing relevant knowledge—tacit knowledge cannot be formally transmitted to other persons. No individual ever possesses full conscious awareness of everything that he actually knows and that actually informs his daily activities; every individual always knows more than he can say. Every individual's daily activities, including economic activities, invariably rely upon continual guidance by both his explicit and tacit knowledge. A society that aims to make the best possible use of scarce resources in service of human needs, constituted as it is by individuals guided in this manner, must make use of all available knowledge, tacit, implicit, and perhaps fleeting, as well as technical, explicit, and more or less stable.

A concrete if homely example may be helpful in recognizing the existence of tacit knowledge and its relevance to the economic problem. Suppose that the kitchen pipes in an individual's residence suddenly spring a major leak; water gushes all over the floor. Such an emergency requires immediate response; a plumber is urgently needed. Recall in this regard that resources are scarce or limited, not only for society as a whole but also for every individual. The individual confronted by the emergency will want to find a plumber who can not only quickly fix the pipes but do so at the lowest cost. He can take his chances with the telephone directory, calling various plumbers and comparing cost estimates. Such, however, is time-consuming and, moreover, his emergency will probably command a premium price for plumbing services.

While contemplating his options, suppose the individual suddenly remembers that his friend has a brother who is an excellent plumber. He calls his friend. She agrees to help him and persuades her brother to fix the pipes at a reasonable price. The brother arrives and repairs the pipes: problem solved, and efficiently. The individual with the broken pipes utilized his knowledge, explicit and implicit, to deal with the unanticipated situation. He explicitly understood, for instance, that a plumber was the proper remedy for the broken pipes. The economically relevant knowledge he utilized, however, was mainly of the tacit kind. The individual was not explicitly aware that he possessed knowledge of the brother-plumber until a particular circumstance—the leak in the pipes—raised it to consciousness. He previously knew of the plumber but only tacitly.

Every human being, as mentioned, possesses similar tacit knowledge relating to myriad topics, and the use of such knowledge is essential to solving the economic problem arising from scarcity. Resources are limited, both individually and for society as a whole. No individual wants to pay more than necessary for any good or service; to do so is to have fewer resources available to obtain other needed or desired items. Nor would this be beneficial from the point of view of society as a whole. To pay more than necessary to repair the pipe is wrong not only from the individual's point of view but also the social point of view, and for the same reason—the additional resources used to pay a more expensive plumber could instead be used to produce items urgently needed or desired by other members of society. Resources are scarce, and both individuals and society at large benefit if they are employed as efficiently as possible, with minimum waste. The individual's tacit knowledge of the brother-plumber assisted him in achieving a more efficient use of intrinsically limited resources, which means a greater availability of resources, individually and socially, for the production and consumption of other needed or desired items. Such is good not only from the individual's point of view but also the point of view of society as a whole. The possibility of achieving such economic efficiencies, however, depends crucially on the effective utilization of tacit knowledge.

A second concrete example will serve to illustrate yet another crucial dimension of human knowledge essential to rational economic activity, so-called fleeting and local knowledge of time, place, and circumstance. Fleeting knowledge is knowledge of immediate circumstances that do not remain stable over time; local knowledge is knowledge confined to one's immediate and particular environment. To perceive the overwhelming significance of such knowledge for solving the economic problem, consider the case of a woman who unexpectedly discovers a hungry kitten on the side of the road. She is confronted with a particular and unanticipated need that is both fleeting (impermanent) and local (within her immediate purview). The Good Samaritan who wants to help the kitten has by chance discovered an urgent need, one that would not have been known to anyone if she had not happened to be driving down that particular road at the precise time the kitten was visible.

A good or rational economic system, one that efficiently employs scarce resources to meet the actual needs and wants of human beings (in this case, cat food), must have some means of satisfying such unanticipated demand in a timely manner. Indeed, many of the goods and services individuals come to demand are contingent in this manner, that is, cannot be foreseen in advance of some unexpected circumstance.

Demand of course can only be satisfied by corresponding supply or production, in this case, supply of cat food. An economic system that provides for the needs and wants of the community thus requires some means of incorporating unanticipated demand into plans of production. As we shall see, and as is attested by daily experience, a market economy is eminently capable of meeting the innumerable contingent needs and desires that inevitably arise within human existence. Every American knows that our Good Samaritan has simply to drive to the nearest grocery store, where she will undoubtedly find a ready supply of cat food awaiting her purchase. Such good fortune is not accidental but an expected feature of capitalism, more or less taken for granted by persons accustomed to life in a market-based society. The ready availability of goods and services to meet both stable and fleeting demand, however, is far from the norm in societies that do not enjoy the benefits of free enterprise. Indeed the inability of non-capitalist economies to respond to contingent needs and desires in a timely manner is among the many reasons for the relative failure of such economic arrangements to promote human wellbeing, as will be further discussed in a following chapter.

Epistemological issues, then, are central to the economic problems of production and distribution, and the alternative solutions to such problems offered by capitalism and socialism must be comprehended in their light. If human beings were omniscient or an omniscient god were immediately to direct all economic activities on earth, there would be no economic problem for any society to solve. An omniscient being, as previously remarked, would know the best means of utilizing scarce resources and would also know who should consume them. Human beings, however, are not in such a position. The extent of human knowledge is constitutionally circumscribed by the inherent limits of the human mind. No human being can know more than an infinitesimal fraction of all the relevant facts that must be taken into account in directing scarce resources toward their optimum allocation. Moreover, certain kinds of knowledge, as we have seen, are held *only* within individual minds and often in a form that cannot be communicated to other persons. Nor can any human being anticipate the ever-changing circumstances of human existence with any precision. The relevant facts that impel economic activity are continually in flux; concrete circumstances change in unpredictable ways (weather, birth and death, accidents, creativity and invention, and so on).

In the face of such irremediable limits to human knowledge, members of society must nevertheless determine which resources are available for production, and in what quantity. They must further determine which goods and services to produce with such resources and, finally, who should receive them, who stands in greatest need or want. Such determinations can only be made rationally and efficiently upon the basis of all relevant knowledge—the actual availability of resources ("supply") and the actual needs and wants of human beings ("demand"). In the absence of such accurate knowledge, a society runs the risk of misallocating resources, that is, wasting scarce resources through either inefficient production or production of goods and services that people do not need or want. Such misallocation is inimical to human welfare; the wasted resources could rather be used to fulfill the real and yet-unsatisfied needs and wants of human beings. In the absence of accurate knowledge, moreover, those who plan for production run the risk not only of waste and inefficiency but also failure to produce goods and services that people do in fact need and want, such as the cat food in the present example. Such problems can only be avoided if producers are able to obtain knowledge of the actual availability of resources and the actual needs and desires of those who will consume the fruits of production. The economic problem, as repeatedly emphasized, is ultimately a knowledge problem.

In conclusion, the optimum solution to the economic problem arising from the fact of scarcity depends on the ability to employ the maximum knowledge possessed by members of society. Such knowledge is not only systematic, technical, and explicit but also tacit, fleeting, and dispersed. The maximal utilization of knowledge cannot be achieved by relying solely on the possession of explicit knowledge because such is only a fraction of the knowledge requisite to solution of the economic problem. Much if not most economically relevant knowledge exists only as tacit or implicit knowledge, and, moreover, relates to fleeting and contingent circumstances. No individual can consciously articulate or transmit the entire body of knowledge that he relies upon in navigating daily activities; the individual mind always possesses, and acts upon, greater knowledge than it can consciously access. The inherent limits to the human mind in the face of the concrete complexity of existence means that the knowledge required to solve the economic problem *cannot* be acquired by any individual or group of individuals, no matter their brilliance or power. No human being does or can possess the capacity to assess or survey every aspect of the immeasurably intricate and ever-changing world. Such irremediable epistemological facts lead to the realization that a wise or rational utilization of the earth's scarce resources cannot be achieved by exclusive reliance on human or personal intellect or will. The solution of the economic problem requires, on the contrary, a *supra-rational* or *supra-personal* process that bypasses or transcends the inherent limits of the human mind. The market process—capitalism—is precisely such a process. Inescapable epistemological facts—the complexity of human knowledge in conjunction with the constitutional limits of the human mind—render the "automatic" or spontaneous coordination of human action achieved by the impersonal and supra-rational market process far superior to any method of coordination based on conscious human direction or centralized planning.

Essential Conditions of a Market Economy

Having explored certain epistemological issues inseparable from the question of rational economic order, we next turn to an examination of the actual process whereby capitalism facilitates solution of the economic problem. We begin with a discussion of the three essential conditions presupposed by, and crucial to the operation of, any market economy, namely, private property, the rule of law, and mutual trust among participants. The market does not operate in a vacuum but rather within a requisite moral, legal, and social framework. The first requirement of a capitalist economy, as the textbook definition makes clear, is the institution of *private property*—the legal recognition and enforcement of individual property rights. A right to private property, as previously noted, is most usefully regarded as a *decision right*. An individual, for instance, who holds a property right in an automobile is morally and legally entitled to decide how that automobile is to be employed. He may choose to leave it sitting in a garage, drive it himself, allow another to drive it, sell or destroy it, and so on. Whatever his choice, his property right in the vehicle legally forbids anyone else to employ it without his permission. It is his, which means that he and he alone decides if and how the automobile, his property, is to be employed; neither other private persons nor the government has anything to say in the matter.[3] The same applies to every other entity regarded as private property. Whoever holds title to property, whatever its nature, holds the ultimate right to decide how that possession is to be employed. That right may be qualified by the bounds of law or governmental regulation (e.g., speed limits) but the essential point remains—only the individual who possesses the property right in an entity is entitled to direct its usage. In a pure or ideal free-market economy, all resources, material and immaterial, belong to, and are thus under the direction of, particular private individuals—those who possess the corresponding property right. The security of private property rights is the first crucial condition or prerequisite of a market system.

The second essential precondition of a market order is the existence of the *rule of law*. The rule of law, discussed in Volume I, establishes an abstract or general legal framework that all persons, including the government, are required to honor in pursuit of their purposes. The rule of law does not concern the ends or goals of human action but rather restricts the means that may be employed in pursuit of such goals. It further provides a framework that secures individual expectations. The establishment of law, as we recall, stabilizes certain features of the environment in a manner that permits individuals more accurately to anticipate certain consequences of their actions. A law prohibiting theft, for instance, permits individuals to rest more or less secure in the expectation that their personal possessions will not be taken from them without their consent. It also informs would-be thieves of the consequence of stealing; if the law is consistently enforced, they can be secure in the expectation that such action will be punished. The protection of private property rights is of course a particular aspect of the general rule of law. Property rights particularly secure the right-holder's expectation that he will be permitted to direct the use of his personal possessions.

Further rules especially relevant to a market economy include contract law and legal prohibition of force and fraud. The enforcement of contract law secures the expectation that all parties to a contract will honor their contractual obligations. Such enhanced certainty facilitates

---

[3] We here exclude general governmental regulations that apply universally to all members of society.

trade and commerce insofar as people are more willing to engage in contractual business relationships if they are certain that contractual agreements will be legally enforced. The handshake of a "gentleman's agreement" is one thing, protection by the full force of law another. Similarly, the legal prohibition of fraud increases the level of trust that buyers can place in the claims of various sellers. Sellers in a market economy are not permitted to lie to or otherwise deliberately deceive their customers regarding the good or service offered and will be punished by law if they do so. Such, again, facilitates trade by securing the buyer's expectation that the good or service he purchases will actually be as advertised. Last but not least, the prohibition of force in market exchange secures the high value of individual freedom. No one, buyer or seller, is permitted to employ coercion toward achievement of his economic ends. No buyer may legally be forced to purchase any particular good or service, and no seller may legally be forced to produce or sell any particular service. The prohibition of coercive force ensures that all economic transactions in a market economy (the "free market") are indeed free, that is, voluntary.

The rule of law, then, is crucial to the operation of a market economy. It serves to ensure that market participants will conduct their affairs in an ethical or just manner (no force, fraud, or theft). It further provides a level of certainty that permits individuals to plan their lives with greater rationality and foresight, with greater knowledge of the consequences of their choices, than is possible in its absence. Such certainty applies to the actions not only of other private individuals but also government. Legal protection of property rights, for instance, assures the individual that the government will not confiscate his resources. He can be certain that any wages, salary, or profits he earns will remain under his own direction and plan his personal economic efforts accordingly.

Tax legislation, as we have seen, serves a similar function. Legislation that establishes fixed tax rates permits individuals to know in advance precisely how much of their income they will be permitted to retain. Such knowledge will factor into many of their personal economic plans and decisions. An individual who desires greater income, for instance, may consider working overtime or taking on a second job. The law informs him in advance of the amount of such additional income he can expect to pay in taxes, information that enables him better to determine whether supplementary employment is worth the effort. Individuals will reach different conclusions, in line with their personal circumstances and values, as to the desirability of additional employment under current tax law. The essential element has nevertheless been achieved, that is, individuals know with certainty the consequences of their decisions and can thus make informed and rational choices, secure in their expectation of retaining a known percentage of any additional income earned. A further example is the recent legislation that requires all employers to provide health insurance to their employees. Both the moral grounds and economic desirability of such legislation may be in question, but it nevertheless provides the security of expectation essential to the operation of the market process. Employers will take the additional cost of health insurance into account each time they consider hiring a new employee. So long as the legislation remains in place and is consistently enforced, they know with certainty the costs involved in expanding their work force and can thus make a rational calculation of whether or not such would serve the interest of the firm.

The rule of law, then, is an essential precondition of a market economy, providing a framework of known and stable rules that every person can depend upon in devising his personal plans. By attaching various known consequences to certain actions, the rule of law provides, again, a "man-made" element of certainty, thereby allowing individuals to formulate personal plans more rationally and confidently than they could in its absence.[4] The security of expectation established by the rule of law facilitates not only the rational development of individual economic plans but also coordination of the simultaneous plans pursued by the millions of individuals who constitute modern society. It is as indispensable to a developed market economy as the institution of private property, itself protected by the rule of law.

The third condition essential for the operation of the market process may be called *mutual trust among participants*. Trust in this regard refers to the expectation that social interaction will be governed in accord with customary moral rules and standards, allowing members of society to depend upon and predict the behavior of their fellows to a considerable extent. Mutual trust, based on a common observance of shared (unwritten) moral values and rules, serves a function similar to the

---

[4] F.A. Hayek, *The Constitution of Liberty* (Chicago: University of Chicago Press, 1960), 153. Hereinafter cited as *Constitution of Liberty*.

formal rule of law, that is, allows people to plan and carry out their plans with a greater degree of certainty than would be possible in its absence. Trust so conceived plays a crucial if implicit role in a market-based society such as the United States.

To perceive its significance to the market process, consider a routine practice such as the consumption of electricity provided by a local utility company. Every month most Americans receive a bill that typically reflects the amount of electricity consumed within the residence over the previous month. The utility companies throughout the nation implicitly *trust* that the vast majority of their millions of customers will in fact pay for the electricity they have used. They typically do not require payment in advance of service but rather trust their customers to honor their financial obligations. Of course the provider of electricity is also protected by the rule of law and has legal recourse in the event of nonpayment. Such legal remedies, however, are reserved for the exceptions to the rule, for those relatively few customers who do not meet their contractual obligations. The courts would be overwhelmed if providers had to sue all or most of their customers to obtain payment for services rendered. The utility companies would also be overwhelmed and unable to operate in the normal manner. Their smooth operation depends, in part, on trust, the expectation that most customers will behave honorably—in accord with received moral norms—and pay their bills. Or consider the situation of an individual who accepts a position with a new employer. Normally a new employee must work several weeks before receiving a paycheck. He trusts that the employer will actually live up to his obligation to pay him for work performed, that the employer will behave decently and honorably. He trusts, in other words, that the employer will observe the implicit rules of just conduct characteristic of the traditional American ethos, which include the moral obligation of an employer to pay an employee for actual work performed. Employers, like utility customers, are also legally obligated to pay for services rendered, but it would be impossible to enforce such law if most employers engaged in unethical behavior and violated their obligation to do so.

All forms of social intercourse involve implicit, tacit, or unspoken ethical rules that everyone counts on their fellows to observe. Such unwritten rules and customs regulate human behavior in every society on earth, varying in accord with its particular cultural and ethical tradition. The implicit moral ethos underlying American social order derives from its particular cultural and religious tradition, namely, the Judeo-Christian or Western ethos that prohibits killing, stealing, lying, breaking promises, and so on. The American people have come to expect such behavior as normal or natural, and it is inseparable from their customary way of life. Such time-honored ethical norms are expected to apply not only within immediate personal relations but impersonal legal, political, and economic relations as well. Traditional American order, including its traditional economic order, depends upon the widespread practice of such customary moral rules, ultimately derived from its religious and cultural inheritance and crucial to the vitality of its characteristic institutions and culture.

A key element of the vibrant market economy historically characteristic of American society, then, is the mutual social trust that emerged from its widespread embrace of Judeo-Christian norms. Such an achievement is the fruit of a particular culture and civilization, Western civilization, and not a universal or permanent aspect of culture in general. Societies that developed on the basis of other moral and cultural traditions certainly possess characteristic and implicit moral and social norms but these may differ substantively from the particular standards crucial to the functioning of a market economy. Such societies may thus lack the requisite moral and cultural preconditions of a market economy—commitment to private property and the rule of law and the ethical norms implicitly governing market exchange. Capitalist economic arrangements are not an autonomous or isolated aspect of a social order but rather dependent on a particular cultural and moral ethos. Western capitalist institutions grew from soil prepared by Judeo-Christian values and presuppositions and cannot simply be transplanted or grafted onto societies that lack the requisite moral, legal, and cultural framework.

Indeed, some observers fear that Western society, including American society, is itself gradually destroying the so-called "moral capital" that nourished its growth over the course of millennia. "Moral capital" in this context refers to the explicit and implicit values, chiefly of biblical inspiration, that definitively shaped the development of Western or Judeo-Christian civilization. The free society, including its economic dimension, capitalism, owes an incalculable debt to the fund of spiritual values invested, so to speak, in its growth. The ongoing erosion of traditional spiritual and religious values—the "moral capital" of Western development—is thus of great significance for the vitality, indeed the preservation, not only of capitalist economic order but traditional American order more generally, including its central value of individual freedom.[5] This important and complex topic—the relation of the free society to its spiritual, religious, and moral heritage—will be extensively explored in Volume III of this study, *The Rise and Fall of Freedom.*

Having identified the three essential conditions or prerequisites of a market or capitalist economy—recognition and protection of individual property rights; enforcement of the rule of law, including prohibition against force, fraud, and theft; and mutual trust among participants— we turn to examine certain other concepts and theoretical constructs central to economic reasoning and practice. Such considerations, in conjunction with the market preconditions and epistemological constraints previously discussed, will leave us prepared to explore the actual operation of the market process, how is, how the market solves the economic problem in practice.

Subjective Value

An appreciation of the market process begins with recognition that individuals vary greatly in their values, needs, desires, tastes, and preferences. In the formal language of economics, every individual is said to possess a unique *scale of values* and preferences, a unique ranking of the particular goods and services personally most valuable or important to that individual. If readers of this book were asked to list the ten particular goods or services they personally regard as most important to their welfare, they would no doubt produce as many different lists as there are readers. We are discussing in this context *economic goods*— items that can be bought and sold on the market. Many personal and social values are certainly desirable "goods," for instance, friendship, love, and justice, but they are not economic goods—goods that can be obtained for a price on the market. Nor may individual rankings contain such generic items as "food, clothing, and shelter." Individuals never desire "food," which is a merely nominal term referring to an abstract

---

[5] Nicholas Capaldi and Theodore Roosevelt Malloch, *America's Spiritual Capital* (South Bend: St. Augustine's Press, 2012).

category of items suitable for the nourishment of human beings, animals, and even plants. They rather desire *particular* kinds of food that suit their individual tastes—McDonald's French fries or celery sticks, ice cream or tofu. Obviously each individual has decided preferences in this regard that are greatly at odds with the preferences of other individuals. In the same way, individuals never desire "clothing" but rather a Perry Ellis cashmere coat or an L.L. Bean hunting jacket, a straw sunhat or a wool skull cap. The particular items of clothing desired by consumers vary dramatically from person to person, depending on age, place of residence, career, the wardrobe a person already possesses, and a host of other factors too numerous to list. Indeed, they vary for a particular individual over time; the clothing desired by Jane the teenager is rarely identical to that desired by Jane the mother or grandmother. "Shelter" varies in the same manner and for the same reasons, from a pup tent erected under a public bridge to a mansion on Palm Beach. People do not want "shelter" but particular and individual forms that suit their needs, tastes, and also their budgets. With such considerations in mind, it is more or less certain that the top ten items on each reader's list of preferences will be unique and particular to each individual reader. It would be astonishing to find even two individuals with identical lists, let alone the more than three hundred million individuals comprised by modern American society.

The formal way to describe the fact that each individual possesses a unique scale of values, specific to himself, is to say that economic value is always and everywhere *subjective value.* That is, the value of any economic good or service is always and everywhere attributed to the good in question by the human person (the "subject") who is perceiving it. Economic value only exists within the mind of the perceiving individual and is thus dependent on human opinion, circumstance, and preference. The second possible form of value, by contrast, is conventionally termed *objective* value, that is, value that is intrinsic to or inherent in the object and thus independent of human opinion. The Judeo-Christian tradition, for instance, teaches that the values embodied in the Ten Commandments are objective values. Killing innocent people, stealing, lying and so on are regarded as objectively wrong, wrong-in-themselves, independent of the opinions or preferences of human beings; an individual's subjective or personal beliefs regarding such actions are irrelevant. Economic value is not of this nature.

Economic value, like beauty, is rather in the eyes of the beholder; it is subjective value. No economic good is intrinsically valuable, valuable in-itself, as truth-telling may be. Economic value is always *imputed* value, imputed to the good or service in question by the individual mind evaluating it. The economic value of particular items to particular individuals always depends on subjective perception shaped by individual beliefs, needs, circumstances, tastes, and so on.

Consider, for example, the economic value of a sixteen-ounce bottle of spring water. For purposes of illustration, assume that its price at a local convenience store is $2. In the language of economics, $2 is the "asking price," which reflects the value of the water to the seller, how much it is personally (subjectively) worth to him or her. The value of the water to potential buyers may be quite different. An individual who already possesses 100,000 bottles of the identical water may not be willing to pay anything at all for an additional bottle; the value to such an individual is zero. Now imagine the same individual buyer under different circumstances. Suppose he finds himself stranded in a desert without food or water; after several days he is on the verge of dehydration or even death. Under such circumstances, the same individual will no doubt be willing to pay far more than $2, perhaps his entire fortune, for the very same bottle of spring water. The bottle of water has undergone no change; it is identical in both sets of circumstances. What has changed is rather the perception of the individual. Under the first set of circumstances, he perceived no value in the bottle of water; under the second set, he perceived inestimable value in the identical bottle (it might save his life). This is only to say that economic value does not inhere in the object, the water in our example. Economic value is never objective, never intrinsic to any good or service, but always and only imputed to a good or service by an individual mind. Economic value is always subjective value, existing always and only in the mind of the evaluating person, the human subject.

Kinds of Order in Society: Spontaneous Order and Organization

An analysis of the operation of the market process proceeds with restatement of the fundamental economic problem confronting every human society: the inescapable fact of scarcity that immediately generates the problem of choice with respect to both production and distribution. Someone must decide *what* is to be produced, and *how,* with what inputs and techniques, and someone must further decide *who* is to receive the fruits of production. In a capitalist economy, no central authority or supervisor, no governmental "planner," "manager," "regulator," "overseer," or "czar," makes such decisions. The direction or utilization of scarce resources is instead guided by the impersonal and decentralized market process. The market exemplifies a particular *kind* of order found in both nature and society, conventionally designated "spontaneous order" and defined as a pattern, system, or structure that emerges indirectly and without conscious or deliberate design. With respect to economic order, such a pattern or structure emerges as an unintended byproduct of the independent decisions and actions of the countless individuals who daily engage in the routine actions of buying and selling.[6] Buyers and sellers are generally unaware that their day-to-day actions contribute to the formation of a supra-personal social order upon which each of them depends for fulfillment of their individual values and goals, namely, the spontaneous order of the market. Such, however, is precisely the case in a society ordered by capitalist exchange. To comprehend capitalism, the market process, then, is to comprehend the process of spontaneous order and how it facilitates solution of the economic problem confronting every society.

Spontaneous order is the technical term for a specific kind of self-generating and self-maintaining pattern or structure of stable and predictable relations among constituent elements. Such a structure is both abstract and purpose-independent, emerging not by intentional human design but rather as an unintended consequence of the regular (rule-governed) behavior of the individual elements forming it. An example of a spontaneous ordering process in the physical realm may shed light on how such forces operate in the social realm. Consider the formation of a crystal. Crystals are found of course in nature but can also be created in a laboratory. To induce the formation of a lab-created crystal, scientists must establish the conditions under which the individual elements that will ultimately form the crystal will so arrange themselves that the overall crystalline structure will emerge. They cannot

---

[6] Famously summarized by Adam Ferguson as "the result of human action, but not the execution of any human design," *An Essay on the History of Civil Society* (London: T. Cadell, 1767).

deliberately arrange the individual elements to produce the desired formation. Under appropriate conditions, however, each rule-governed element, adapting itself to its initial position and particular circumstances, will arrange itself in a way consistent with the formation of the more complex structure of a crystal. The "order" of a crystalline structure can emerge under appropriate laboratory conditions, but it "grows" spontaneously, without conscious arrangement of the individual constituent elements by human design. The most scientists can do is induce its formation by establishing the requisite conditions for growth.

The market process that coordinates human action within modern liberal society is precisely such a process of spontaneous ordering or "growth." Its character is perhaps most clearly seen in contrast to a second type of ordering technique also utilized in modern society—organization or "made order." Unlike the purpose-independent order that emerges spontaneously and unintentionally from the activities of market participants, an organization is a purpose-or end-dependent order, that is, a structure deliberately designed to achieve a particular purpose. Such an order is created, moreover, by the deliberate arrangement of its constituent elements according to the conscious intention of a designing human mind. A watch or computer microchip exemplify such "constructed" or "made" order within the physical realm. A watch is made for a specific purpose (end-dependent) and each component is deliberately positioned in accordance with the maker's knowledge and purpose and in accordance with his preconceived design.

A social "organization" or "made order," such as a business firm or a university, is similarly constructed. It too is made to fulfill a particular purpose (e.g., profit, education) and each particular element of the structure is deliberately positioned in accordance with the maker's knowledge and purpose and in accordance with his preconceived design (e.g., staff composition, organizational flow charts, position descriptions, and so on). In other words, every social organization is consciously made or constructed by one or more human beings who position its constituent elements in their places and direct their movements toward fulfillment of a particular known purpose. Organization is an indispensable ordering technique for the achievement of *known* and specific goals. If one's purpose is to educate university students, the deliberate construction of an organization known as a university will greatly assist realization of that goal. If one's purpose is to produce automobiles that customers will desire to purchase, it would be most useful to construct a manufacturing organization dedicated to that end. If one's purpose is to rescue homeless animals, one may better achieve that goal by constructing an organization specifically dedicated to achieving that purpose, that is, an animal-shelter administered by persons with clearly defined roles and responsibilities.

The overarching spontaneous order of liberal society, however, is not an organization so conceived. Certain members of liberal society do employ the ordering technique of deliberate organization toward fulfillment of known purposes. American society, as we have seen, is constituted in part by numerous organizations—governmental institutions, business corporations, religious institutions, and other voluntary associations, all of which are deliberately created to pursue particular known ends. The coordination of activities among such organized institutions, and among individuals within society as a whole, however, is achieved not by conscious human design or arrangement but rather by an impersonal and spontaneous process that no one designed and that does not serve to achieve known and particular purposes. Such of course is the market process or capitalism. Coordination of human activity by means of market forces is achieved not by conscious, deliberate, centralized human direction but rather the widespread observance and enforcement of certain types of general moral and legal rules. Organization and spontaneous order are not only distinct kinds of order but, as we shall see, structured by distinct kinds of rules.

The distinction between organization and spontaneous order is more formally characterized as the distinction between *teleocratic* and *nomocratic* order. An organization is a *teleocratic* order—one that aims to realize a *telos* or known purpose. Modern liberal society, as said, is constituted in part by many such organizations or teleocratic orders. Society as a whole, however, is not a teleocratic order, not an organization deliberately designed by a human agent to realize a particular known purpose, but rather a *nomocratic* order (from the Greek *telos* [purpose], and *nomos* [law or convention], respectively).[7] A

---

[7] According to Hayek, the conceptions of spontaneous order and organization are more or less equivalent to Michael Oakeshott's conceptions of the "nomocratic," purpose-independent, "civil association" (societas) and the "teleocratic," end-dependent, "enterprise association" (universitas). Hayek, *Rules and Order*, 15.

nomocratic order such as traditional American society does not possess an overarching *telos* or purpose that every individual and group is expected or required to pursue. Within such an order, individuals and groups are rather expected and entitled to pursue their own freely chosen purposes and values. No human authority assigns their particular positions or directs their actions by specific orders or commands; their activity is self-directed. Individual self-direction is obviously the antithesis of rule by human command or order.

Such holds true, moreover, not only for a single individual but also the coordination of the individually self-directed activities of the hundreds of millions of persons who constitute American society as a whole. In a free society, the ordering or coordination of their activities is achieved not by command or directive of authority. No one orders the managers of Microsoft to sell its products to Starbucks or any private individual. No one orders Starbucks or any private individual to purchase Microsoft products. Coordination of the self-directed activities of Microsoft, Starbucks, and millions of American producers and consumers is rather achieved by mutual observance of a different kind of rule, namely, law proper (*nomos*). We have previously discussed the distinct and opposing nature of law and command. As we recall, an ideal command, command proper, is an authoritative order, a precise and detailed directive that mandates certain specified action. Law proper, by contrast, is a general, abstract, purpose-independent rule that structures the *means* individuals (and firms) may employ in pursuing their individual (or corporate) purposes but, unlike a command, does not define or specify those means or purposes. Starbucks is permitted to strive to obtain Microsoft products if such is its self-chosen goal, but the means it may employ in that effort are restricted by law (Starbucks may not, for instance, steal Microsoft products but must obtain them in a legal manner). The general rule that prohibits theft restricts the means the firm may employ to realize its self-directed purpose but says nothing about the purpose itself. No one, as said, directs or commands Starbucks to buy Microsoft products.

The two kinds of ordering techniques, organization and spontaneous order, are further distinguished, then, by the *kinds* of rules that necessarily structure their operation—purpose-dependent commands or directives and general purpose-independent rules (law proper), respectively. As we recall from previous discussion, only end-independent general rules, true law, permit individuals (and individuals voluntarily associated as organizations) to use their own knowledge for their own purposes. The knowledge embodied in end-dependent commands or directives is necessarily limited to the knowledge possessed by the commander or director; the knowledge of the person(s) commanded is not and cannot be utilized if the order is strictly followed. Organizations necessarily rely on such purpose-dependent directives to order their internal operations. They are designed to fulfill particular purposes, and all members of an organization are expected to contribute to the achievement of its particular known goal. Any employee hired by a business organization, for instance, is expected to fulfill a role or task specified in advance by the employer. Employees are expected to use their knowledge not to fulfill their own purposes but rather those associated with their particular position within the organization. Their positions are defined by specific directives devised by the organization's managers and thus embody the latter's knowledge and purpose; employees are hired to assist in fulfilling that specified purpose. All organizations rely on such internal ordering techniques. All organizations aim to achieve particular known purposes, and each member must be assigned his part in achieving them.

The technique of organization, however, while indispensable to the achievement of known and specific purposes, involves an inherent drawback. The individual elements of the organization (the "employees") are deliberately arranged by a designing mind toward achievement of the particular purpose established by its creators. Employees, as we have seen, are expected to pursue the goal of the organization, which means they are expected to use their knowledge, not to fulfill their own purposes but rather those established by the organization's directors. This can only be accomplished if they are required to follow specific directives or commands and not general purpose-independent rules ("thou shalt not steal"). As we recall, however, every command or specific directive necessarily restricts the knowledge employed to the imperfect knowledge possessed by those who issue the directives, in a business organization, typically owners, managers, or supervisors. The knowledge possessed by the individual employees who must obey such directives may be lost or wasted, depending on the generality or specificity of the directives they are under. Such, however, is the price paid for utilizing the otherwise valuable ordering technique of organization.

The fact that organizations must employ teleocratic rules in their internal operation has significant implications for liberal society as a whole and, in particular, its ability to solve the economic or knowledge problem as described. The crucial difference between the respective ordering techniques of organization and spontaneous order, that is, the ordering of human action by command (directive) or general rules, is the extent of knowledge utilized by either technique. We have seen that purpose-dependent directives or commands necessarily restrict the knowledge employed to that of the person or persons issuing the directive or command. A legal framework constituted by general, purpose-independent rules, by contrast, permits maximum utilization of the knowledge possessed in a society.

The inherent epistemological difficulties involved in order achieved by personal command rather than impersonal general rules may be illustrated by the following hypothetical example. Imagine a university professor who wishes to distribute a particular scholarly article to students in her class. She only has one copy of the article at hand. She thus issues a directive to her work-study student, as follows: "Take this article. Go to the Xerox machine down the hall. Make fifty copies, collated and stapled, and return them to me within an hour." Such a directive exemplifies a perfect or ideal command: it not only orders action toward fulfillment of the specific purpose established by the commander (the professor) but also specifies the precise means by which it is to be fulfilled. Such a command, like any command, embodies only the knowledge possessed by the commander-professor. Whatever knowledge the student may possess is irrelevant; his sole task is to follow orders. The student under command, like the driver under command in Volume I, is essentially a tool, like a hammer or nail, whose utilization is utterly controlled by the commander. Indeed the particular student could probably be replaced by any other able-bodied student to no effect. Hammers are largely interchangeable; a tool is a tool.

Consider the possibility, however, that the student actually possesses knowledge relevant to the task at hand. Perhaps he knows that another professor previously distributed the same article and that fifty extra copies already exist for the taking. In the situation under discussion, such knowledge is utterly wasted, lost to the social or economic process. The student under command is constrained to follow the specific orders of the professor which, under the circumstances, proves wasteful and irrational; scarce resources are needlessly used to produce copies that already exist. Such is wrong from an economic point of view, both for the particular organization, the university, and society at large. The resources used to produce the fifty unnecessary copies could rather have been used to meet other needs and wants, either within the university or elsewhere. Such waste of knowledge and resources, however, is a predictable outcome of the type of rule employed in this situation, a specific command or directive. We have seen that any and every command necessarily embodies only the limited knowledge of the commander. In the present case, the professor's limited knowledge led to a needless waste of resources which could have been avoided if the student had been permitted to contribute his personal knowledge toward accomplishing his assigned goal (acquiring the fifty copies). Such could only have been achieved, however, by permitting him a greater measure of self-direction than is possible under command.

Our example is merely a particular instance of a more general problem arising from order produced by command: the inevitable restriction of knowledge involved in such a technique, a restriction proportionate to the degree of specificity involved in a directive. The more specific a directive, the more knowledge is restricted to that possessed by the issuer. The more general a directive, on the other hand, the greater the possibility of utilizing knowledge wider than that possessed by the issuer. The professor in the present example could have avoided the negative outcome by giving the student more general instructions, telling him, for instance, simply to obtain fifty copies of the article, leaving aside specification of the means he must employ in achieving that end. The advantage of utilizing a more general directive is that it leaves the student free to personally devise the means of realizing the given end. In our case, he would have been free to use his knowledge of the existence of the fifty copies to meet the directive, eliminating the unnecessary waste involved in producing the extra copies as ordered.

We have repeatedly emphasized that the economic problem is ultimately a knowledge problem. An understanding of the different *kinds* of rules and order in society leads to the recognition that its solution involves the ordering of human action by the widespread use of general rules rather than commands or directives of authority. Only a society governed by the rule of law proper—the enforcement of general rules possessing the attributes described in a previous volume—is capable of potentially eliciting and utilizing *all* the economically relevant knowledge and information possessed by *all* its members, even the least among them. A society ordered by commands and directives, on the other hand, necessarily restricts the knowledge brought to bear on the solution of the economic problem to that possessed by those who devise the commands and directives. The problems that arise from employing human directives in place of general rules are identical to those that arise from attempts to order a society's economic arrangements by means of deliberate direction by political authority rather than the spontaneous ordering forces of the market. A market economy, and the coordination of individual pursuits in a free society more generally, is necessarily ordered not by commands or directives of government (a planned or command economy) but rather impersonal general rules of conduct applicable to all persons, that is, the rule of law.

In conclusion, the coordination of human activity by means of general rules of law is among the chief reasons for the manifest superiority of capitalism over socialism and other forms of planned economy. It is superior precisely because it is ordered not by conscious central direction involving personal command or human directive but rather impersonal rules. A society ordered by general rules of conduct encourages the emergence and utilization of far greater knowledge than is possible in any order fashioned by specific directives of authority. Individuals in a market economy are not forced to obey authoritative commands but rather permitted to "use their own knowledge for their own purposes," within the limits of law that merely restricts but does not compel action. Accordingly, every individual, whatever his social or economic position, is able to contribute all his many kinds of knowledge—technical, tacit, and the all-important fleeting knowledge of time, place, and circumstance—toward solution of the overarching economic problem confronting every society.

Order achieved by the observance of general rules has the further benefit of encouraging not only discovery and utilization of knowledge but also more flexible adaptation to the ever-changing and unanticipated circumstances of existence. Moreover, and not least of its many advantages, only an economic order achieved on the basis of general rules of law permits the exercise of individual freedom; order achieved by command, by definition, eliminates the capacity for voluntary choice. Such are the reasons—the superior knowledge informing decisions regarding both production and consumption and the ability flexibly to adapt to the flux of circumstance—why the spontaneous order of the market has been more successful in solving the economic problem than any other form of economic organization heretofore discovered.

The great modern competitor to capitalism has of course been the planned or command economy of communism and its variants. A planned economy, by definition, attempts to consciously and deliberately order economic activity across society by conscious human design, the technique of organization. Centralized planning necessarily relies upon command and directive, which means that it necessarily rests upon the inevitably limited knowledge possessed by the planners, usually politically appointed directors, managers, or other bureaucrats. Insofar as the economic problem is ultimately a knowledge problem, such a fact has tremendous consequences for the ability of any planned or command economy to achieve a rational, let alone optimal, allocation of resources. Such is evident not only in consideration of the various epistemological issues under discussion but also historical experience—the universal failure of collectivized economies to achieve the prosperity and plenty promised by their designers. We return to a discussion of the problems inherent to all forms of planned economy in a subsequent chapter.

SEVEN

CAPITALISM: THE MARKET PROCESS

The price system is an evolved medium of communication . . . a language of a kind.   —F.A. Hayek

Underlying most arguments against the free market is a lack of belief in freedom itself.   —Milton Friedman

Every functioning society exhibits some orderly pattern of activities. In the absence of order existence would be chaos, and no one could go about their daily affairs or satisfy even basic needs. In modern American society each person pursues his individual aims within a comprehensive order that most people take more or less for granted, namely, the set of abstract social relations called "the market."[8] Although many persons are not consciously aware of its existence, the smooth functioning of the overarching or background market order is crucial to the realization of every person's plans. The spontaneous order of the market is not of course a concrete entity that can be seen or touched. It is rather an abstract or intangible order that manifests as the matching or coincidence of expectations and plans across individuals who are necessarily ignorant of most of the factors that influence the success of

---

[8] Hayek (1973) defines the concept of order as a "state of affairs in which a multiplicity of elements of various kinds are so related to each other that we may learn from our acquaintance with some spatial or temporal part of the whole to form correct expectations concerning the rest, or at least expectations which have a good chance of proving correct" (*Rules and Order*, 36). The relations that structure a spontaneous social order include such abstract social relations as buyer and seller; lessor and lessee; lender and borrower; producer and consumer; judge and litigant; and so on.

their personal plans. Members of a geographically extensive social order such as American society know little if anything of either the concrete circumstances prevailing throughout society (such as conditions of "supply" and "demand") or the concrete aims pursued by their (mostly unknown) fellows. Such knowledge, however, is crucial to the realization of any individual's plans and goals, involving as it does the availability of the material resources required for their fulfillment.

Such inevitable facts of modern social existence raise several interesting questions. First, how do strangers who possess no explicit knowledge of their fellows' concrete needs and wants nevertheless manage to provide the means—the material goods and services—required to fulfill them? How is the evident order each person experiences in the course of a day generated and maintained even though most persons are only tacitly aware of its existence and do not deliberately aim to produce it? More concretely, why can every American confidently assume he can purchase a loaf of bread at the local grocery store whenever he so desires? He can do so because contemporary American society largely secures the abstract or general conditions that allow the activities of millions of persons— buyers and sellers who do not and cannot know one another's concrete circumstances and intentions—to "dovetail" or mesh rather than come into conflict. He can do so because American society is ordered by the widespread observance of certain general rules, perceptual, behavioral, moral, and legal, that structure the spontaneous ordering process called the market.

The Ordering Principle of the Market

The market comprises a complex of social relations, institutions, and practices that may be regarded as historically developed solutions to the economic or knowledge problem as described—how to elicit, utilize, and coordinate relevant economic knowledge, explicit, tacit, and fleeting, most of which is necessarily fragmented and dispersed among the numerous members of any complex society. Capitalism, as we have seen, goes by many names: free enterprise, the market economy, system, order, process, and so on. Perhaps the most accurate of all such descriptions, however, is the term preferred by Nobel Laureate economist F. A. Hayek and other economists associated with the so-called Austrian school, namely, the "price system." Such a designation highlights the all-important function of prices in a market economy, especially their role in the social transmission of relevant economic knowledge and information. Hayek underscores that function by characterizing the market or price system as essentially an evolved "information system," "medium of communicati[on]," or "system of telecommunications."[9]

The vast majority of market participants are relatively blind to the crucial function of prices in a capitalist economy. Their interest in prices is typically limited to the affordability of various needed or desired goods and services. Market prices, however, bear significance far beyond such individual concerns, constituting, indeed, the very linchpin of capitalist economic arrangements. Comprehension of the crucial role played by prices in a market economy begins with a discussion of the nature and meaning of a "price." A price is an abstract symbol—a language of a kind—that embodies or summarizes knowledge and information garnered by means of the transpersonal social process conventionally termed the market. More particularly, the prevailing structure of relative prices in a market economy indicates the relative scarcity or abundance of resources available for production and consumption at any point in time. Such knowledge, collectively acquired via the actions of market participants, transcends the knowledge available to any individual human mind, which is constitutionally incapable of mastering the infinite concrete complexity of the social environment.

The price system represents a culturally evolved adaptation to such irremediable limits of the human mind, one made possible by the mind's ability to employ abstract thought and symbols (such as a "price"). The ability to read and speak the abstract language of prices permits human beings to navigate in a world of scarce resources and unimaginable concrete intricacy. Such an ability, as mentioned, permits individuals to bypass their irremediable ignorance of the innumerable facts upon which the success of their individual plans inevitably depends, namely, the concrete or material circumstances prevailing throughout society and indeed the world. Prices are indispensable guides to human action, one that each person, whether as producer or consumer, relies upon on a daily basis. Only the guidance provided by the prevailing structure of relative prices permits individuals to orient their actions in a way that

---

[9] F. A. Hayek, "The Use of Knowledge in Society," *American Economic Review* (American Economic Association Association) XXXV (4): 519-30.

coordinates or meshes with the actions of the millions and billions of other individuals with whom he must share the scarce resources of the earth and who also plan to utilize them in fulfillment of their purposes. In the absence of an accurate structure of relative prices, human beings would have no means of knowing whether their personal plans and goals are consistent with the plans and goals simultaneously pursued by their fellow human beings. Without the guidance of prices, human beings would have no way of knowing whether the (scarce) resources requisite to fulfillment of their myriad personal plans are actually available for use.

The information conveyed by relative prices, moreover, is crucial not only to solving the economic problem, both individually and socially, but also to the exercise of individual freedom. The prevailing structure of relative prices in a market economy, as said, indicates the relative scarcity or abundance of resources available for production and consumption. Without the guiding function of prices, individuals could not know how to employ their productive efforts (contribute to "supply") in a manner compatible with the plans and actions, the needs and desires, of other human beings ("demand"). In the absence of an accurate structure of relative prices, production, which of course is essential to human survival, could not be undertaken on a voluntary basis but would have to be directed by command.[10]

Capital

The next task is to examine more closely the actual process by which capitalism or the price system leads toward solution of the economic problem in practice. Analysis of the market process must first address the problem of production; there can be no distribution or consumption of what has not yet been produced. We have seen that the nature of things—the inescapable fact of limited resources or scarcity—forces upon every society the question of choice: someone must decide, in the first instance, what is to be produced, and how. In a market economy, that function is performed by private individuals (business owners, entrepreneurs) and groups of voluntarily associated individuals (business firms, corporations). Individuals, either singly or jointly, decide to

---

[10] As I write, the press is reporting the forced labor mandated by Maduro in socialist Venezuela.

employ their personal resources—their "capital"—in the production of goods and services that they believe will be desired by other people—the potential consumers or buyers of their goods and services. In the formal language of economics, producers generate "supply" and consumers generate "demand."[11]

Capitalism, of course, derives its name from the essential role of capital in its manner of operation. The concept of economic capital is perhaps most readily grasped by perceiving its identity with "savings" employed or "invested" in the production of goods and services. Capital initially arises from an individual's ability to produce more than he or she needs for subsistence. The "capitalist" is the person who not only manages to raise his production above subsistence level but further decides to "save" and then "invest" such savings in the production of a good or service.[12]

To simplify matters, consider the hypothetical situation of Robinson Crusoe alone on his desert island. Crusoe, like every human being, is confronted by the economic problem arising from scarcity. He must thus decide how he is to employ his personally limited resources, which in his case largely consist of labor and time, to meet his needs. He must first of all decide what to produce, and how. Suppose he identifies food as his most urgent need and decides to spend his time and labor attempting to catch a fish. We shall assume that, after some practice, he manages to catch a fish and, further, that he requires one fish per day to survive. Day after day he successfully catches a fish and thus is able to sustain his existence.

Suppose that one day, however, Crusoe manages to catch two fish. Such a seemingly simple if fortunate event will have significant bearing on Crusoe's prospects—it raises the possibility of capitalist development on his little island. Such development is not certain but rather will depend on Crusoe's next decision: whether immediately to feast on the two fish or instead delay his gratification and save the second fish for the following day's meal. If he decides immediately to consume both fish, potential capitalist development is halted in its tracks. On the next day, Crusoe is "back to Go," that is, he must continue to expend all his resources, his labor and time, in the attempt to catch the daily fish he

---

[11] Although producers also generate demand for the specific inputs they utilize in the production of their final goods.

[12] See also "The Function of the Capitalist," pp. 131-139.

needs for survival. If, however, Crusoe is more self-disciplined and far-sighted, he will choose not to eat the second fish but rather save it. In that event, he begins to build his "capital" (savings), thereby enlarging the personal resources—the time and labor—he has at his disposal. On the following day, he will not have to use all his limited resources to catch a fish, as was the case up to this point. His decision to save the second fish means that he can now "invest" the time and labor he would normally expend toward catching his daily fish toward production of another good, that is, satisfaction of another need.

If he is truly wise, moreover, Crusoe will choose to invest his savings (capital) in the production of what economists call "producer" goods, that is, goods such as tools that are not suitable for immediate consumption but rather useful in the production of consumption goods. If Crusoe is a good capitalist, then, he will use the time and labor he has gained by delaying consumption of the second fish to, say, scour the island for material suitable for building a net. He cannot consume the net, but it will greatly facilitate his attempts to catch (consumable) fish in the future. Suppose, then, that Crusoe uses his savings—his additional time and labor—to build a net and manages on the following day to catch half a dozen fish with his new tool. He is now well on the way to even further capitalist development. The net, the tool, has enormously increased the productivity of his labor, and he reaps the benefits of such productivity as additional "wealth," in his case, additional time and labor. Now released from the daily necessity of catching a fish, Crusoe can employ such resources in the production of yet other goods that will further improve his condition, perhaps shelter, clothing, and so on. By choosing to save the second fish—the fruit of production beyond his subsistence needs—and further choosing to invest the additional time and labor so gained in the production of a non-consumable tool, Crusoe has increased his wealth and wellbeing. Indeed he has become a successful capitalist.

The Language of Price

We are now better prepared to resume discussion of the manner in which capitalism leads toward solution of the economic problem. As we recall, the right to private property presupposed by a market economy entitles both producers and consumers to make decisions regarding production and consumption. All production in a market economy is financed by the entrepreneur's personal savings (his "capital") or resources he can persuade other private individuals to lend him. Such capital, as we have seen, is acquired by raising personal productivity above the level of subsistence and saving rather than consuming the surplus so produced. Resources, however, including capital resources, are scarce by nature. Producers must thus be vigilant in employing their personally limited resources—their savings or capital—in the production of only such goods as are actually demanded by market participants, that is, consumers. In a market economy, producers are free, within the bounds of law, to produce as they see fit. Those who produce goods and services that consumers do not want, however, will be unable to sell them. Such production errors are undesirable from both the individual producer's point of view and that of society as a whole. A producer who makes wrong production decisions will personally suffer negative consequences. More particularly, he will suffer a loss rather than earn a profit, which means he will partially or totally lose his capital—the initial resources he invested to produce the goods in question. Such a producer, however, harms not only himself but also the greater good: he has wasted scarce resources that could rather have been employed in the production of goods or services that meet the actual needs and desires of his fellows.

Every production decision thus entails *risk*. Producers in a market economy can never be certain that their goods or services will in fact be desired by consumers. If potential buyers reject their offerings, they stand to suffer loss, loss of their personal resources. Producers thus have every incentive to make correct decisions, that is, produce goods and services that other individuals will voluntarily purchase. The risk inherent in every production decision is countered by the potential of reward. A producer who makes the right decisions—produces goods and services that other persons actually want and do purchase—stands to earn the reward of profit. Indeed, in a market economy, the possibility of earning profit is the principal motivation for production in general; the principal disincentive is of course the ever-accompanying threat of loss. Such incentives and disincentives are crucial elements of the market process. They foster rationality in economic decision-making by providing a self-regulating or self-enforcing mechanism that encourages careful utilization of scarce resources and discourages their waste. Profit and loss play a central role in the discovery of the "best" possible utilization of limited resources, defined, as we recall, as the most efficient or least-cost method of producing goods and services that consumers, in their own subjective judgment, actually need or want.

The question, however, remains—how is the producer to *know* which goods and services to produce, that is, which of myriad possibilities will actually be desired and purchased by consumers and whose production will yield profit rather than loss. In a free market, consumers cannot be forced to purchase any good or service; voluntariness, freedom, is the essence of market exchange. The prohibition of force means that no seller is permitted to put a gun, literal or figurative, to a potential buyer's head and demand his business; every buyer is free to purchase or not purchase as he wills. Thus producers must take care to bring to market only those items that appeal to consumers in such a way that they will voluntarily exchange their personal, and limited, resources for the sellers' wares. For this reason a market economy generates an astonishingly wide variety of goods and services, tailored to the individual preferences of consumers with dramatically different tastes. Producers, motivated by the possibility of profit (and fear of loss), strive to fill every possible niche for which there may exist potential buyers. The success of their efforts, however, depends not only on creativity and foresight but also the indispensable guidance provided by the impersonal forces of the market. More particularly, producers in a market economy are invariably guided in their production decisions by the key such force—the existence of a freely formed structure of relative prices.

"Prices," as previously observed, represent a kind of language, one that every normal person comes to understand without formal training or study. As the economic problem, at bottom, is a knowledge problem, so the price system, at bottom, is a carrier of knowledge, a system of communication that transmits relevant economic information spontaneously throughout society by means of the abstract signals or symbols called prices. The information summarized or condensed in relative prices is precisely what permits producers to know which goods and services to produce and consumers to know which goods and services will best meet their individual needs and wants, in line with the constraints imposed by their personally limited resources. Moreover, it is fair to assume that most people want to be good stewards of the earth. The knowledge and information embodied in prices serve that end by encouraging the optimum utilization of the scarce resources of the earth, that is, production of the goods and services most highly valued by members of society and, moreover, by the least-cost, most efficient method, with minimum waste of limited resources. Such can only be achieved if market participants, producer and consumer, possess accurate information regarding the relative scarcity or abundance of resources as well as the level of demand for particular goods and services. The only means to obtain such crucial information in the complex extended order of modern society is the language of price.

Price Formation

The next important issue concerns the manner in which prices are formed in a market economy. The prevailing relative price structure in a capitalist economy is formed as an unintended consequence of the independent actions of millions of individuals, those who participate in any form of market exchange, whether as consumer or producer or both. Indeed the vast majority of individuals wear both hats, that of consumer or buyer, and, if employed, that of producer or seller. Whenever an individual purchases or sells any good or service, he is not only affected by, but also affects, its price. It is obvious that every individual is affected by the price of an item when acting as a consumer; price is almost always taken into consideration when contemplating the purchase of any good or service. It is perhaps not as obvious, but just as true, that the price of any item is also affected by the action of the consumer, by his decision to purchase or not to purchase a particular good or service. The greater the number of individuals who purchase a particular item at any point in time, the greater the upward pressure on the price of the item in question, at least in the short run. In the formal language of economics, *ceteris paribus* (all other things remaining equal), increased demand leads to an increase in price. Conversely, the fewer the number of individuals who purchase a particular item at any given time, the greater the downward pressure on the price of the item in question, at least in the short run; *ceteris paribus*, decreased demand leads to a decrease in price. The source of the price movements in both cases, increase and decrease, is the voluntary choice—to buy or not to buy—made by individuals in their role as consumers. When consumers increase their demand for a product, its price tends to increase; when they no longer want it, its price tends to decrease.

Demand, however, is not the sole determinant of price; supply considerations also play a major role. Initiation of a change in relative prices can arise from either the "demand side" or the "supply side," from either buyers or sellers. Buyers exert upward pressure on prices, as said, when the general demand for a product increases and also through competitive bidding (offering a price higher than the seller's asking price). Sellers can affect prices by raising or lowering the asking prices for the particular products they sell, within limits. Producers are not absolutely autonomous in this regard; they cannot charge any price they want if they hope to remain in business. Most producers, for instance, have little control over the price of the inputs they use to produce their final product. They are "price takers" who must purchase the necessary inputs at prevailing market prices, which are affected by various factors beyond the control of an individual producer.

Suppose, for instance, that the price of an essential input rises due to a decrease in its availability (supply). Perhaps unfavorable weather has caused an unexpected failure of the Columbian coffee crop, decreasing this year's world supply of raw coffee beans. There are not as many coffee beans available for purchase this year as last year; not everyone who purchased them last year will be able to purchase them this year. Supply has decreased. One response will be competitive bidding among purchasers. Those buyers who most urgently desire the coffee beans may offer a higher price than those whose desire is less urgent, thereby exerting upward pressure on their price. Such an increase in price can also arise from the actions of sellers or producers of the beans. The unanticipated decrease in supply means that demand now exceeds supply, that is, more buyers exist than can be accommodated by the existing supply. Sellers thus can reasonably expect that some buyers will be willing to pay more to obtain the relatively limited supply and raise their price accordingly. In either case, whether the upward pressure on the price of coffee beans arises from buyers or sellers, all firms that use coffee beans in the production of their final product will have to pay more to obtain that input. Starbucks's production costs will increase. A producer such as Starbucks will usually attempt to pass such additional costs on to their customers, resulting in an increase in the retail price of the final product; consumers will have to pay more for Starbucks coffee. In the language of economics, *ceteris paribus*, a decrease in supply leads to an increase in price. Conversely, the price of an important input may fall. Perhaps exceptionally favorable weather produces a bumper crop of coffee beans, increasing the world supply and thus decreasing the cost. In a competitive market, sellers will pass these reduced costs on to the consumer and the price of the final good will fall. *Ceteris paribus,* an increase in supply leads to a decrease in price.

Price formation, then, results from the ongoing daily activities of market participants, in their roles as both producer and consumer. All consumers and producers of any good or service fluently read and speak the language of prices. In their role as consumers (a role simultaneously played by most producers, who are consumers of the inputs employed in their production processes), individuals announce, through their purchase or lack of purchase, their approval or disapproval of the manner in which scarce resources are being employed. Every individual who actually purchases a good or service is implicitly expressing approval of such usage, evidenced by his voluntary purchase of the good in question. The joint purchase of the same good or service by many individuals expresses widespread social approval of this particular use of scarce resources, an approval which manifests as upward pressure on the price of the good or service in question. In the same manner, every individual who refuses to purchase a particular good or service is implicitly expressing disapproval of the manner in which scarce resources are being employed, a judgment which manifests as downward pressure on the price of the unwanted item. Through the language of prices, consumers tacitly speak their minds. They tell producers either to "stop" or to "go," whether they want or do not want the fruits of his production, whether they approve or disapprove of the manner in which he is employing scarce resources.

Producers, also fluent in the language of prices, will hear their customers loud and clear. In a market economy, they heed such complaints not because of benevolence or concern with the common good but because they have no other choice. In a capitalist economy, the income of each and every producer is derived solely from the voluntary purchases made by his customers. If individuals utterly refuse to purchase his good or service, his income will fall to zero. Reduced sales will result in reduced income, possibly to the point of actual loss. The only way producers can avoid such loss is to produce goods or services that other persons actually want to purchase, the knowledge of which is conveyed to them through the language of relative prices.

Further Price Considerations

It is worth repeating that in a free market all purchases are voluntary; people cannot be coerced or forced to buy a good or service they do not want. We have also seen that employing scarce resources to produce goods and services that members of society do not value is wrong and wasteful from both an economic and social point of view and should be discouraged. Such a disciplinary function is admirably performed by a market economy. An individual or firm that wastes scarce resources by producing goods and services that other individuals do not value will be penalized not by government or law but rather the impersonal forces of the market. More specifically, such producers will incur losses (costs greater than revenue), which, if continued over time, will eventually force closure of the business. This spontaneous or automatic feature of the market process has been described as a self-regulating "feedback" mechanism that permits producers to know whether they are utilizing scarce resources wisely or foolishly. A seller who is doing the right thing—using scarce resources to produce goods and services people actually want—will be rewarded by increased sales and profits. A seller who is doing the wrong thing—wasting resources by producing goods and services people do not want—will be punished by decreased sales and losses and eventually forced out of business. Such is highly beneficial, if not for the individual producer, then for society as a whole. Producers who consistently make losses have proven by that very fact that they are not capable of directing scarce resources toward their best possible uses. Such producers should not be permitted to continue such resource misallocation, such waste of scarce resources, and market forces ensure their inability to do so. They will suffer losses, perhaps consume their capital, which means they no longer possess personal resources available for investment and production. The harm they have done is limited to their previous malinvestment.

Moreover, producers in a competitive market economy must strive for efficiency, that is, to produce their goods at the least possible cost. The concern with efficiency, like the concern with consumer taste and preference, is not due to kindness or benevolence but rather market necessity. A producer who is able to produce a particular good or service at lower cost has a competitive advantage over producers who use higher-cost inputs or methods: the former can charge a lower price for the good in question. *Ceteris paribus,* a decrease in price leads to an increase in demand; consumers will switch from the higher-cost producer to the lower-cost producer. No one must force or command producers in a market economy to make the right decisions—produce the goods and services people actually want with the least waste of scarce resources. They are led precisely in this direction by the impersonal forces of the market, in particular, the signal of profit or loss conveyed by freely forming relative prices, themselves a product of subjective human preference in conjunction with existing conditions of supply.

Capitalism or the market economy is often said to be characterized by *consumer sovereignty.* Such a concept refers to the fact that, ultimately, consumers guide production decisions by signaling their desire or aversion for particular goods and services via the language of prices. In a market economy, as mentioned, producers are of course free to produce whatever they want (within the bounds of law or regulation) but there is no guarantee they will be able to sell their goods and thus stay in business. Producers in a market economy must strive for profit, which is crucial to survival of their firm. Profit is certainly in the interest of the producer, but it can only be achieved by considering the interests, indeed catering to the preferences, of the consumer. Producers who fail to take their customers' preferences into account are punished by lack of sales and, ultimately, losses. Only those who correctly anticipate consumer needs and wants, and can satisfy them at the least possible cost, will flourish in a market economy. This is good from the perspective of both individual consumers and society as a whole—scarce resources should not be wasted by producing items that people do not value or at higher-than-necessary cost. The beneficent harmony of interest between producer and consumer characteristic of market exchange arises from the fact that profit can only be gained by accommodating the tastes and preferences of the buyer.

Let us recapitulate the argument thus far. The information conveyed through the language of relative prices permits "the market" to solve the first aspect of the economic problem—what to produce, and how. Producers know *what* they should produce, and with *what* inputs, because they can base such decisions on accurate information regarding conditions of demand and supply conveyed by the abstract language of relative prices. Prices tell producers *what* consumers actually value and also provide information about the relative scarcity or abundance of the inputs needed to produce the final goods and services. The information condensed in the relative price structure, moreover, permits producers to calculate profit and loss, the signals that indicate whether or not a given good or service is economically desirable to produce. An economically desirable good is one whose production yields a profit, that is, whose cost (the value of the resources necessary to produce it) is less than the revenue yielded by its sale (the value imputed to the good by the consumers). Producers can only perform their function—the direction of scarce resources toward least-cost production of the goods and services desired by consumers—if they have access to the information embodied in a freely formed structure of relative prices. Without the guidance of relative prices, producers would have no way of knowing either the needs and desires of consumers or the best—least wasteful—methods of producing them. They would be operating in the dark.

*

We previously noted that the language of prices is relied upon not only by producers but also individuals in their role as consumers. However little they may be aware of the fact, price considerations play a crucial role in orienting human action in daily life. Prices guide such action at every level, and a moment's reflection makes clear that price considerations of one kind or another are never far from the human mind. As always, the starting part of economic analysis begins with the fundamental fact from which all economic behavior and reasoning flow—the fact of scarcity. In the case of the consumer, it is clear that the resources held by any individual, like the resources of society at large and of nature itself, are characterized by scarcity. No human being possesses unlimited resources. Consequently, each individual confronts a personal economic problem similar to the economic problem of society as a whole. That is, the scarcity of individual resources forces each individual to choose—to decide among the myriad goods and services available on the market which he will actually purchase. Resources are limited; no one can have it all. Every individual must decide how to employ his personal scarce resources in a manner that will best meet his individual needs and preferences, with minimum expense. Such can only be achieved if the individual possesses relevant knowledge of available possibilities, knowledge again transmitted through the language of price.

No one wants to pay more for an item than necessary. The less one spends on any particular item, the more is available to purchase other goods and services, to fulfill other needs or desires. Such a fact may seem mere common sense, insultingly simple and elementary. It is only common knowledge, however, because everyone knows how to read the language of prices, whether they know anything of the laws of economics or not.

To further highlight the indispensable role of prices in guiding human action, consider the role of price considerations in one of the most fundamental of all life decisions—the choice of profession or career. In the absence of the information conveyed by a society's prevailing structure of relative prices, individuals would have little means of determining the best use of their talents and abilities in a manner compatible with the facts of social existence, that is, the relative scarcity and abundance of limited resources and the value placed upon such resources by their fellow men. When considering possible career choices, most persons attempt to find a profession they will enjoy and that permits development of their individual potential. Various options, however, always exist; rarely are a person's abilities so specialized that there is only one possible choice of profession open to him or her. Most people, moreover, not only want to find enjoyment in their work but also enjoy a secure income. To do so requires the development of skills that can be sold or traded on the market. Individuals entering the workforce must have something to offer to others, a good or service that other persons sufficiently value to be willing voluntarily to offer their own resources in exchange. An individual's choice of profession, then, is greatly facilitated by possessing knowledge of the value that other people place on various skills and services. Such information is embodied in relative prices, in particular, the salaries typically earned in various professions. Should a person aim for a career as a dishwasher at McDonald's or an accountant at Price Waterhouse? Such a question may seem silly—everyone knows the latter position would not only be more fulfilling but also more lucrative. Again, however, how does everyone know this? They know it because everyone understands the language of price. Everyone knows that accountants earn more than dishwashers precisely because they have more or less effortlessly learned to read and speak the language of prices.

In the absence of the information conveyed by market prices, individuals would have no way of knowing the relative financial reward of developing the skills of a dishwasher or an accountant. They would have no way of knowing how their particular talents and abilities can be employed in a manner compatible with the values of their fellows, as indicated by the amount the latter are willing to pay for the skill in question. Nor would they have any way of knowing how their particular talents and skills mesh with the facts of existence, in this case, the relative scarcity or abundance of dishwashing and accounting skills. They would have no way of knowing how to incorporate their own abilities into the more comprehensive economic and social order within which each person necessarily exists; no man is an island. A salary is a price like any other price, and the labor market a market like any other market. Relative salaries reflect both the scarcity or abundance of particular skills and the value placed on them by members of society; the higher the salary, the greater its value to one's fellows or the greater its scarcity. Moreover, certain types of work are essential for human survival. In the absence of relative price signals that serve to guide individuals into professions of greatest value to their fellows, individuals would have to be directed toward essential professions or occupations by some external authority. In other words, there could be no free or voluntary choice of profession without the indispensable guidance provided by the prevailing structure of relative prices.

Prices, then, represent a universal language that guides every individual's personal and professional decisions in a profound manner. They are a means of enabling individuals to exercise freedom—voluntary choice—with respect to both everyday needs and wants and larger concerns such as choice of profession. In the absence of freely forming relative prices in a world characterized by scarcity, people would be unable to orient their individual actions in a manner consistent with either the facts of existence or the values and actions of their fellows. Price considerations cannot be avoided. Every person, like the world as a whole, has limited resources and an interest in choosing the least-cost means of satisfying his needs and desires. The information conveyed by prices permits human beings to do so with minimum effort and in a manner that takes account of the relative scarcity or abundance of resources. The price system not only permits individuals to make sound economic decisions regarding their own limited resources but also serves a wider social function. Through its operation, individuals, whether acting as consumers or producers, are led, quite without conscious awareness, to behave precisely as they should behave from the point of view of society as a whole, that is, efficiently employing scarce resources in the production of goods and services that people subjectively value. Last but not least among such considerations, the guidance of relative prices also permits them to do so in freedom.

The Market Process in Action

We have said that the market provides a solution to the economic problem arising from scarcity. It should be clear, however, that such can only be true in a metaphorical sense. The market is not a "thing" or a conscious, willing entity capable of devising solutions or, indeed, of any form of agency. It is rather a metaphor for an impersonal social process that unfolds over time within a framework of general rules and institutional arrangements and leads individual human beings to contribute to the solution of the economic problem.

The operation of such a process may be further elucidated by considering a second hypothetical (if fanciful) example of how market relations lead market participants to solve the economic problem in practice, spontaneously, without conscious direction by central or political authority. Imagine that the American people awake one morning to news of an astonishing scientific breakthrough: it has been discovered that persons who drink eight ounces of orange juice a day will live to the age of 150 while maintaining the beauty and vigor of a thirty-year-old. Assume that such a finding is now regarded as established, unquestionable, scientific fact; the "fountain of youth" has at long last been discovered, and it is orange juice. This is certainly an unexpected change of circumstance. New knowledge has been acquired which, like most forms of knowledge, will entail significant economic consequences.

The remarkable scientific discovery will significantly impact the social process called the market, both immediately and over time, in both the short-run and long-run. Consider, first, the immediate and short-run effects. As news of the discovery gradually spreads throughout the nation, more and more people learn of the newfound benefits of orange juice. Local stores will soon be swamped with customers seeking to buy a gallon or two; demand for orange juice suddenly and dramatically increases. If the market is permitted to operate, the unanticipated increase in demand will initially be expressed through upward pressure on the retail price of orange juice. The rise in price can be initiated in several ways. Suppose a crowd of people descend on the local Walmart to purchase orange juice. Everyone wants to purchase the juice, but the shelves are rapidly emptying and immediate supply is limited (Walmart and other retailers had no advance warning of the sudden and huge increase in demand). Further suppose the existence of a customer who is particularly eager to obtain a gallon of juice. He wants the juice *today* but is concerned about the rapidly diminishing supply. In order to ensure that he will be obtain a gallon, he offers the salesclerk a price higher than the listed or asking price. The seller has no reason to reject such an offer. Other people follow suit and offer even higher prices for the juice. The price will continue to rise until it reaches a level beyond which there are no further bids; no one is willing to pay more. Alternatively, the increase in price can arise from the seller's side. An alert store clerk may notice that juice at the initial (pre-news release) price is disappearing from the shelves. He may decide to raise the price of the existing supply and observe whether customers continue to purchase it. If buying proceeds despite the price rise, he will continue to raise the price up to the point beyond which it no longer sells. No one— buyer or seller—knows in advance the ultimate price of the juice, only that it will be higher than the initial price. Precise quantitative changes in relative prices can never be predicted with certainty but only general patterns, in this case, that increase in demand will manifest as increase in price.

In the short run, the existing supply of orange juice is necessarily limited. Producers cannot snap their fingers and instantaneously produce more at will; the production of any particular good or service, like the market order more generally, is also a process, that is, unfolds over time. Consequently, not everyone who wants orange juice in the short run will be able to buy it. The existing (limited) supply of orange juice will be obtained by the highest bidders, that is, those persons who place the greatest value on the juice as demonstrated by their willingness to pay a higher price for it. Recall, again, that economic value is always subjective value. What is the value of a gallon of orange juice? It depends. In the case under consideration, the perceived subjective value of the juice may be lower for a twenty-year-old than for a person of advanced years. The elderly may long to recapture youth as soon as possible and thus willing to pay more for the juice than young adults. In any event, the existing juice supply will be distributed to those persons who value it most highly, as they themselves subjectively evaluate the good and as evidenced by their willingness to pay the highest price.

The initial rise in the retail price of orange juice, however, only begins the story of how the market process spontaneously adapts to the ever-changing circumstances of existence, including discovery of knowledge. The market, again, is a process, and processes, unfolding over time, necessarily involve both short-run and long-run considerations. Day One of the new discovery will be followed by Days Two and Three and so on, into the long-run. On Day One, as we have seen, the sudden increase in demand will put upward pressure on the price of orange juice at the retail level, and the existing supply of orange juice will be obtained by those who value it most highly. At the end of Day One, the shelves are empty of orange juice. Every retail store that carries the product is in more or less the same situation as Walmart, and all of them will try to replenish their stocks. Most retailers do not themselves produce orange juice but rather purchase it from a wholesaler or distributor; they will undoubtedly be contacting their suppliers to order more juice to restock their shelves. No one must command or force them to do so. Sellers are in business to make a profit, and, *ceteris paribus*, an increase in the price of the products they sell leads, in the short run, to increase in their profits.[13] Retail sellers of orange juice thus have every personal incentive to meet the increased demand for orange juice by increasing their supply: they personally stand to benefit through increased profit.

The actions of individual retailers are motivated by individual self-interest, but such self-regarding actions nevertheless, unwittingly and simultaneously, also serve both the interests of their particular customers and the common interest of society as a whole. That is, retailers, along with all others involved in the production and distribution of orange juice, are led by impersonal market forces to do precisely what they *should* do, not only for their own benefit but also that of their customers and the community at large, namely, increase the supply of orange juice to meet the newly increased demand. Indeed, one of the many celebrated achievements of a market economy is the spontaneous coincidence of individual and social well-being, a feature notably highlighted by Adam Smith and explored more thoroughly in a following section.

On Day Two of the market process, the experience of the retailers on Day One will be duplicated in the experience of wholesale sellers of orange juice. Wholesalers will experience an unexpected increase in demand for their product, suddenly receiving far more orders than usual. As occurred with retail sales of the previous day, the increase in demand at the wholesale level will lead to an increase in the wholesale price of orange juice. Again, either potential buyers (Walmart, et al.) will offer more than the seller's asking price or sellers will raise the price in the face of the sudden increase in demand. However initiated, the wholesale price of orange juice will rise. Moreover, the existing supply of orange juice at the wholesale level, like that at the retail level, is limited in the short run. The retailers who will obtain a portion of this limited supply will be those willing to pay the highest price for it, the price that reflects their subjective judgment of its value. Those who value the juice more highly will offer a higher price than those who value it less. At the end of Day Two, the wholesalers, like the retailers on the preceding day, will find their warehouses empty of orange juice. The wholesalers, motivated like the retailers by the possibility of increased profit, can thus be expected to contact their suppliers, perhaps firms that specialize in bottling orange juice.

On Day Three, the bottlers will thus experience, like the retailers and wholesalers on Days One and Two respectively, an unexpected increase in demand for their product, which will lead to an increase in the price of bottled orange juice. Motivated by the possibility of profit, these producers will try to increase the existing supply of bottled juice to meet the increased demand. On Day Four they will be placing additional orders with their suppliers, say, firms that produce concentrated orange pulp to make into juice. Such increased demand will lead to an increase in the price of orange pulp, just as previously occurred for orange juice at the retail and wholesale levels and for bottled juice. Motivated by the possibility of profit, producers of orange pulp will try to meet the increased demand for their product by increasing production. They will no doubt place additional orders with orange growers (oranges are of course a major input in the production of orange pulp), and the price of oranges will tend to rise. Orange growers, motivated by the possibility of increased profit due to the rise in the price of their product, will attempt to expand production of oranges, perhaps purchasing additional farmland or hiring additional workers which, in turn, will lead to a rise in the price of those factors of production. The initial rise in price at the retail level will engender similar changes all along the complex chain of production typical of modern capitalist production processes.

An extensive and intricate process has been set in motion that spreads itself spontaneously throughout the market economy. The initial impetus was the discovery of the health benefits of orange juice. This led to an increase in demand for orange juice, manifested and communicated throughout the chain of production via the simple language of prices, first at the retail and later at the wholesale level, through the bottlers and other intermediaries, down to the orange growers and field hands themselves. At every link in the chain of production, producers know precisely how to read this language—an increase in the price of their respective product means an increase in their respective profit. The possibility of further profit motivates producers and leads each firm to do precisely what it should do—take steps to increase the quantity of its particular product. The overarching goal is to increase the supply of retail orange juice in order to meet increased consumer demand. The extensive specialization and division of labor that characterize a market economy, however, means that such a goal can only be realized by the cooperation of many different producers, as well as a rational coordination of their individual activities (e.g., the quantity of orange juice should not exceed or fall short of the available number of plastic jugs). At every stage of the market process, each individual producer of any input involved in the production of a gallon of orange juice is led by impersonal market forces (price movements) and his individual self-interest (profit) to behave precisely as he should behave from the point of view of consumers and society at large, that is, direct scarce resources toward production of goods most highly valued by consumers, in this case, the various inputs involved in the production and distribution of orange juice.

The complexity of the process cannot be overstated. The retailers, wholesalers, bottlers, pulp manufacturers, and orange growers will not be the only producers to experience sudden and unexpected demand for their products, initiated by the increased demand for orange juice at the retail level. It is difficult if not impossible to trace all of the individuals and industries involved in bringing additional supplies of juice to consumers at the local grocery store. The producers of orange pulp, for instance, may have to purchase new machines if they wish to increase production. This will increase demand for such machines and thus their price, which in turn will lead manufacturers of the machines to increase production. The machine-manufacturers may have to hire additional labor to do so, as will the orange growers and pulp producers, who will need additional workers to plant and pick the oranges and process the pulp. The increased demand for workers will put upward pressure on the price of labor; wages relating to employment in the orange-juice industry will increase to attract the workers needed to meet the increased demand for the final product. Firms that make plastic jugs will similarly experience an unexpected increase in demand for their product, which in turn will increase demand for the chemicals used in the production of plastic. The same will hold true for firms that produce paper labels; firms that make the ink used to print the paper labels and the glue that attaches them to the jug; firms that produce the wood pulp used to make the paper labels; transportation firms that carry the juice to the retail stores; manufacturers of tires used on such trucks; producers of the rubber used as an input for tires; tool makers who produce the machines necessary for juice processing; machinists who operate them, and so on. It is scarcely possible for the human mind to identify all of the thousands if not millions of people who will ultimately be involved in the seemingly simple act of increasing the supply of orange juice at the local grocery store.

Moreover, the knowledge required to initiate and guide the market process is minimal and spontaneously transmitted to all relevant parties. For instance, none of the individuals and firms involved in the production process need know anything about the newly discovered benefits of orange juice. The market process efficiently summarizes all knowledge relevant to their activities in the abstract symbol of a "price." The only information needed by individual producers is that the price of their particular good or service, for whatever reason, has increased. The increase in the price of their particular product, whether orange pulp, trucking services, manual labor, processing of chemicals for plastic, and so on, means a potential increase in the profitability of their individual activity. Their self-interested desire to earn greater income leads them to take precisely the action the market "requests." The ultimate result of the intricate process will be an increased supply of orange juice at the retail stores, precisely as demanded by consumers. Along with the essential preconditions of the market previously discussed, all that is required to achieve such a result is the spontaneous transmission of the information condensed in relative prices, information accumulated and transmitted through individual acts of buying and selling, and the fact that human nature is so constituted that, *ceteris paribus*, every person would prefer a higher to a lower income.[14]

Surplus and Shortage

The next issue to consider is how market forces lead to the production not only of more orange juice but the correct *quantity* of orange juice, that is, the amount consumers actually wish to purchase, no more and no less. More formally stated, the issue is how market forces prevent surplus (quantity supplied exceeds consumer demand) and shortage (quantity supplied insufficient to meet consumer demand). The market, as we shall see, is self-regulating in this regard as in others. In the long run, the spontaneous forces of the market tend toward the elimination of both surplus and shortage and this without need for intervention of authority. The market process will lead spontaneously not only to production of more orange juice, as demanded, but also in the quantity demanded by consumers.

To explain this aspect of the market process, it is necessary to introduce a formal economic term, what economists refer to as a "normal rate of return."[15] Profit and loss are calculated, of course, by subtracting total costs of production from total revenue (earnings received from sales). The "normal rate of return" is the percentage of profit an investor expects to earn ("return on investment") by investing his capital (savings) in a relatively risk-free asset, such as a bank certificate of deposit or a

---

[14] Assuming that the institutional requirements of the market—private property, the rule of law, and mutual trust—are in place.

[15] In finance, rate of return (ROR), also known as return on investment (ROI), rate of profit or sometimes just return, is the ratio of money gained or lost on an investment relative to the amount of money invested. The amount of money gained or lost may be referred to as interest, profit/loss, gain/loss, or net income/loss. The money invested may be referred to as the asset, capital, principal, or the cost basis of the investment. ROI is usually expressed as a percentage rather than a fraction.

stable and mature industry not experiencing growth or decline. The normal rate of return can vary *across* industries. Over time, however, the rate of return *within* various industries tends to stabilize—to become the "normal" return expected from investing in a particular business or industry. In our example, prior to the unexpected increase in demand for orange juice, investors in the production of orange juice earned more or less the same rate of return, the "normal rate" for investment in the long-established and stable orange-juice industry. The sudden change in demand, however, led to upward pressure on prices of goods and services related to orange-juice production, price movements that changed—increased—the rate of return on investment in the orange-juice industry. As we have seen, in the short run, producers in every firm directly or indirectly involved in the production of the final retail good, orange juice, experience a rise in the price of their respective products. This means that their profits will rise and thus the rate of return on investment in their firms will rise. The fortunate producers and investors who initially experience an unexpected increase in demand for their products will, in the short run, earn a greater-than-normal return. In everyday language, they are now earning greater profits than before. Such economic actors are in an enviable position, but their good fortune is transitory. Such short-run effects will not endure over the long run.

In every developed market economy, people seek profitable opportunities for investment. Capitalist investors want to earn the maximum possible rate of return, and they scour the earth looking for the best—most profitable—investment opportunities. They are guided in such investment decisions by the price system. In our example, the increased profitability of investment in the orange-juice industry will quickly become public knowledge, entering the social process through changes in the structure of relative prices. Investors will compare the now-higher rate of return in the orange-juice industry with rates of return in other industries. They learn that investment in orange juice and related industries is now more profitable than investment in industries that have not experienced a comparable rise in demand. We have seen that all producers involved in the orange-juice industry have experienced increased profitability due to the increase in demand for their products, which means they are temporarily earning higher-than-normal rates of return. Other investors will want a share of this newly enlarged pie. Capital resources will flow into production of orange juice

57

and related industries, eventually resulting in the production of more orange juice (as well as more oranges, pulp machines, plastic jugs, and so on).

Such investment is motivated, once again, by the self-interested desire for profit. Once again, however, it is also precisely what is desired from the point of view of consumers and society as a whole. The market process was set in motion precisely because consumers want more orange juice than formerly, and this requires that scarce resources be directed or redirected toward its production. Over time, the market responds by increasing investment in the orange-juice industry through the lure of potentially increased profit, thereby increasing the supply of the juice and necessary inputs.

Such an increase in investment and supply, however, is not infinite. It is safe to assume that demand will eventually stabilize at the point where enough orange juice is produced to satisfy the desires of all market participants. As supply increases over time, in conjunction with stable demand, the price of orange juice and related factors will tend to fall from their initial high (*ceteris paribus*, an increase in supply leads to a decrease in price). As such prices begin to fall, so does the rate of return on their production. Additional resources will continue to be invested in orange-juice production so long as the rate of return in that industry remains above the normal rate. As more and more supply enters the market, however, enticed by the above-normal rates of return, the price of orange juice and its inputs will continue to decline. Additional investment in orange-juice production will ultimately cease when prices fall to such a level that investors earn no more than the normal rate of return. The orange-juice industry will stabilize at this point. The final result of the market process will be an increased supply of orange juice, in more or less the correct quantity relative to demand, and at the lowest price necessary to produce it. All consumers who want orange juice will be able to purchase it; there will be no shortage. Sellers will not be saddled with lakes of orange juice they cannot sell; there will be no surplus. If a shortage should exist (demand exceeds supply), prices will rise and producers, in pursuit of profit, will be led to increase production, as discussed. If a surplus should exist (supply exceeds demand), prices will fall, and producers, aiming to minimize their losses, will be led to cut back on production. The self-regulating forces intrinsic to the market spontaneously tend toward elimination of both shortage and surplus.

Such, then, is the market process, the manner in which the market operates over time to adjust production to consumer demand and with the least possible waste of scarce resources. It should again be emphasized that the entire chain of events proceeds spontaneously, that is, without the conscious oversight or direction of any central authority. There is no need for a government "czar" to direct the orange-juice industry to meet the increase in demand. Each and every individual and firm involved is led to do precisely what it should do by pursuing individual self-interest, secured by property rights and guided by the movement of relative prices. Prices tell the producers *what* to produce—the orange juice the consumers urgently want, reflected in the increase in its price. Prices also tell producers *how* to efficiently produce the orange juice and related factors. In determining the best, most economic, way of producing an item, producers calculate their costs in terms of prevailing market prices. In order to increase their profitability, they will strive to use the lowest-priced inputs whenever possible. No one has to force them to conserve scarce resources; it is in their own interest to do so, since their profit depends in part on their costs of production. Moreover, all producers in a market economy seek to reduce the price of their good or service so far as possible; *ceteris paribus*, the lower the final price, the greater the demand for their product.

That is only to say that the market process is characterized by *competition*. Market competition, contrary to popular misconception, does not involve battle or conflict. Competition among producers serves both society in general and the consumer in particular. The threat to a firm's profitability posed by the superior skill of existing competitors or potential entrance of new competitors ensures that any producer not utilizing least-cost methods of production, in service of actual consumer needs and wants, will be challenged by another firm that does so. A producer who faces competition from a rival who can produce the same good at lower cost, or a higher quality good at the same cost, will lose customers and sales, and perhaps be forced out of business. Market competition ensures that consumers do not have to settle for inferior goods or pay more for a good or service than is necessary to produce it. It further serves to ensure that scarce resources are used as efficiently as possible, an outcome that benefits not only consumers but society as a whole. All that is required is that potential competitors are free to enter or exit a given industry at will.

Finally, the price system also facilitates resolution of the third aspect of the economic problem: the problem of "distribution"—*who* is to receive the fruits of production. We have seen that in a market economy, the goods and services produced will be obtained by those persons willing to pay the highest price for them or, in venues that do not permit competitive bidding, by those willing to pay the price asked by the seller. No one is forced to purchase or prohibited from purchasing an item legally for sale in the market. Each individual evaluates the asking price of a good or service and decides for himself whether, in his own subjective judgment, the item is worth the price. That is only to say that in a market economy, individual consumers themselves solve the problem of distribution; they themselves determine "who gets what." Indeed the very concept of economic "distribution" of goods and services is meaningless within a market economy. The concept of "distribution" of course implies a "distributor," that is, an agent capable of conscious selection or choice. In a market economy, however, no one "distributes" any economic good to anyone (with the possible exception of intra-familial relations).[16] As will be further discussed in the following chapter, the concept of economic distribution is only meaningful within a planned or command economy controlled and directed by centralized political authority, for instance, communist and quasi-communist forms of economic organization. In a capitalist or market economy, on the contrary, no central authority consciously or deliberately "distributes" material goods or services to any particular person or group, that is, no governmental administrator decides which particular members of society shall receive which particular fruits of production. In a market order, each individual decides for himself.

The Invisible Hand

In 1776 Adam Smith published his seminal treatise on the operation of the market system, *An Inquiry into the Nature and Causes of the Wealth of Nations*. Among other major contributions, Smith highlighted the

---

[16] Parents may engage in the conscious selection of goods that they subsequently "distribute" among their children.

remarkable self-regulating and self-coordinating aspects of the market process, encapsulated in his celebrated metaphor of the "Invisible Hand." We have seen how the guidance of prices permits human beings to employ scarce resources efficiently and toward production of items most highly valued by consumers. Smith perceived a further beneficent feature of the market process. As he observed the daily interaction of buyers and sellers in his small Scottish town, he was struck by the fact that market participants, as previously noted, were led, in their own self-interest, unintentionally and simultaneously to serve both their fellows' interests and those of society as a whole, and this without any explicit direction from authority. The market order thus seemed to him marked by Providence, guided by an "invisible hand" that spontaneously produces harmony of interest among buyers and sellers as an unintended consequence of their individually self-interested motivations and actions.

Smith further perceived that the market system is not only efficient, rational, and conducive of interpersonal harmony but also commendable in a moral sense. More specifically, it provides the additional *moral* benefit of transforming or channeling purely self-regarding interests into actions beneficial to others. A market economy particularly serves to restrain the human propensity for selfishness—the tendency to consider only one's self and one's personal well-being and not also the wellbeing of others. Smith, like the American Founders, accepted human nature as it is. Neither he nor the Americans dreamed of attempting the impossible—transforming human beings into angels or selfless "servants of Humanity." Human nature was regarded as given and fixed. Human beings are constitutionally self-directing and self-regarding, and this is not subject to change. "Self-interest rightly understood," as Tocqueville later expressed the general idea, is a sure spring of human action—a core motivation of every human being—and rightly so.[17] Human beings always strive to pursue their own purposes and further their own wellbeing, and there is nothing intrinsically immoral about that fact. Smith's great discovery, however, was that individual self-interest, while inevitable, can also be made to serve the interest and wellbeing of other

---

[17] Alexis de Tocqueville, *Democracy in America*, trans, ed, intro, Harvey C. Mansfield and Delba Winthrop (Chicago: University of Chicago Press, 2000 [1835]), p. 500.

human beings, a harmony spontaneously achieved through the "invisible hand" of the market.

It is thus ironic that one of the chief moral allegations raised against capitalism in subsequent centuries is its purported encouragement of "selfishness." Modern society is saturated with caricatures of the market economy drawn by its enemies. Most Americans, for instance, are familiar with the figures of the heartless "capitalist pig" and "fat cats" of Wall Street motivated solely by greedy and selfish desire for personal profit and gain. The anti-capitalist animus conveyed by such images is a commonplace of modern culture at least since the time of Karl Marx. The irony stems from the fact that early theorists of the market, including Smith, regarded capitalism not as conducive to selfishness but rather ameliorative of that moral propensity. One of the special virtues of the market, Smith suggests, is precisely its ability to restrain the human propensity for selfishness while, moreover, simultaneously channeling selfish motives into actions that enhance the wellbeing of other persons.

The following example will illustrate the manner by which the market yields such a moral benefit. Imagine a young man contemplating his life plan, searching for a way to achieve happiness for himself and perhaps also his loved ones. The young man, like most persons, will be confronted by the need to earn a living. Everyone understands that fulfillment of their values requires certain material means; it is difficult to live a happy life if continually on the verge of starvation. Unless a person has inherited significant wealth, his attention is thus immediately drawn to choice of profession. Human beings, moreover, desire more than mere survival; they further want to thrive and flourish. They seek not only to earn an income but also a trade or profession that will allow pursuit of personal interests and propensities, development of their unique potential. Human beings are not interchangeable cogs in a wheel, but individuals who vary widely in values, abilities, and interests. They will generally consider such personal characteristics in light of their potential ability to obtain a source of income.

Suppose our young man has a talent for baking and greatly enjoys that activity. He thus conceives the idea of becoming a baker and eventually owning his own bakery and sets his mind to realizing that goal. His motivation is entirely self-interested. The young man desires personal happiness and financial wellbeing and hopes to fulfill such desires by means of a congenial profession that also generates sufficient income to live a pleasant life. He is not considering the welfare of others but solely his own; some might call this "selfish." Further assume that the young baker eventually succeeds in establishing his own bakery. While he been successful in achieving his intermediary goal (owning a bake store), he has not yet realized his ultimate goal (happiness and financial wellbeing). Owning a bakery is a necessary but not sufficient condition of his ultimate success. Whether or not he achieves personal and material wellbeing depends not only upon his own skill and determination to pursue a profession he loves, but also upon his fellow men. No man is an island, least of all those who live in modern liberal society wherein human activity is coordinated by market exchange. In a market economy, the realization of the young man's personal life plan will depend not only on the establishment of his bakery but also his ability to thereby make a living. The interdependence among members of a market economy means that his ultimate success depends only in part on his personal dedication, skills, and preferences. To achieve ultimate success he will also have to take into account his fellow men.

To better perceive the situation, let us assume the young baker particularly enjoys making cheesecake and wants to specialize in its production. He himself loves cheesecake, takes great pleasure in its creation and is highly skilled in its production. In a market economy, such factors may or may not be helpful to our aspiring baker but, in either case, they will not alone ensure his success. His personal tastes and skills in this regard are not decisive. In the market, as we have seen, the consumer is sovereign. That is, the young baker who hopes to achieve his life plan—happiness and material security—must not only possess relevant skills and motivation but also produce goods that other persons, his customers, actually and voluntarily purchase. In a free society ordered by market exchange, as said, no person can be forced to purchase any seller's goods, however high their quality or however important they may seem to the producer. It is possible that people simply do not care for cheesecake and refuse to purchase it. In that case, our baker must overcome his self-interested or even "selfish" desire to produce cheesecake. He may in fact produce the best cheesecake in the world, and love doing so, but such is irrelevant if his potential customers do not want it. If he aims to earn a living as a baker, then, he must put aside personal tastes and preferences and consider instead the subjective preferences of other persons, what *they* might want. Such, according to Smith, is more or less the manner in which the market serves to restrain rather than encourage selfishness. Producers who want to be successful are forced to consider not their own needs and desires but those of their potential customers. There is no other way for our baker (or any other producer in a market economy) to achieve his personal goal—the profit through which he hopes to gain happiness and material security.

The young baker in a market economy faces the further problem of competition from other bakers or potential bakers. His goal of earning a living through operating his own bakery can only be achieved by offering his customers products that they both subjectively value *and* prefer over those of his competitors. In order to win their business, he must produce either better products, better in the subjective judgment of the consumer, or items identical to his competitors' but at a lower price. Producers certainly do not welcome such competition. Smith, in fact, was among the first economic theorists to highlight the fact that capitalism, contrary to popular misconception, chiefly serves the interests not of producers or "businessmen" but rather consumers. Market competition spontaneously leads producers to further benefit their fellow men by providing them with opportunities to purchase either better products or identical products at lower cost. Such is generally not the intention of any producer, whose aim is not to help his fellows but rather further his personal self-interest, that is, gain profit. In a market economy, however, a producer can only further his own self-interest by serving the consumers; as we shall see, there is no other way to earn income or profit in a society ordered by market exchange. Every producer's income is entirely dependent on the value that *other* persons place on the goods or services he provides.[18] Producers can only realize their personal goals by successfully meeting their customers' needs and desires, providing them with products superior to that which they can find elsewhere, in their own subjective judgment.

Such is the relation that spontaneously produces the harmony of interest among buyers and sellers in a market economy so brilliantly captured by Smith's famous metaphor. Observing such unintended harmony, it seemed to Smith as if producers in a market economy are guided by an "invisible hand" that leads them to channel their self-

---

[18] Again, leaving aside inherited wealth.

interested and even selfish desires, such as the desire for personal profit, into actions beneficial to their fellow men, namely, providing them with the particular goods and services they themselves (subjectively) value. It seemed to Smith as though a higher power, nature or God, were involved in the design of a system as beneficent as the market order, a system that spontaneously, without conscious intent, leads to social harmony and mutual wellbeing among members of society.

The Determination of Income

We next turn to explore yet another important if frequently misunderstood dimension of capitalism, namely, the manner in which individual income is determined in a market economy. Why do celebrated basketball players such as Michael Jordan earn multimillions of dollars and a fast-food worker at McDonald's barely enough to sustain his existence? Critics of capitalism commonly allege that an economic system that permits such wide disparities of income is somehow unfair or otherwise morally suspect. In order to evaluate the justice of such charges, it is essential to understand how income is determined in a free society ordered by market exchange.

We have seen that the income of the baker in the prior example is ultimately determined by the value that other persons, his customers, place on the goods and services he provides. His income consists solely in the revenue he derives from voluntary purchase of his products. Such holds true not only for the baker but for every person employed in a market economy. There is basically one, and only one, way to earn income in a capitalist economy—to produce a good or service that other persons will voluntarily purchase because they subjectively perceive its value as equal to or greater than its asking or purchase price. We have repeatedly emphasized that in a market economy *all* exchange is voluntary; force is prohibited by definition. No one is permitted to put a literal or metaphorical gun to another person's head and coerce him to purchase a particular good or service, whether a concrete material item or the skills and abilities embodied in another person's "labor." An individual who does not want to purchase a particular item may simply refrain from purchasing it, which of course happens on a daily basis. An individual who chooses, on the contrary, to purchase an item demonstrates by the very act of purchase that he would rather have that item than the resources (usually money) he must exchange for it. His partner in trade—the seller on the other side of the transaction—demonstrates the converse, that he would rather have the money than the item in question. A market exchange will occur if, and only if, both conditions are met. If either buyer or seller is unhappy with the proposed terms of trade, either of them can, and often do, refuse to trade.

Exchange on the free market *always* benefits both buyer and seller, in their own subjective judgment; otherwise it would not occur. Such mutual benefit is of the essence of market exchange; provided that the previously discussed preconditions of a market economy are met, it *always* results in a "win-win" situation. Market exchange or trade improves the subjective wellbeing of both parties to a transaction and does so in a manner that honors the individual freedom—the ability to act in a voluntary manner—of both buyer and seller. This of course is one of the principal reasons why valorization of individual freedom typically involves concurrent valorization of the market economy.

In a society ordered by market exchange, we have seen that the income of any individual is only partially a consequence of his own abilities and efforts. Individual income is also dependent upon the values and choices of other persons, in particular, the subjective value that market participants, buyers or consumers, place upon the individual producer's skill or ability. More specifically, the income of every individual is impersonally, unintentionally, and jointly determined by all those consumers who purchase the good or service in whose production the individual is directly or indirectly involved. Producers or sellers may of course be either self-employed or employees of a firm owned by other persons. The category includes not only individuals who personally provide concrete goods to consumers (such as the baker) but also those who provide nonmaterial skills and talents ("labor," knowledge, and other immaterial services). "Employees" of all kinds are producers or sellers in this sense and "employers" the corresponding buyers of their skills and talents. The income of an employee, like that of all producers in a market economy, is determined by the value that *other persons* place on his particular skills or services—the proximate value perceived by the employer which, in turn, is a function of the ultimate value perceived by the consumer of the final good or service produced by the firm.

The fact that individual income is ultimately determined by consumers is most readily perceived in the case of a person who is self-employed, whose sole source of income is the payment he receives from his customers for the good or service he directly provides to them. The baker in our previous example is a case in point. It is obvious that one hundred percent of the self-employed baker's income is derived from sale of his baked goods to his customers. If they are pleased with his products he may attract more customers and his income will increase. If customers are dissatisfied, they will no longer purchase from him, and his income will decrease. He is of course free to offer his goods at whatever price he chooses but, again, no one can be forced to purchase them. Customers will only do so if they regard the value of the baker's goods as equal to or greater than his asking price. In the final analysis, the income of the baker is entirely dependent upon the perceived or subjective value of his goods to those who purchase them. His customers determine his income.

The baker's income, like the income of every individual in a capitalist economy, is not intentionally "distributed" to him by any conscious human agent but is rather an impersonal and largely unintended byproduct of market exchange. The baker's customers jointly determine his income as a consequence of their decision to purchase his goods. Buyers, like sellers, are generally self-interested; they generally purchase a product because they need or want it, not to provide income to its producer.[19] Indeed, even if one's aim were to increase the income of a particular producer, it would be difficult to do so in an advanced capitalist order. It is rarely possible to know the identity of those responsible for the production of most goods and services, especially those indirectly involved in their production, in the spatially extended order of the modern market. We have discussed the complexity of the market process, involving as it does thousands if not millions of individuals in the mere production of a gallon of orange juice. The intricacy of a far-flung global market order means that income determination in a developed market economy is not, and cannot be, the result of conscious decision on the part of any person or persons. It is rather an unintended and impersonal outcome of voluntary market exchange. The prevailing pattern of income distribution in a market-based society is a spontaneous consequence of the actions of countless individuals pursuing their own self-interest, purchasing goods and

---

[19] There may of course be occasional exceptions, cases in which customers deliberately purchase from a given seller in order to assist that person financially

services to which they subjectively attach value, individuals who possess neither knowledge of the particular persons responsible for production nor the intent to affect their income.

We previously noted the relative ease of perceiving the relation between the income of a self-employed individual and the value placed on his goods or services by his customers. It is not as easy to perceive the same relation in the case of an individual employed by a firm or other large organization. Nevertheless, the same factors determine individual income in either case—self-employment or employment in a business owned by others. The income of individual employees, like the income of the self-employed, is ultimately determined by the value imputed by the firm's customers to the final good or service produced by the firm. The self-employed personally retain one hundred percent of total receipts from sales to customers. Individual employees of a business firm, by contrast, receive only a portion of the proceeds from all sales of the final good or service, one proportionate to the value of their particular contributions to the production of the final good or service.

*

A concrete example may clarify the impersonal process of income determination in a complex market economy that includes not only the self-employed but also numerous firms and corporate enterprises, large and small. Consider a common everyday event: an individual stops by the grocery store after work to pick up a few items, say, a gallon of milk and Fancy Feast cat food. His intention is simply to fulfill a personal need or desire, certainly not to determine another person's income. Such, however, is precisely the unintended outcome of his action, in conjunction with the action of every other individual making similar purchases. However little he or she may be aware of the fact, such indeed is the effect of every individual's action any time he or she makes a purchase on the market.

The relation between individual consumption and the determination of income is more clearly perceived by exploring both short-and long-run dimensions of the market process. We begin with an individual who purchases a can of Fancy Feast cat food at a local grocery store, paying for the item by cash or credit card. The money or purchase price is received, in the first instance, by the retail store. The retailer, however, does not retain the entire amount. He does not personally manufacture the cat food but typically purchases it from a wholesaler or distributor. A portion of the price the customer paid for the Fancy Feast, then, is distributed by the retailer to the wholesaler to pay for the cat food. The wholesaler, however, is also a middleman who does not personally produce the cat food but rather purchases it from the manufacturer, the Fancy Feast firm. Thus a portion of the money the original retail customer paid for the cat food, transmitted by the retailer to the wholesaler, will in turn be distributed by the wholesaler to Fancy Feast. Nor will the Fancy Feast firm retain all the money received from the wholesaler. It will rather spend a portion of its proceeds from sales to purchase the inputs necessary to make its cat food. Thus another portion of the retail purchase price is distributed by Fancy Feast to firms that produce meat, grains, and other ingredients used to make the cat food. Fancy Feast will also distribute portions of the original customer's purchase price to pay for its capital and operating expenses, for instance, wages of workers and other staff hired by Fancy Feast; costs of the machines used in the Fancy Feast factory and electricity to operate the plant, and so on. Yet other portions of the original retail purchase price will be distributed, by Fancy Feast or its direct suppliers, to firms or workers indirectly involved in bringing Fancy Feast to the retail shelves—the truckers who transport the cases of cat food to the wholesalers and retailers, the butchers, miners, farmers, manufacturers of paper labels, ink, glue, and so on.

Innumerable individuals, then, are involved, directly or indirectly, in bringing a simple can of Fancy Feast cat food to the retail shelves. The income of every person involved in that process is partly determined by every consumer who purchases a can of Fancy Feast cat food at the local grocery store. Their income is determined, in the end, by the value that consumers place on the final product, the Fancy Feast cat food. If consumers do not want to purchase this product, there will be no money to distribute to the retailer, wholesaler, manufacturer, or workers in all the myriad industries involved in its production. If all consumers were to stop purchasing Fancy Feast, the income of the owners and all other persons directly employed by the Fancy Feast firm would fall to zero, and the income of all other persons employed throughout the chain of its production would decline. The Fancy Feast firm would have no revenue because no one is purchasing the product it manufactures. Because the salaries of all employees of the Fancy Feast firm are paid from the revenue derived from sales of its product, the firm's owners would be unable to pay them. In the total absence of customers, the Fancy Feast workers would have to be laid off and the factory closed. Such an outcome is the inevitable result of the market process, driven as it is by consumer demand. In the end, the income received by every person involved in the production of Fancy Feast cat food, directly or indirectly, is determined, wholly or partly, by the consumers who purchase that particular brand of cat food. Each individual purchaser is partially responsible, and all such purchasers jointly and fully responsible, for the total income earned by the Fancy Feast firm, the income of workers as well as owners and managers, and also for a portion of the income of all those individuals and firms indirectly involved in bringing Fancy Feast to market (truckers, miners, butchers, and so on).

The complexity of capitalist production, in conjunction with the spatially extended reach of modern market exchange, makes it impossible to know precisely *whose* income is determined, and in precisely what manner, by the individual actions of the millions of consumers in an advanced market economy, such as that of the United States. It is usually impossible for the consumer to know or learn which particular individuals will receive a portion of the price he pays for his various retail purchases. In the case under discussion, the individual purchaser of Fancy Feast knows in principle that he, along with all other customers who purchase Fancy Feast, ultimately determine the income of all those persons directly employed by the Fancy Feast firm. It would be difficult if not impossible, however, to know precisely how each of the firm's individual workers is affected or even to know their identity. It is even less conceivable that any individual could know the identity of the innumerable persons whose income is also affected by his decision to purchase a can of Fancy Feast.

That is only to say that individual income in an extended market order is not, and cannot be, the consequence of any person's deliberate choice. Any individual's income in a market economy is ultimately determined, on the contrary, by the *impersonal* decisions of the millions of people who buy one another's goods and services. Their aim in purchasing such goods is to satisfy their personal needs and wants. In so doing, however, they unintentionally and simultaneously contribute to the determination of the income of every person involved, directly or indirectly, in producing the goods and services they purchase, persons whose individual identity is largely and necessarily unknown to them.

Such are the inescapable facts that lead to our previously stated conclusion: no one distributes income in a market economy. The concept of "distribution," as mentioned, implies a "distributor," that is, a conscious mind that decides to arrange things in a particular manner. Such is emphatically not the manner in which income is determined in a market economy. No one consciously or deliberately decided to "distribute" billions of dollars a year to Michael Jordan or, say, $15,000 a year to the worker at McDonald's. Such results follow from the impersonal decisions of all those consumers who chose to purchase goods or services produced by Jordan and McDonald's. Such consumers are not generally concerned with the basketball player or the fast-food worker but rather with satisfying their personal needs and desires. Indeed, as previously observed, even if their purchases were motivated not by self-interest but rather the altruistic desire to raise the income of particular persons or groups, they could not do so in a complex market order: they have no way of knowing precisely whose income is affected by their purchases. As has been discussed, contemporary market exchange extends across a far-flung global economy. No one can ever know all the particular individuals whose income he is partially determining by his purchases; they may be his neighbors or people living in the most remote regions of the world.

This aspect of modern market exchange is often difficult to accept, conflicting as it does with a widespread and understandable emotional propensity and yearning. Many if not most people would undoubtedly prefer that their individual purchases, say of cat food, support the income of a deserving and poverty-stricken mother of five rather than a wealthy person of means. Such might be possible in a local village economy, where people can know of individual need and direct their purchases accordingly, but it is impossible in the modern market order that unites people across the world. We have seen that individual participants in modern market exchange have no way of knowing who will ultimately receive the proceeds of their purchases; the items at the local grocery store could have been manufactured anywhere in the United States and indeed almost anywhere in the world. Modern society involves participation in a global economy, and the income derived from most individual purchases is impersonally distributed to the four corners of the earth, beyond the range of conscious knowledge.

In conclusion, the reason why Michael Jordan is a billionaire and the worker at McDonald's is relatively poor is that Jordan succeeded in producing goods and services highly valued by millions and millions of people and the fast-food worker did not. Millions of customers have been willing voluntarily to exchange their personal resources for Jordan's goods and services because they value them at least as much as they value the money they exchanged for them. Jordan obviously possessed talent, creative insight, and the skill to produce goods and services that many people want to possess and with few ready equivalents or substitutes. Not only his personal income but also the income of the numerous individuals he employs is ultimately determined by the value that Jordan's customers place on the final products he supplies to the market. If customers stopped purchasing his products, Jordan's income and that of all his employees would fall to zero.

The same market forces are responsible for determining the income of the McDonald's worker. The relatively low income of such a worker is a consequence of the fact that other persons do not place a relatively high value on the limited skill he brings to market. The limited skills required for fast-food service are not in great demand and, moreover, in abundant supply (many people possess them). The relatively low demand for fast-food workers, in conjunction with the abundant supply of such unskilled labor, means that the market price offered for their service will be relatively low; *ceteris paribus*, both decrease in demand and increase in supply lead to reduction in price, including the price of fast-food service. The disparity of income between Michael Jordan and the dishwasher is not the result of anyone's deliberate choice—any act of "distribution"— but rather the spontaneous and unintended consequence of impersonal market forces.

For precisely this reason, moreover, one must conclude that the common criticism of income distribution in a market economy—that it is unfair or unjust—is unfounded. It is true that market exchange inevitably results in an unequal distribution of income; some persons will be relatively richer and some relatively poorer. The pattern of income distribution produced by the market process, however, is not the consequence of anyone's deliberate intention or decision but rather the impersonal choices of market participants in accord with their subjective values. Those persons with skills more highly valued by fellow members of society will earn relatively higher income and those with skills less highly valued will earn relatively lower income. Such an outcome is unintentional, insofar as market participants generally do not and cannot know the effects of their consumption choices on the economic position of particular human beings.

For that reason—the impersonal and unintentional manner by which income is determined in a market economy—the pattern of distribution that results from market exchange is not and cannot be a matter of justice. Strictly speaking, there is no such entity as a "just society" or an "unjust society." We have previously discussed in another context the merely nominal character of the term "society." As we have seen, the abstraction "society" is not a conscious, thinking, willing entity capable of bearing or exercising moral agency. There is no concrete entity called "society," which is rather a name for an association of individuals united by common values and experiences. Only such individuals bear the capacity for moral agency, for acting justly or unjustly. It is true that careless use of language does commonly lead to a description of society as "just" or "unjust," but such can only be true in a metaphorical and not a literal sense. Society in itself is incapable of acting justly or unjustly or in any conceivable manner. To speak of a society as "just" or "unjust" can only meaningfully refer to the actions of the individuals comprised by that society. The joint actions of individuals who behave justly may thus be said, loosely and metaphorically, to produce a "just" society. Accordingly, the pattern of income distribution that results from market exchange must be regarded as "just" so long as individual market participants behave justly in conducting their personal economic activity (and "unjust" to the extent they behave unjustly). There is no other possible measure of the justice of an abstract entity such as "society." We will return to this crucial question—the morality and justice of a market economy—in a following chapter, in which we also examine the justice of planned or collectivized economic organization.

The Broken Window Fallacy

The chief difference between sound and unsound economic reasoning may be summarized in two short statements. First, sound economic reasoning considers not only the immediate or short-run effects of a given act or policy but also attempts to trace its long-term consequences; second, it considers the effects of an act or policy not only on one person or group but on all persons and groups in society.[20] Errors in economic reasoning typically stem from failure to consider one or the other of such considerations, errors which can, and do, lead to advocacy of unsound and even irrational economic policy by government officials, academics, journalists, and members of the general public. It is not difficult to understand why human beings are prone to such errors. Human beings are often short-sighted: our tendency is to perceive that which is immediately before our eyes and that which affects us directly and personally. It takes mental and imaginative effort, on the other hand, to perceive beyond our immediate range of experience, to trace direct and indirect effects on persons other than ourselves, and to consider the longer-term consequences of action.

Such a common human propensity is classically illustrated by the so-called "Broken Window Fallacy."[21] The story opens on a sunny afternoon in a major American city. A small group of teenagers stroll along the sidewalk of a busy city street. One of them impulsively throws a rock through the plate-glass window of a tailoring shop; the window shatters and the kids run away. Passers-by soon begin to gather outside the tailor's shop, expressing indignation at the destructiveness of the teenager's action. At some point, however, one of them attempts to brighten the mood by suggesting that the seemingly negative situation may actually have a silver lining:

> "Cheer up," he says to the crowd. "Yes, I agree that the boy should not have acted so recklessly and destructively. But if you think about it, the damage he wrought may, in truth, be a good thing, beneficial to society. The window that was broken must now be replaced and that means the glassmaker down the street will receive an order he would not otherwise have received. His sales will increase and thus his profit. The act of destruction, one might say, is "stimulating the

---

[20] Henry Hazlitt, *Economics in One Lesson* (New York: Crown Business, 1988). Hereinafter cited as *Economics*.
[21] Frederic Bastiat, "That Which is Seen, and That Which is Not Seen" (1850), cited in Hazlitt, *Economics*.

economy'—encouraging economic activity by increasing demand, in this case, for a plate-glass window. The boy's motivation may have been wrong but he seems inadvertently to have done society a favor. Things may not be as bad as they appear!"

The passerby's remarks are comforting but they defy common sense, which regards wanton destruction of property as wrong. Perhaps, however, common sense is not a reliable guide in this instance and the passerby is correct: the teenager's action will ultimately benefit society as a whole and should thus inspire gratitude, not anger or contempt. Unfortunately, however, such is not the case. The cheerful passerby's conclusion, which may seem plausible at first glance, is fallacious. Its plausibility derives from the fact that certain elements of the reasoning involved are sound. It is true that the glassmaker will benefit from destruction of the window; he will indeed receive an additional and unexpected order that will increase his sales and income. Contrary to the passerby, however, other members of society have no reason to rejoice, for there is no benefit to society as a whole. The passerby's judgement is flawed because he fell victim to the common human propensity to perceive only the immediate effects of an act and only its effects on one person or group. A careful analysis of the actual situation, including its long-term effects and effects on all persons involved, confirms the common-sense judgment that reckless destruction is intrinsically undesirable and harmful.

The passerby's first error was to consider the effects of the broken window on only one person—the glassmaker. The glassmaker, however, is far from the only person affected by the teenager's action. Consider, first and foremost, the situation of the tailor. Let us assume that prior to the destruction of his property he was in possession of a plate-glass window and other assets, including, say, $3,000 in savings intended for purchase of a new computer. The teenager broke his window. In the aftermath of the destruction, the tailor's situation has changed, and for the worse. He still possesses the $3,000 and other assets but no longer the window, which will have to be replaced. Assume for ease of illustration that the replacement cost is about $3,000. Accordingly, the tailor must now spend his $3,000 savings, not to buy a computer as intended but instead to replace the broken window. He will once again possess a window but have lost his $3,000 savings. The rock-thrower's action certainly brought the tailor no benefit but, on the contrary, an absolute loss equal to the $3,000 cost of replacing the window. He is without question economically worse off than before the incident.

The tailor, moreover, is not the only person worse off than before the act of destruction. Consider the situation of a second "forgotten man," namely, the seller of computers.[22] Prior to destruction of his window, the tailor had planned to use his $3,000 savings to purchase a new computer. He can no longer do so because those funds were spent to replace the window. That means the seller of computers has lost a sale that would have occurred if the window had remained intact; his income is consequently lower than it would have been if the destruction had not taken place. The teenager's action has resulted in the decline not only of the tailor's economic wellbeing but the computer seller's as well.

The passerby's analysis is flawed because he neglected to consider the effects of the destructive act on *all* persons involved, the tailor and seller of computers, as well as the glassmaker. Such an error derives from the previously mentioned human propensity to short-sightedness. Everyone *sees* the broken window right before their eyes and can readily relate it to the glassmaker. It is more difficult, however, to identify the unseen but nevertheless real effects on the tailor and seller of computers. Such requires imaginative effort, tracing the consequences of the teenager's action beyond the immediate and short-run effects. It further requires consideration not only of the effects on one party—the glassmaker—but on all parties affected, directly or indirectly, by the incident—the tailor and computer seller. The passerby failed in both respects, leading to his erroneous conclusion. Acts of destruction do not and cannot produce net gain for society as a whole; the glassmaker's gain is offset by the losses of the other two parties involved. In the final analysis, the teenager's action has at best effected a mere redirection of resources, that is, a redistribution of wealth from the tailor and computer seller to the glassmaker. Destruction of things of real economic value can never produce net benefits for society at large.

The Broken Window fallacy is classic because it perfectly illustrates the two main causes of faulty economic reasoning, again, the failure to

---

[22] Amity Shales, *The Forgotten Man: A New History of the Great Depression* (NY: Harper Perennial, 2008).

consider both indirect and long-term effects and effects on all persons, not only those immediately impacted by any act or policy. Despite repeated demonstrations of the errors embodied in the fallacy, it nevertheless continues to distort economic reasoning, not merely among the general public but also influential persons such as journalists and politicians.

A few contemporary examples will demonstrate the stubborn persistence of the fallacy in the public mind. Several years ago a series of hurricanes struck the Palm Beaches in Florida and caused significant damage to personal property such as homes, roofs, cars, and much else. Both common sense and personal experience affirm that such destruction is bad or harmful; any person who experienced damage to his personal property knows quite well he is worse off than prior to the hurricane. Nevertheless, the hurricane destruction brought renewed life to an old fallacy, the Broken Window Fallacy—the idea that acts of destruction can produce net economic benefits for society as a whole. The local newspaper ran an editorial that cheerfully anticipated the economic boom that was sure to follow in the wake of the hurricanes. Readers were reassured that the recent destruction would soon be met by expansive and vigorous economic activity in the Palm Beach community, stimulated by the need to rebuild and repair damaged property. The hurricanes (like the rock thrown through the tailor's window), they were told, will increase demand, in this case for roofers, glassmakers, debris-removal firms, and a host of construction workers, all of whom will experience a rise in sales and income. The newspaper account did involve an element of truth: such firms and industries do indeed gain from destruction, as did the glassmaker. But it neglected to mention that the gains of construction and allied firms are offset by the real losses experienced by those whose property has been damaged or destroyed and who must pay for needed reconstruction. Hurricane damage produces no net gain to the community as a whole but rather, at best, only a redistribution of wealth from those who suffer the damage to those who repair the damage. Even journalists seem unable to extricate themselves from the tenacious hold of the fallacy.

Indeed the aftermath of the 9/11 attack on the World Trade Center in New York City met with a similar response. Newspapers of the period published similarly cheerful editorials anticipating the amazing economic boom that was bound to follow the destruction of the

Towers.[23] The act of terror, readers were informed, had a silver lining—the powerful economic stimulus it will provide to the local community. Firms involved in reconstruction will experience an enormous increase in demand for their services, as will individual New Yorkers employed in such trades. The identical argument was made with respect to the German economy in the aftermath of World War II. The wartime destruction of the German infrastructure was said to promise massive economic benefits for industries involved in rebuilding and reconstruction, in particular, American construction firms contracted by the U.S. government for the task. The anticipation of economic benefits was similarly touted in the destruction of the Iraqi infrastructure in the early years of the Iraq war. Such destruction, it was suggested, would benefit the U.S. economy by raising demand for American firms and workers involved in subsequent reconstruction. The Broken Window Fallacy is alive and well to the present day.

In every case, whether the destruction is caused by natural disasters, wanton violence, or war, writers of such optimistic editorials reach the same false conclusion, based on the same flawed reasoning, as the passerby on the street observing the broken window. In all cases they perceive merely the immediate and direct effects of the destruction and ignore the long-term and indirect effects. They perceive only the benefits that will accrue to one group of all those affected and ignore the effect on other persons and groups. The element of truth in all of the examples presented is that certain types of industries do indeed benefit from destruction. Roofers will benefit in the wake of a hurricane; construction workers would have benefitted had the World Trade Center been rebuilt; and corporate giants like Halliburton do benefit from rebuilding infrastructure in war-torn lands. The gains of construction workers and firms, however, are offset by the losses of others—those whose property is destroyed—eliminating any possibility of net benefit to society as a whole. The money that homeowners must pay roofers to repair storm damage is comparable to the money the tailor had to pay the glassmaker to replace his broken window. The roofers gain, but their gain is offset by the absolute loss of the homeowners, just as the glassmaker's gain was offset by the tailor's absolute loss. Moreover, the money that

---

[23] Paul Krugman, "Reckonings; After the Horror," Opinion Page, *New York Times*, Sept. 14, 2001.

homeowners must pay to replace their damaged roofs is no longer available for other purchases, say, a new washing machine, precisely as the tailor's savings were no longer available to purchase a new computer. The washing-machine manufacturer, like the computer company in the original example, also suffers a loss—the loss of revenue the firm would have earned had the hurricane not damaged the roof.

The identical analysis applies to destruction of property caused by war. Certain industries, again, do gain from such destruction, mainly governmental contractors in the building and construction trades. Their gain, however, like that of the glassmaker, is offset by the losses of others, those, like the tailor, whose property is destroyed and those who must pay to rebuild it. These are usually but not always the same entities. In the case of postwar Germany and Iraq, for instance, German and Iraqi property owners certainly suffered a loss equal to the value of their destroyed property. But American taxpayers—those required to repair the ravages of war—also suffered a loss. Postwar reconstruction is largely funded by the American government. Government spending, however, is chiefly funded by American taxpayers, who thus suffer a loss equal to the total amount of taxes appropriated for the purpose of postwar reconstruction. Moreover, the resources used to replace destroyed property, whether private funds or funds obtained by taxation, are no longer available to purchase other goods and services, whose producers, like the computer seller, also suffer economic losses. Those who tout the alleged economic benefits of war are victims of the Broken Window Fallacy, failing to consider the direct loss experienced by American taxpayers, equal to the amount taxed to rebuild Germany and Iraq, and the indirect loss of sales and revenue experienced by producers of computers, cars, washing machines, and so on, all those goods and services that American citizens would have purchased had they not been taxed to restore infrastructure ravaged by war. They fail to consider effects beyond the immediate and apparent (the benefit to the reconstruction trades). To recognize the plight of the invisible actors requires imagination and reason, the ability to perceive both "what is seen and what is unseen," to mentally trace both the long-term and indirect consequences of economic acts or policy.[24]

---

[24] Indeed, the benefits of war to corporate giants such as Halliburton, Boeing, and others, the chief recipients of government contracts, has led to the rise of

what President Dwight Eisenhower famously called the "military-industrial complex." The term refers to the corporate enterprises who stand to gain from rebuilding infrastructure in war-torn lands and who thus have every incentive to promote war by means of lobbying and so on. They are joined by military lobbyists who also have an interest in war, ensuring that the largess of the American taxpayers is directed toward their establishments.

EIGHT

SOCIALISM: THE PLANNED ECONOMY

The characteristic error of the constructive rationalists . . . is that they tend to base their argument on what has been called the synoptic delusion, that is, on the fiction that all the relevant facts are known to some one mind, and that it is possible to construct from this knowledge of the particulars a desirable social order.   —F.A. Hayek

The most significant political dimension of the modern era has been the great contest between liberal democracy and the so-called "ideological movements" that arose in the nineteenth and twentieth centuries as alternatives and rivals to Western liberal society. Ideological in this regard refers to the fact that movements such as communism, socialism, and fascism were based on a comprehensive and consistent set of ideas—a belief system, worldview or *Weltanschauung*—that provided both the inspiration and justification for the revolutionary movement in question.[25] Indeed the widespread appeal and impact of such ideologies throughout the twentieth century has led to its dual characterization as both the "Age of Ideology" and "Age of Totalitarianism," highlighting the relation between modern ideology and the rise of totalitarian government that further marked that period. The general nature and meaning of the ideological movements will be examined in a subsequent chapter. The present chapter explores a more particular but highly significant dimension of such movements, namely, the fact that their goals were cast not only in political but also economic terms. The express

---

[25] Hayek maintains that classical liberalism is an ideology in the sense that it is a consistent set of principles and beliefs that constitute a worldview. Most scholars, however, reserve the term for the totalitarian movements as discussed above. See Hayek, "Why I am Not a Conservative," in *Constitution*, 397-411.

aim was to replace capitalism with an alternative form of economic arrangement—one variant or other of a centralized, socialized, or "planned" economy. The twentieth-century experiments in planned economy were elaborately organized and conducted in various nations and regions, including the Soviet Union, Eastern Europe, Cuba, China, and others. One benefit of such experience has been an advance of knowledge concerning both the theory and practice of socialism and other forms of planned economy, knowledge unavailable to their original proponents.

We begin with socialism and its central economic aim—to replace the spontaneous order of the market with the "organization of society as a whole," as early French socialists such as the St. Simonians and Auguste Comte expressed the goal.[26] In contemporary terminology, such an aim involves the replacement of capitalism with one form or other of planned or command economy characterized by centralization or collectivization of economic decision-making. The textbook definition of socialism is an economic system based on "collective or governmental ownership and administration of the means of production and distribution of goods" or, less formally, "public ownership of the means of production."

The conventional definition, while not entirely satisfactory, does successfully highlight the key difference between capitalism and socialism, namely, and as we recall, the locus of property or decision rights in the two systems (private and public ownership, respectively). The private ownership of resources that defines capitalism, as we have seen, means that private individuals decide if and how resources are to be employed. Modern capitalist decision-making, based on the universal right to private property, is decentralized among millions of people, permitting individuals directly to respond to the particular circumstances encountered in their local and immediate environments. The accompanying rule of law, as we further recall, including the security of private property, provides both the institutional certainty and incentives needed to elicit such response, to encourage individuals to act in the face of local and immediate circumstances, informed by the information condensed in the prevailing structure of relative prices. The result is an efficient and rational use of limited resources, adapted to the ever-changing circumstances of human existence and in service of the

---

[26] Cited in Hayek, *Rules and Order*, 53.

fluid needs and wants of the people. Such an outcome is made possible by capitalist decentralization of decision-making with respect to both production and consumption. Such, as we have seen, is crucial to the discovery and utilization of all relevant economic knowledge in society, including the tacit and fleeting knowledge requisite to the careful use of scarce resources and that only exists dispersed among countless individual minds.

Early advocates of economic centralization or socialization well recognized that the institution of private property, securing individual and decentralized decision rights over resources, is the cornerstone of a capitalist economy. For that reason, said Karl Marx (1818-1883), the most prominent advocate of modern socialism, the replacement of capitalism with socialism requires, first and foremost, the abolition of private property.[27] As he says in the *Communist Manifesto*, "the theory of the Communists may be summed up in the single sentence: Abolition of private [*bourgeois*] property."[28] Accordingly, he and fellow travelers called for the transfer of property rights—ownership and direction of resources—from the private to the public domain, in effect, from private persons to government or "the state." Such is the decisive move in the transformation of capitalism to socialism, summarized in the conventional definitions previously stated. Classic socialism involves the transfer of decision rights over resources from the private to the public realm. In terms of our discussion, this means that the responsibility for solving the economic problem confronting society is transferred from private individuals to centralized public authority of one form or another. We have seen that the fundamental fact of scarcity requires every society to reach decisions regarding what is to be produced, and *how,* as well as decisions regarding distribution of the fruits of production. In a socialized or planned economy, such decision rights are held by government. Government, and not private individuals, decides *what* is to be produced, and *how* to produce it; and government also decides, directly or indirectly, how the fruits of production are distributed.

Economic planning by government can assume a variety of forms and embrace various degrees of control, more or less extensive or restricted.

---

[27] *Communist Manifesto*, 486.
[28] Ibid., 484.

All such variants, however, from pure communism to socialism, fascism, modern-liberal progressivism, Keynesian "demand management," and others, share certain essential attributes characteristic of all forms of planned economy. The differences among them, as we shall see, largely involve either the *methods* or *extent* of governmental planning and control and not the question of governmental control per se.

Central Planning

Having identified the defining attribute of all forms of planned or socialized economy—governmental control or direction of resources— the next task is to explore how a planned economy operates both in theory and in practice. To provide the clearest illustration of the dynamics involved, we shall use as our model the classic form of socialized economy, namely, pure or ideal communism, wherein government assumes centralized control over all resources in society. Communism so conceived is best regarded as a Weberian "ideal type." Few if any actual modern societies practice or have practiced pure communism, just as few if any modern societies practice or have practiced pure or ideal capitalism as described in the previous chapter. The economic arrangements found in most modern societies, as we shall see, represent some mixture of capitalist and socialist elements. The use of ideal types, however, in both the present and preceding chapters, is particularly helpful for our purpose, that is, theoretical clarification of the basic operational principles and methods by which the two rival systems propose to solve the economic problem.

Keeping such analytic constraints in mind, pure or ideal communism may be defined as *exclusive* public ownership of the means of production and other social resources. Government is solely and directly responsible for the allocation of resources with respect to both production and distribution. Production and distribution decisions are typically embodied in comprehensive economic "plans" devised by a central authority and aiming, in principle, to further the wellbeing of all members of society. (The more specific aims of economic socialization, practical and moral, will be explored in a following section.) The method is appealingly simple and straightforward. Government assumes ownership of all resources in society. It then establishes various planning boards or committees divided among particular sectors of the economy—agriculture, housing, health care, education, and so on. Committee members are expected to centralize within their purview all relevant economic knowledge held within society, that is, survey all available resources and all needs and desires of members of the community. By such means, it is believed, planners can develop a "big picture" of economic and social conditions (supply and demand) that will assist them in devising rational and efficient production plans that meet the needs of all people. Such plans typically embody various time horizons, such as the Five-Year Plans developed in the early Soviet Union. Planners devise quotas and time lines for the production of various goods and services, which are given in turn to managers of state-owned firms. Managers are expected to fulfill their assigned quotas by appropriate administration of the human and material resources allocated by the committees for their production. Upon production, the goods and services are to be distributed by political authority in a fair and equitable manner. The celebrated Marxist slogan summarizes the ethos underlying such collectivized production and distribution: "From each according to his ability, to each according to his need."[29] Each member of society is to contribute, in accord with his particular abilities, toward fulfillment of the production plans devised by the central government. The collective fruits of their individual contributions are to be distributed by government for consumption "according to need."

Centralized governmental planning so conceived is portrayed by its advocates as a decided advance in economic practice. The rational "organization of society as a whole"—the creation of an overarching economic blueprint ostensibly embodying all relevant economic knowledge found within society—is the collectivist alternative to the alleged irrationality of the spontaneous market process. Advocates of economic socialization are typically marked by the inability to perceive the order intrinsic to a market economy, achieved as it is by observance of abstract or general rules and not specific commands or directives of an identifiable human authority. Indeed such critics of capitalism typically perceive its processes as disorderly and even reckless, without

---

[29] The slogan is conventionally attributed to Marx (*"Jeder nach seinen Faehigkeiten, jedem nach seinen Beduerfnissen"* (*Critique of the Gotha Program* [*Marx-Engels Reader*, 531]), but it was common to the socialist movement and employed by earlier socialists such as Etienne-Gabriel Morelly and Louis Blanc.

rhyme or reason, and its outcomes the product of chance, luck, or some other random or irrational phenomenon.[30] Economic socialization is invariably portrayed as a far more intelligent and rational manner of resolving the economic problem confronting society.

As we shall see, however, the socialist demand, while generally cast in economic terms, is not, at bottom, an economic demand, that is, concerned with rational allocation of scarce resources in service of subjective human needs and wants. It is rather a moral demand asserted in the idiom of economics. The impetus for the replacement of capitalism with one form or other of socialized economy largely derives from the conviction that the distribution of resources that results from the market process is unjust. A market economy, as has been discussed, is inevitably characterized by wide disparities in relative income—some people are richer and some poorer. Collectivists of various persuasions regard such an outcome as morally unacceptable, and all forms of socialized economy thus aim to establish a more "even" distribution of wealth. The socialist moral imperative demands that every person have access to certain material goods and services, regardless of individual income. Such universal access is to be achieved by governmental production and distribution of the requisite goods and services. Contrary to the rhetoric often associated with central planning, its purpose is not a more rational or efficient utilization of the earth's scarce resources but rather a more "equitable" distribution of resources than that achieved by a market economy. The importance of this topic—the competing moral visions embodied within socialism and capitalism—justifies an extended discussion, and it will be explored more fully in subsequent chapters.

Our main concern at this juncture is to examine the actual operational methods typically employed in a highly centralized economy. The classic procedure, as we have seen, involves the abolition of private property and subsequent establishment of state planning committees charged with the responsibility of devising economic plans encompassing society as a whole. Such comprehensive central planning necessarily involves plans for production of particular goods and services, both "final" or consumer goods, such as automobiles and orange juice, and so-called "intermediate" and "producer" goods (sometimes referred to as "capital"

---

[30] Accidents of birth, luck, chance, "animal spirits," booms, and busts, and so on.

goods). The production of any consumer good, say, an automobile, requires both "intermediate" goods or inputs (tires, engines, steel, paint, labor, and so on) and "producer" goods (non-consumable machines and other tools required to produce both intermediate and final goods). The particular plans for all such goods are devised by the committees and given, as said, to public firms for fulfillment. State-owned automobile firms are instructed to produce so many automobiles. State-owned tire firms are instructed to produce so many tires. State-owned manufacturers of steel receive similar orders. Every aspect of production—final, intermediate, and producer goods—must be planned for and organized in this fashion. Governmental planners may be intricately involved in the details of production or their oversight may be confined to assigning target production quotas, omitting precise specification of the manner of production, in which case firm managers may have some flexibility in devising individual ways of meeting their targets.

Whatever the specific provisions detailed in the plans, however, the point of overwhelming significance is the enormity of such an endeavor. To grasp what is involved in centralized economic planning, consider the thousands, if not hundreds of thousands, of items sitting on the shelves of a local Home Depot or Lowe's. Consumers can purchase everything from lighting fixtures to gardening supplies to drywall bolts of numerous kinds and sizes. They can do so, however, only because someone had the foresight to plan for their production. In a planned economy, a relatively small number of people, the state planning committees, must be able to fulfill the function performed in a capitalist economy by countless private entrepreneurs and business firms. The central planners alone must anticipate the need for each and every item that may arise over the time horizon established by the plan, as well as plan for all the intermediate and producer goods required for their production. Obviously a tremendous amount of knowledge and information is required to fulfill such a daunting task.

*

Such considerations lead back to the central issue involved in every attempt to solve the economic problem arising from scarcity—how to *know* what to produce, and how, and how to *know* who should receive the fruits of production? We have seen that a decentralized market economy facilitates the solution of the economic problem by maximizing the potential discovery and utilization of relevant knowledge. Every market participant is able to bring his individual knowledge to bear on its solution, communicating his particular knowledge of conditions of demand and/or supply through his actions as buyer and/or seller, anchored in the right to private property. Knowledge of demand preferences is communicated through consumer purchases (or lack thereof), and knowledge of supply or production possibilities through the actions of producers and investors. Both kinds of knowledge, as discussed, are transmitted and coordinated through the spontaneous movement of prices. The knowledge embodied in the resulting structure of relative prices permits producers to know what consumers want (final goods), as well as the relative scarcity or abundance of needed factors of production (intermediate and producer goods). It further permits consumers and producers to know the least-cost method of fulfilling their particular needs and desires. The price system not only conveys accurate knowledge regarding the relative scarcity or abundance of resources and guides their usage accordingly but also allocates the fruits of production in accord with the subjective preferences of the consumer. As we have seen, these are impersonally "distributed" to those individuals who value them most highly, as demonstrated by their willingness to pay for them with their own resources.

The chief and insurmountable obstacle faced by central planners in a socialized economy is that the information conveyed by prices in a free-market economy is unavailable to them. As we have seen, a radically centralized economy, by definition, eliminates or circumscribes private property and transfers ultimate decisions rights over resources to public or governmental authority. The problem inherent to that form of economic organization arises from the absence of private property, which prohibits the formation of an accurate structure of relative prices. Relative prices, as we have seen, serve a crucial economic and social function: communicating accurate knowledge of the conditions of supply and demand and thereby guiding decisions relating to both production and consumption. Price signals can only perform such a function if they reflect actual conditions of supply and the actual value that people place on particular resources (demand). Such essential knowledge, however, cannot be acquired in the absence of private property. Hypothetical supply—what resources might be available for production—is of no use to economic decision makers. They must know which resources are actually available, and such information is impossible to garner in the absence of freely formed market prices that embody the dispersed knowledge of relevant sources of supply held by market participants across the globe. Similarly, hypothetical demand—what individuals might want if resources were unlimited or if they themselves did not personally have to pay for it—is illusionary demand. Such is never the human condition, characterized as it is by the inescapable fact of scarcity. What people might like to have if resources were unlimited and what they can actually afford, as a society and as individuals, are distinct issues.

In a free market freely formed relative prices reflect the truth of reality—actual demand and actual supply—but only because the institution of private property requires people to use their own limited resources every time they purchase or produce a good or service. Consumers are forced carefully to evaluate the actual value they place on contemplated purchases because they themselves will personally experience the consequences of their choice—either an increase in their subjective wellbeing or careless waste of their own scarce resources. Producers are similarly forced carefully to evaluate the actual value of the scarce resources they employ in their production decisions, since they too personally experience the consequences of their choices. If they make the correct decision—employ scarce resources efficiently in the production of items that consumers actually want—they will be rewarded with profit; if they make a mistake, they must personally suffer the loss. The discipline of the market process is crucial to a rational allocation of scarce resources, and it is utterly dependent on the institution of private property. Human beings, including governmental planners, have little incentive to be rational when spending other people's money.

Nor is it possible for human beings, central planners again included, to behave rationally if their plans are based on imaginary resources. Rational economic decisions depend on accurate information regarding relevant conditions of supply and demand and such can only be acquired by the means of relative prices formed on the basis of private property. It is impossible to produce goods and services economically, that is, with minimum waste of scarce resources and in service of subjective human needs and wants, in the absence of accurate price information. In a socialized economy, however, the necessary condition for the formation of accurate or truthful prices—the institution of private property—is absent or truncated. The absence of freely forming relative prices means that government planners have no way of knowing the prevailing conditions of supply and demand; they must plan in the dark. They are constrained merely to guess or estimate the resources that might be available to fulfill their production plans. They must also guess or estimate the goods and services that people might want produced; they have no way of knowing their actual, and ever-changing, needs and wants. Such indeed is the fatal flaw of all highly centralized economic planning—the impossibility of rational economic calculation in the absence of accurate information regarding conditions of supply and demand. For this reason centralized economic organization has failed wherever and whenever instituted, a failure proportionate to the attempted degree of centralization or collectivization, that is, the degree to which private property rights have been curtailed. Failure in this regard means the inability to achieve the goals—the economic plans—established by the central authority. Such failure is not a result of the personal characteristics, intentions, or competence of the planners. Mother Teresa herself would be unable to acquire requisite information concerning relative scarcity and actual demand in a society without private property and thus without the ability to form an accurate structure of relative prices.

Planning without Prices

We next consider the manner in which government planners in a centralized economic system must actually prepare their plans in the absence of an accurate structure of relative prices. Planners may attempt to base such planning on historic price information, on the relative prices for resources that prevailed in the recent past, prior to establishment of the socialized economy. Alternatively, they may use certain kinds of publicly available information regarding relative prices, for instance, current world market prices for commodities such as oil, corn, copper, and so on routinely published in major newspapers. (In this regard, centrally planned systems are parasitic on the existence of free markets in other parts of the world.) Such methods, however, can never be more than makeshift approximations that do not and cannot embody existing conditions of supply and demand in a particular society. The attempt to employ historical information regarding demand (what people have valued in the past) or supply (the resources available for production in the past) to guide present production decisions is fraught with peril. Neither demand nor supply is static or constant. Every individual recognizes that his past consumption choices will not necessarily, or even probably, correspond with his future needs and wants. What people may need or want tomorrow is not necessarily what they needed or wanted yesterday. Not only do tastes change, but many other aspects of human life change continually as well. People are born and they die. They marry and have children. They divorce and live alone. They acquire pets or lose pets. They become ill or regain health. Their interests change or develop in new directions; out of the blue an individual develops an interest in learning to paint or play the piano. Neither historical nor current world-market prices can provide requisite information concerning the intrinsically unpredictable future circumstances of human existence.

Conditions of supply change continuously and unexpectedly as well. No one can control the weather; floods, droughts, and other natural disasters can and do lead to unanticipated crop failure. To illustrate the problems involved, suppose central planners devise a plan to produce ethanol for fuel. A major input into such production is corn, and thus they also incorporate a specific amount of corn into their production plans. Further suppose that the corn crop unexpectedly fails due to drought. As a result of the unforeseen weather conditions, corn producers cannot fulfill their production quotas, and this means that the ethanol producers will not be able to obtain sufficient corn to fulfill their assigned quotas. The unexpected shortages of corn and ethanol will affect numerous other industries as well—all industries whose production plans include either corn or ethanol as an input into the production of the final good. The expected inputs are not available, and all such industries will consequently be unable to fulfill their individual plans or quotas. Shortages begin to spread throughout the economy. The success of the master economic plan is dependent upon the validity of the assumption that all necessary inputs will actually be available and the further assumption that demand will remain stable and unchanging over the relevant time horizon. Both assumptions may defy reality. Many conditions of human existence are not subject to human control; moreover, they continually change and often in unanticipated ways.

Human survival and wellbeing depend upon the ability flexibly and rapidly to adapt to the ever-changing conditions of existence. A planned economy cannot readily do so. The information required to become aware of changing conditions, as well as the incentives required to elicit appropriate response—freely forming relative prices and the institution of private property, respectively—either do not exist at all or, in an imperfectly centralized economy, only to a limited extent.

In a market economy, by contrast, a drought that causes failure of the corn crop will quickly manifest as a rise in the price of corn. The rise in price, as we have seen, means a rise in the potential profitability of producing corn. Private producers, seeking profit as always, have every personal incentive to shift capital resources into production of corn. Moreover, they will be able and willing to do so as rapidly as possible. Not only do they themselves possess decision rights over their personal resources but those producers first to increase production stand the best chance of earning higher-than-normal profit. Additional resources will soon be directed toward corn production, precisely what is required in response to the weather-related shortage. Planned economies do not and cannot adapt to change in a similarly swift and flexible manner. The requisite movement of relative prices is suppressed in a society that does not secure a full-throated right to private property, as are the requisite incentives for increased production (the possibility of profit, secured by property rights). For such reasons centrally planned economies are invariably characterized by chronic shortages and surpluses, chronic underproduction or overproduction. No human mind or minds, however great the political control, can identify the concrete circumstances that will prevail in the future, neither conditions of demand nor supply. All of this is to emphasize, yet again, that the economic problem, at bottom, is a knowledge problem. No human mind can foresee future events with certainty let alone attain the omniscience presupposed by central economic planning.

*

Given such inevitable epistemological constraints, the question nevertheless remains: how do central planners in a socialized economy actually devise their plans in the face of their irremediable ignorance of the actual conditions of supply and demand? Their goal of course is to determine what "should" be produced and this, we shall assume, toward the end of maximizing human welfare. Such, however, is a thorny issue impervious to rational resolution. In a society of any degree of complexity, it is not possible to achieve universal agreement on what "should" be produced because universal demand for particular goods and services, in particular quantities, simply does not exist. Moreover, what "should" be produced is inevitably dependent not only on demand but also the relative scarcity or abundance of resources (supply). Because central planners have no way of acquiring accurate knowledge of either demand or supply, their plans, in the end, must be based on mere arbitrary preference, not the actual availability of limited resources or actual preferences of ultimate consumers.

To perceive more clearly the intractable problems confronting would-be central planners, assume the perspective of a governmental official assigned the task of devising plans for the production of food, a basic necessity that must of course be foremost in any economic plan. The first leg of the planning process must involve decisions concerning which food products to produce, and in what quantity. Planners will immediately encounter the fact, however, that human beings never desire or consume "food" but rather particular concrete items that fall within that abstract category—rice or potatoes, chocolate bars or chicken. From the innumerable items subsumed within the general category of "food," planners must somehow choose which concrete items to actually produce and in what quantity. Moreover, resources are limited in a planned economy as in any other form of economic organization, and it is fair to assume that planners will aim to fulfill their plans in the least wasteful manner. To do so, they must have some means of knowing the relative availability of the various inputs involved in the production of the food items included in their plans.

For the sake of argument, further assume that the planners are benevolent and kind human beings who sincerely aim to identify food items that will be needed or desired by everyone in society. One of the first items to come to mind might be "water," a fundamental necessity for human survival. In the language of economics, planners can confidently anticipate a universal demand for water and will thus want to include it in their production plans. We shall see, however, that even the production of an item as basic as water is not as simple as it appears. Planners must determine not only to produce water but also decide *how much* water and *what kind* of water to produce, *how* to produce it and *who* should receive it. There may exist a universal demand for water in a general and biological sense, but the quantity and kind of water demanded varies greatly from person to person. Some people love water and drink it incessantly; others hate water and drink it only under duress. Some people crave pure mineral water; others are happy with water from the tap. Some people take showers; others prefer baths. Some wash large amounts of laundry, others very little. Some water their lawns and gardens (an unpredictable need that depends on the weather); others have no lawns or gardens. Even the amount of water consumed by a particular individual will vary over time, and unpredictably; an unusually hot summer will unexpectedly increase the demand for water. And so on. In short, there is no "universal demand" for any concrete good or service, even a good as universally essential as water.

Yet planners must somehow determine the quantity and kind of water to include in their production plans, and they must do so without the guiding signals of freely formed relative prices. We assume that planners actually desire to make rational economic decisions—to employ scarce resources only in the production of goods and services that consumers actually need or want and in the least wasteful manner. Despite such good intentions, however, they cannot do so. In the absence of information conveyed by the price system, they have no means of knowing either the relative scarcity or abundance of water or the actual demand for water among the populace. We have previously discussed the problems involved is basing economic plans on historical data. In the end, the planners will have to arbitrarily decide, guess or estimate, how much and what kind of water to produce, whether or not their decision meets the actual conditions of supply (their plan may prove impossible to fulfill) or proves to satisfy actual consumer demand. Consumers will have to "make do" with whatever water is ultimately provided; one cannot consume something that has not been produced.

A second example will further drive home this crucial point. Assume our planner next decides to include a breakfast beverage in his plan; most people begin their day with some form of liquid nourishment. Again, however, individual tastes vary considerably in this regard; one person likes coffee, another tea, a third cocoa, a fourth milk, a fifth orange juice, and so on. How does a planner decide which of these alternatives to produce, by what method and in what quantity? Perhaps he allows majority rule to prevail and submits the issue to the public for a vote.

Such a process may satisfy the majority but only the majority. If the majority prefers tea, there will be no coffee, orange juice, cocoa, or milk to satisfy minority tastes. Indeed, any form of individual and minority taste will be difficult to satisfy in a planned economy. Central planning is a system of "one-size fits all," tailored at best to majority tastes and, at worst, simply to the personal preferences of the planners.

A market economy, by contrast, will produce any item so long as it is profitable to do so, that is, so long as the price anyone is willing to pay for it covers its cost of production. There is no need to restrict production to only those items desired by the majority; indeed, and on the contrary, the market provides incentives for specifically catering to minority tastes. A producer can make a good living producing items demanded by relatively few consumers, such as Rolls-Royce automobiles, neon-purple nail polish, or scholarly books on freedom. All that is necessary to bring such items to market is the existence of buyers, however few, willing to pay a price that covers the cost of production, including sufficient profit to make it worth the producer's effort and risk. Such is precisely why a market economy generates such a remarkable variety of goods and services, tailored to every conceivable taste. A centrally planned economy, by contrast, is characterized by uniformity. One cannot consume what has not been produced, and planners, if at all concerned with matching production to demand, will generally try to produce those items that will satisfy majority taste. Minorities will simply have to do without. Homogenized mass production, in the quantity determined by the central planners, is the fate of all.

To avoid such a fate, benevolent planners might resort to one final option, that is, a direct survey of each individual member of society regarding his personal needs and wants. Perhaps they establish a website and instruct every individual to convey to the authorities everything he knows regarding his preferences (his "demand"), as well as his knowledge of local circumstances relating to conditions of supply. By such means the planners hope to collect all relevant knowledge dispersed among the populace and incorporate it into the economic plans they formulate for society as a whole. Assume for purposes of illustration that all members of society eagerly support the government's goal and conscientiously strive to ensure its success. Each individual earnestly pursues his personal project of trying to transmit all his relevant knowledge to the central planners in Havana or Washington. Most people would probably begin by communicating their own specialized or technical knowledge, for instance, plumbing, automobile mechanics, hairdressing, web design, and so on. They might also include their knowledge of particular local resources, for instance, the availability of physicians or cat food in their communities, that is, their personal knowledge of available supply. Each person would further attempt to identify his personal demand, his individual needs, desires, tastes, and preferences.

A moment's reflection, however, should reveal the impossibility of obtaining relevant economic knowledge and information in such a manner. We have discussed the fact that an economic system serving the actual needs and wants of the populace must have a means of incorporating into production plans *all* relevant kinds of knowledge, not only explicit or conscious but also fleeting and tacit. Neither of these latter forms of knowledge are transmissible in advance to a central authority devising plans for the future. The discovery and utilization of fleeting knowledge requires a man-on-the-spot able to perceive and then respond to a largely opportunistic situation, one that, by definition, does not endure over time. Tacit knowledge is of a kind that cannot be articulated in advance of some triggering event that raises it to consciousness. Even the most zealous comrade would be incapable of communicating such kinds of knowledge to a central authority, both of which are crucial to a rational allocation of scarce resources.

A further difficulty arises from the very nature of things: the fact that human existence is inseparable from unpredictability and ever-changing circumstance. The difficulty arises not from lack of intelligence or will but rather factors beyond human control: the inherent limitations of the human mind in a world characterized by contingency and unexpected turns of events. Human beings are constitutionally incapable of foreseeing the future with any degree of certainty, from knowing in advance the particular goods and services they will need to deal with existence in a world such as ours. No one can be certain that the items he needs or desires today will be the same items he needs or desires in six months, let alone over a more extended time horizon. Indeed, it is not always possible to know in advance everything an individual may need even to get through a single day. Unforeseen circumstances continually arise in the life of every person—pipes leak; a car breaks down; a new romance develops; a hungry kitten appears in the roadway. Few if any people would have the foresight to include plumbing equipment, automobile parts, a dozen roses, or cat food in the list they prepare for the planner. Even those who possess such foresight, however, cannot be certain they will actually need such items. Perhaps the car will not break down or the existing pipes will hold up fine. The production of items that subsequently prove unnecessary is a waste of scarce resources. Well-meaning government planners will undoubtedly want to ensure access to roses or cat food should the need for such items unexpectedly arise, but it is highly unlikely such aims will be realized in practice. The future cannot be predicted with certainty, and the possible need for any particular good or service depends on largely unforeseeable future circumstances. The relevant facts of economic activity are continually in flux, changing in unpredictable ways. All forms of centralized economic planning encounter the irremediable fact that human existence is not static. We have seen the difficulty if not impossibility of precisely anticipating even one's own future needs and wants with any specificity.

It is thus simply inconceivable that government planners could achieve a corresponding feat for a complex modern society composed of millions upon millions of individuals. Such a conclusion follows from the impossibility of centralizing relevant economic knowledge. Individual knowledge of present and future conditions of demand and supply cannot be transmitted to a central authority because, first, such knowledge is often held by individual minds only as tacit knowledge, inaccessible to the conscious mind unless and until evoked by a particular concrete circumstance; second, fleeting knowledge, by definition, is of a kind that cannot be incorporated into future plans; and, third, the contingency of human experience renders it impossible accurately to foresee either future demand or future sources of supply, both of which depend on unforeseeable future conditions. The inevitable conclusion derived from such epistemological facts is that centralized economic planning, even if motivated by the best intentions, cannot lead to solution of the economic problem. Such a method of economic organization has no means of garnering the knowledge and information requisite to the efficient allocation of scarce resources in service of actual human needs and wants.

The Pretense of Knowledge

The simplest way of expressing the fundamental flaw of all centrally planned economic systems, then, is that planners simply do not possess, and cannot acquire, the relevant knowledge and information required for rational economic planning. Such information can only be acquired through the free and spontaneous formation of a structure of relative prices, which, as we have seen, depends upon the institution of private property. No mind or group of minds can possibly grasp the enormous concrete complexity of modern society. It is impossible to know the actual needs and wants of millions and millions of individuals, needs and wants, moreover, which do not remain stable over time and which individuals themselves may not recognize until some circumstance raises them to consciousness. Nor can planners possess more than an insignificant fraction of relevant knowledge concerning actual and potential supply of scarce resources. An overwhelming portion of such knowledge is dispersed throughout society, held only in the minds of millions of individuals, and of a kind, as we have seen, that cannot be consciously communicated. Central planners feel confident in the wisdom of their plans only because they are blind to the extent of their own ignorance. Their confidence is a false confidence, based on illusion or self-deception, on the mere "pretense of knowledge," in Hayek's well-known phrase.[31] Advocates of central planning are victims of what he calls the "synoptic delusion"—"the fiction that all the relevant economic facts are known to some one mind, and that it is possible to construct from this knowledge of the particulars a desirable social order."[32] Such, as we have seen, is impossible.

The reason why the market economy has generated the greatest prosperity ever known in human history is its superior ability to facilitate the solution of the economic problem that, in the end, is a problem of knowledge. The decentralization of decision processes permits the potential discovery and utilization of all relevant economic knowledge existing in society while a centralized or planned system can only utilize the limited knowledge possessed or acquired by the planners. In the absence of accurate price signals, planners have no means of obtaining

---

[31] F. A. Hayek, "The Pretence of Knowledge," Lecture at the reception at which Hayek, jointly with Gunnar Myrdal, received the Sveriges Riksbank prize in memory of Alfred Nobel, 1974. (Dec. 11, 1974)
[32] Hayek, *Rules and Order*, 14.

knowledge of relevant sources of supply or actual demand. Neither tacit nor fleeting knowledge of local time, place, and circumstance nor knowledge of subjective personal preference can guide the direction of scarce resources. For such reasons centralized or socialized economies invariably fail to produce the results intended by their planners, oblivious as they must be to the limits of their own knowledge.

The market process, by contrast, represents a humble acquiescence to the intractable complexity of actual human experience and the irremediable limits of the human mind. In this instance, the meek do indeed inherit the earth. For accepting the guidance of supra-rational market forces permits individuals to bypass the inherent limits of their minds and limited range of their concrete perception. Their ability to read and speak the abstract language of prices grants access to the vastly greater supra-personal knowledge and information summarized in the simple symbol of a market price—knowledge of real conditions prevailing not only within individual societies but across the world. Centralized or planned systems, by contrast, are characterized by the hubristic refusal to acknowledge the constitutional limits of the human mind—the inherently circumscribed range of any individual's possible knowledge—in the face of the complexity of human existence. However well-meaning the intentions, the socialist endeavor to "organize society as a whole" must, in the end, be regarded as an arrogant and illusory presumption of knowledge and dangerous disregard for the nature of things—the actual conditions of human existence. Adam Smith was among the first to recognize such unfortunate human propensities:

> The man of system . . . is apt to be very wise in his own conceit; and is often so enamoured with the supposed beauty of his own ideal plan of government, that he cannot suffer the smallest deviation from any part of it. . . . He seems to imagine that he can arrange the different members of a great society with as much ease as the hand arranges the different pieces upon a chess-board. He does not consider that in the great chess-board of human society, every single piece has a

principle of motion of its own, altogether different from that
which the legislature might choose to impress upon it.[33]

The "Mixed Economy"

The goal of classic communism, as we have seen, is the replacement of
capitalism with an economic system controlled and administered by
central authority, that is, transfer of the direction of resources from
private to public hands. As previously observed, however, such a goal is
not an end-in-itself, desirable for its own sake, but rather a means toward
realization of the ultimate goal of all collectivized economic systems,
namely, the moral goal of establishing a putatively more just and
equitable society. Collectivists of all persuasions regard significant
disparities in income or wealth as inconsistent with justice. A just society
is said, on the contrary, to require a relatively even distribution of wealth
among members of society; capitalism, which fails to meet such a
requirement, is thus condemned as unjust. The early modern champions
of economic collectivism, such as Marx, believed that the best way to
achieve justice so conceived was the outright appropriation and transfer
of the means of production from private to public ownership, the so-
called "nationalization" of industry. Classic communism or "hot
socialism" on the Marxian model, however, has fallen from favor in the
wake of the uniformly dismal results of the communist and socialist
experiments of the twentieth century. Even proponents of collectivist
ideology have come to recognize that direct nationalization of industry
and complete elimination of private ownership produces disastrous
economic and social consequences.

Despite the dismal performance of actual socialized economies in the
twentieth century and beyond, Marx's prodigious efforts did not prove
in vain. Although his economic theory has been successfully refuted both
theoretically and in practice, by both reason and history, Marx
nevertheless has grounds to claim victory. His triumph, however, would
ultimately relate not to economics but rather morality, more particularly,
the successful transmission of his moral vision to succeeding generations.
Marx vigorously asserted the moral superiority of economic collectivism

---

[33] Adam Smith, *The Theory Of Moral Sentiments*, Part VI, Section II, Chapter
II, 233-4

over capitalism. His most important legacy is to have won the moral high ground for socialist ideals. The views he championed have been widely assimilated throughout Western society and, to the present day, millions of people are convinced that socialism embodies a morality superior to that embodied in capitalism. The validity of such a conviction will be thoroughly explored in a subsequent chapter.

Our present interest involves the simple fact that many individuals in modern society came to embrace, and continue to embrace, the socialist moral ideal: a society is often adjudged more or less just to the extent it achieves or fails to achieve greater equalization of wealth. Marx himself believed that violent revolution would be necessary to realize a just society so conceived.[34] Capitalists, he assumed, would not voluntarily relinquish their privileges. The overthrow of existing capitalist arrangements must therefore entail revolutionary violence and indeed a temporary "dictatorship of the proletariat."[35] Numerous Western converts to socialism, however, were discomforted by the violence Marx regarded as necessary to institute socialized economic organization in formerly capitalist societies. Fellow travelers such as the British Fabians, among others, embraced the Marxian goal but disavowed violence as a means of achieving it. They came to believe, moreover, that violent revolution was not only undesirable but also unnecessary. The establishment of socialism, they recognized, need not require violence or dictatorship but can rather be achieved by peaceful and democratic means, through political evolution, not revolution. They further recognized that pure communism ("hot socialism")—outright confiscation of private property and nationalization of industry—was far from necessary to achieve socialist economic and moral goals. Such could also be achieved by permitting nominal private ownership of resources but regulating and taxing such resources in a way that would further the realization of the overarching moral-economic ideal—greater equalization of material wealth. Yet others who embraced the Marxian

---

[34] ". . . [T]here is only one way in which the murderous death agonies of the old society and the bloody birth throes of the new society can be shortened, simplified and concentrated, and that way is revolutionary terror." Karl Marx, "The Victory of the Counter-Revolution in Vienna," *Neue Rheinische Zeitung*, November 7, 1848.
[35] The phrase was coined by communist journalist Joseph Wedemeyer in 1852 and adopted by Marx and Engels.

moral vision but disavowed Marxian violence came to champion the so-called "mixed economy" or "Third Way," one combination or another of capitalist and socialist economic methods. An economy that united the two principles of economic arrangement, it was argued, could preserve the engine of capitalist productivity and prosperity and simultaneously employ its material achievements to effectuate a more even distribution of wealth.

The contemporary economic system of the United States is a classic instance of such a "mixed economy." Although American economic order relies upon market forces to a significant degree, it is far from a purely capitalist system ordered exclusively through voluntary exchange. Throughout the course of American history, numerous measures were enacted by government that grafted various socialistic programs onto the infrastructure of the market system, a process that continues to the present day.

The narrow textbook definition of socialism as "public ownership of the means of production" does not adequately capture the essence of socialist economic organization, namely, direction of resources by government. The fundamental distinction between capitalism and socialism is not the merely nominal assignment of property rights, private or public, but rather *actual* and *ultimate* decision rights—*who* actually and ultimately decides how resources shall be employed, private individuals or political authority. Socialism exists, in practice if not in name, wherever government assumes authority to direct the use of resources rather than permitting private individuals to direct their use in accord with their individual purposes. Governmental direction or control of such resources does not, as radical communism anticipated, require outright nationalization of industry and confiscation of private property. Such control may rather be achieved by far less draconian methods. It can be accomplished, for instance, by tax and regulatory policy and other kinds of legislation that transfer, in one way or another, ultimate decision rights over nominally private resources from private individuals to public officials.

A conventional measure of the degree of socialization of a nation's economy is the percentage of its so-called Gross Domestic Product (GDP)—the total dollar amount of the goods and services produced within a given society in a given time frame, usually one year—spent, controlled, or otherwise directed by government. In the United States, government expenditure as a percentage of GDP has continuously increased over the course of the twentieth century. At its turn, researchers estimate that the federal government controlled or spent approximately 3% of the GDP of the United States; as of 2014, this percentage is estimated at 21%. Total government spending, including federal, state, and local governments, during the early twentieth century is estimated at about 7% of GDP; as of 2014, that percentage had risen to about 38%.[36] This means that 38% of all resources measured by GDP are ultimately controlled and directed not by private individuals but rather government. In a pure or ideal communist society, government of course directs or controls one hundred percent of all resources; all "spending" is "government spending." As a general rule, the higher the percentage of government spending as a portion of GDP, the greater the socialization of an economy. By such a measure, economic order within the United States is moving ever further away from capitalism and ever closer toward full-fledged socialization. Individuals who are required by law to transfer 38% of their income or other resources to government via taxation no longer possess decision rights over 38% of their personal resources. Government officials decide how such resources are to be employed.

Outright government spending, moreover, is not the only measure of economic socialization and taxation not the only means of controlling nominally private resources. Governmental control of resources can also be achieved by regulatory policy and legislation not directly related to taxation. Recent Congressional legislation, for instance, requires every individual to purchase health insurance by penalty of law.[37] This means that individuals no longer possess decision rights over that portion of personal income that must be spent for the mandated purchase of medical insurance; government has decided how their personal resources are to be employed. There is little difference between such policy and outright confiscation of an individual's property, even if such a "taking" of personal property leads to provision of governmental benefits of one kind or another. In either case, the individual's right to decide how his personal resources are to be employed, that is, his right to property, has

---

[36] Source: OECD (2016), General government spending (indicator). doi: 10.1787/a31cbf4d-en; www.usgovernmentspending.com
[37] The Affordable Care Act of 2010.

been compromised if not invalidated. The defining attribute of socialism or economic socialization is governmental control and direction of resources. Such control is of course direct and explicit in the draconian methods of classic communism, that is, utter abolition of private property and total confiscation of the personal assets of the populace. Similar governmental control and direction of resources, however, is achieved indirectly and implicitly by the methods employed in many nominally capitalist societies, that is, tax and regulatory policy and other legislative enactments. The latter is the procedure employed by most "Progressive" governments in the Western democracies throughout the twentieth century, including the United States.

Socialism and Democracy

We previously noted that Marx's aim—governmental control of resources in the interest of achieving a more equitable distribution of wealth—was widely embraced in the latter half of the nineteenth and early part of the twentieth century. Many converts to socialism, as said, accepted Marx's end but rejected his proposed means—violent revolution—believing instead that socialism could be peacefully established.

In the late nineteenth century, one group of such converts organized to establish the aforementioned and highly influential English Fabian Society.[38] The Fabians were socialists who also regarded themselves politically as democrats, disavowing authoritarian or forceful imposition of socialism in any society. The Fabians, moreover, clearly perceived the potential contribution of democracy to the achievement of socialist goals. They recognized, in particular, that the democratic electoral process provides an ideal vehicle for the peaceful, nonviolent, and legal achievement of socialism toward which they aimed. Greater democratization would serve the achievement of such a purpose by widening the electorate, ideally to the point of universal suffrage. Such an extension of the franchise was to be combined with an educational agenda designed to lead the masses to embrace socialist values and aspirations. Fabians believed that such a combination of means— elections and education—would lead to the formation of democratic

---

[38] G. Bernard Shaw, *Fabian Essays in Socialism* (London: Fabian Society, 1889).

majorities persuaded to vote for candidates committed to various forms of socialistic legislation and regulatory policy, including progressive taxation. Socialism would thus be achieved not immediately and at a stroke but rather gradually and over time. Its movement would proceed not through violence but rather piecemeal and democratic enactment of socialistic policy. Both the celebrated slogan of the Fabian Society—"Make Haste Slowly"—and its adopted symbol—the turtle—clearly expressed its conviction that socialism would eventually be established in Western society through the slow-but-steady evolution of the democratic political process.[39]

Democracy, as we recall, is one traditional Western answer to the question of *who shall rule*—who shall be permitted to participate in the political process, determine law and policy, and hold office. The wider the democracy, the greater the range and number of individuals permitted to vote. The ultimate democratic goal, universal suffrage, was achieved in the United States in 1920 and Britain in 1928. As previously mentioned, Fabians and fellow travelers, such as American Progressives of the era, clearly perceived the potential means-end relation between democracy (majority rule) and socialism. The majority in any society is always comprised by the less-well-to-do members of society, the so-called "have-nots." Wealthier members of society—the "haves"—are always a minority of the total population. It could thus confidently be expected that an ever-wider democratization of society—ever-wider participation of the masses in the political process—would enable ever-greater numbers of "have nots" to exert influence on electoral and legislative outcomes.

Fabians and Progressives further believed that the majority of a democratic electorate can readily be persuaded to vote for socialistic legislation that serves to redistribute or transfer wealth from the "haves" toward themselves. Toward that end, they advocated a policy of progressive taxation: individuals with relatively higher income are taxed at a higher rate than those with relatively lower income. By such means, wealth can be withdrawn from the "haves" and used to fund government programs ("entitlements") that transfer income, goods, or services to the

---

[39] The Fabians took their name from the Roman general Fabius, who developed carefully planned strategies to achieve ultimate victory by slowly wear down his enemies over a long period of time.

"have-nots." Expanding democracy to the point of universal suffrage would more or less ensure that the relatively "poor" would constitute a majority of voters. Such a majority, educated to embrace socialistic values, could be expected to support legislation that transfers material resources from the "rich" to themselves, thereby indirectly, legally, and peacefully serving the socialist goal of equalizing the distribution of wealth across society. Fabians, Progressives, and fellow travelers were indeed correct: the achievement of socialist goals requires neither violence nor the drastic methods of pure communism but can rather be achieved by thoroughgoing democratization of the political process. Democratic majorities can (and do) achieve the political redistribution of wealth by supporting progressive taxation and redistributive legislation and regulation while simultaneously permitting private property and the rule of law more generally to remain nominally intact. We have previously discussed the modern phenomenon of totalitarian democracy.

Fabian or Progressive gradualism is one aspect of the process that has led to the transformation of the American economic order from a predominantly capitalist to a "mixed" economy. As mentioned, significant and vibrant elements of a market economy continue to exist in the United States, but such are intermingled with various socialistic measures that operate on principles incompatible with the principles of the market. The question is whether the simultaneous application of opposing economic principles—capitalism and socialism—can sustain a flourishing and prosperous society over time. In his celebrated book *The Road to Serfdom*, Hayek argues against the stability and long-run viability of such a "mixed" economy.[40] He maintains, on the contrary, that the tendency of an economic system that confounds contradictory principles is toward the gradual elimination of one or the other of the opposing elements. Either the socialistic elements will give way to market principles, or the reverse, the free economy will gradually find itself overwhelmed by collectivist command and control.

Fascism

---

[40] F. A. Hayek, *The Road to Serfdom,* ed, Bruce Caldwell (Chicago: University of Chicago Press. 2007).

The attempt to combine capitalistic and socialistic practices is also a prominent feature of another type of collectivized economy that shares important attributes with socialism, namely, fascism. The term fascism is widely if inappropriately employed in contemporary discourse as a potent emotional symbol, usually associated with various political evils such as dictatorship, authoritarianism, fanatic nationalism, racism, militarism, and so on. Such usage no doubt stems from its popular association with the image of Adolph Hitler and the German Nazi Party (National Socialist Party), the most infamous face of fascism in the twentieth century. Such careless and emotionally charged usage, however, should be avoided. The term fascism is more than a mere emotional epithet. It designates an objective concept whose meaning is essential to analytic clarity.

Modern fascism is of Italian origin, first emerging in the totalitarian regime of Benito Mussolini (1883-1945). The term derives from the Latin *fascis*—a bundle of bound rods containing an axe and blade protruding from the center. In ancient Rome the *fasces* was employed as a symbol of the power and jurisdiction of a magistrate (legal administrator). It was revived in modern Italy in conjunction with the regime established by Mussolini, whose symbol was the *fasces* and whose slogan was "strength through unity." Hitler and the Nazis later adopted the term fascism and reinterpreted it in line with their particular purposes.

With respect to economics, the term fascism, like the terms socialism and capitalism, refers to a distinctive set of economic arrangements, namely, a collectivist organization of economic activity sometimes called *corporatism* or *syndicalism*. It is akin to communism and other forms of economic socialization in that it too involves governmental or state control of resources within society. Unlike classic communism, however, and somewhat like the conception of a mixed economy, it does not involve the abolition of private property. Property remains nominally private but industries and workers are organized into large associations— corporations and unions. Individual entrepreneurship is discouraged or prohibited. Ideally, every individual and association of individuals is grouped within one of three massively organized entities—what Americans call "Big Business," "Big Labor," and "Big Government." Representatives of the three organized sectors participate in the formation of economic plans for society as a whole, planning that involves government in every instance. Government officials more or less issue directives to corporate and union leaders, perhaps with some negotiation of benefits for particular economic sectors, and corporations and unions carry out the resulting plans. Individual property is no longer under exclusive direction of its owners but rather must be employed to fulfill the purposes established or approved by government in conjunction with the other two organized sectors. Government ultimately directs the allocation of resources but in a roundabout manner. By such indirect methods, however, government may potentially gain control of resources as effectively as the direct control exercised under communism proper.

"Crony Capitalism"

Over time, the United States has come to adopt economic arrangements that combine capitalist, socialist, and corporatist elements, a form of mixed economy variously referred to as "crony capitalism," "political capitalism," "state capitalism," and, most recently, "participatory fascism."[41] Crony capitalism, like fascist corporatism, must be sharply distinguished from authentic capitalism. Capitalism, as we have seen, is based upon private direction of personally owned resources, guided by market prices and regulated by the discipline of profit and loss. Its successful operation depends upon the existence of both freely forming relative prices and authentically competitive markets. Market competition means that any person is free to enter or exit any industry or business at any time. Such competition or even potential competition serves to ensure that resources are employed in the least wasteful manner and toward fulfillment of actual consumer demand. A firm that is wasting resources, charging unnecessarily high prices, or not fulfilling consumer demand, may be, and typically is, challenged by a newcomer with a better idea. Business leaders often dislike capitalism precisely for this reason; however successful they may have been in the past, they are always threatened by the possibility of new competition. Contrary to popular belief, capitalism does not primarily serve "capitalists"— producers, investors, and entrepreneurs—but rather consumers. The

---

[41] Such a politico-economic system is sometimes referred to as "special interest liberalism" or the "corporate-welfare state."

forces of competitive markets serve to ensure least-cost production and tailoring of production to the specific needs and wants of consumers, not the wellbeing of producers.

Business firms, then, especially large and well established organizations ("Big Business"), often seek means to shield themselves from the forces of market competition. The most common approach is to seek political and legal protection from such competition, as evidenced by the more than 7,000 so-called "lobbying" firms headquartered in Washington D.C. The mission of such lobbyists is generally to influence the federal legislative process toward the end of obtaining political privileges for the firms, industries, and interests they represent. Such privileges take various forms but they all serve to shield producers from market competition. Among the historically most common forms of "special-interest" pleading is the attempt to obtain monopolistic privileges for a particular firm or industry, that is, gain the exclusive right to produce a particular good or service. Monopoly ("one" producer) is not necessarily sinister-in-itself. Benign monopolies may in fact develop in a free-market economy. Such could occur, for instance, if one producer possesses such superior knowledge and expertise that others simply cannot compete in terms of cost and quality. The only way to know, however, whether a monopolist is benign, that is, actually serving the best interests of the consumer in the most efficient manner, is the existence of potential competition. In a free economy, a monopolist that charges exorbitant and unjustified prices, "gouging" the consumer, will eventually be challenged by competitors. If the price charged by the monopolist is actually higher than necessary to produce a given item, other producers have every incentive (potential profit) to enter the market and sell the item at lower cost. If a monopolist remains unchallenged in a market economy, on the other hand, it is probably because no one can do better.

Such monopolistic superiority is possible but relatively rare in a capitalist economy; most monopolies have been, and are, the result not of market forces but rather political intervention or favoritism. "Crony capitalism" is the result of successful efforts, whether of industries, firms, or individuals, to influence governmental policy in their favor and at the expense of other producers, consumers, and taxpayers. In the case of monopoly, the aim is to obtain exclusive privilege to produce a particular good or service by legally prohibiting competitors from entering the market. Political actors, seeking to reward past supporters or win future support, can and do grant such favors to their friends or "cronies." Economic history clearly demonstrates that the vast majority of historical monopolies result not from capitalist processes but rather government intervention in the market process.[42]

Outright monopoly, however, is not the only form of political protection sought by corporate and business interests. Such protection can also be obtained by various forms of governmental regulation that similarly serve to shield such interests from competitive market forces. Historically, regulated industries have often been involved in designing the very regulations under which they must operate, regulations that typically benefit larger and established producers at the expense of smaller producers and potential newcomers to the field. A typical example is recent financial legislation (the so-called "Dodd-Frank" bill) that establishes onerous capital requirements for banks and other lenders. Such requirements penalize smaller community banks and benefit corporate giants such as Bank of America and Citibank. An account of crony or political capitalism should also mention the legions of quasi-independent contractors who lobby legislators to win lucrative government contracts, often without competitive bidding. As early as the 1950s, President Dwight Eisenhower warned Americans of the growth of what he called the "military-industrial complex"—the "conjunction of an immense military establishment and a large arms industry"—that not only potentially threatens our "liberties or democratic processes" but also parasitically feeds on government at the expense of other businesses and taxpayers in general.[43]

Licensing regulations are another form of special-interest pleading that serves to buffer existing producers from competition at the expense of both unlicensed producers and consumers. The history of licensing laws

---

[42] Milton Friedman, *Capitalism & Freedom* (Chicago: University of Chicago Press, 1962); Dominick T. Armentano, *Antitrust and Monopoly: Anatomy of a Policy Failure* (Oakland, CA: Independent Institute, 1996; Yale Brozen, *Is Government the Source of Monopoly? And Other Essays* (Washington DC: Cato Institute, 1980); Sylvester Petro, "Competition, Monopoly, and the Role of Government" (Irvington-on-Hudson, NY: Foundation for Economic Education, 1959).

[43] Dwight D. Eisenhower, "Military-Industrial Complex Speech," 1961. *Public Papers of the Presidents,* Dwight D. Eisenhower (Washington DC: National Archives [Federal Depository Library] 1960), 1035-1040.

shows that the demand for such laws is often initiated by practicing members of the occupation in question. The aim is to shield the license holder from competition from unlicensed businesses offering the same good or service. Professions that win political privilege in the form of licensing laws force losses on both unlicensed producers, who may no longer practice their trade, and consumers. Licensing laws decrease the supply of providers and restrict competition within the licensed industry or profession, which means that consumer choice is limited to fewer suppliers. The reduction in competitive pressure also means that suppliers have less incentive either to improve quality or reduce cost (and thus price) of the good or service in question. *Ceteris paribus*, a reduction in supply, whether of producers or produced goods, tends to lead to an increase in price. As Nobel Laureate economist Milton Friedman noted, "[trade licensing] almost inevitably becomes a tool in the hands of a special producer group to maintain a monopoly position at the expense of the rest of the public. There is no way to avoid this result."[44]

Crony capitalism and other forms of governmental privilege or favoritism benefit politically influential industries in other ways as well. Huge corporate "agribusiness," for instance, lobbies for agricultural subsidies that enable producers to stay in business even if total sales from their products are not sufficient to cover costs of production. In recent years, Americans have witnessed governmental "bail-out" after bail-out, from giant insurance companies like AIG to General Motors to labor unions unable to meet their pension and health-care obligations. A "bail-out" to industry is nothing more than a government subsidy, funded by present or future taxpayers (if the funds are obtained by borrowing). It is a reward to politically connected and organized interests at the expense of unorganized interests, such as individual taxpayers and small business.

Bail-outs, like agricultural subsidies, permit nonviable firms to remain in business despite the fact that they are unable to win a number of customers sufficient to pay the costs of their operation. In an authentic market economy, such producers would suffer losses and go out of business. Such indeed is the proper and rational economic consequence, difficult as it may be for those directly involved in a failing business or industry. We have seen that "losses," in the language of price, mean that

---

[44] Milton Friedman, *Capitalism & Freedom*, 148. Awarded Nobel Prize in economics in 1976.

consumers do not want the products offered by the producer or at least not at the seller's asking price. Losses signal to producers that they are doing something wrong—wasting scarce resources to produce unwanted items—and must change course. Governmental bailouts, however, override such price signals and encourage wasteful production of items that consumers do not value. Such bailouts, moreover, are generally paid for by taxation, which means that resources of productive workers are taken and politically redistributed to firms with a *demonstrated* inability to allocate limited resources efficiently and wisely (demonstrated by the very fact of economic losses). Such economic irrationality benefits the privileged firms but harms taxpayers, other businesses, and society at large. Resources are scarce and should not be used to produce uneconomic goods and services, that is, goods that cost more to produce than people are willing to pay. In the modern American economy, however, the market process that serves rationally and spontaneously to allocate scarce resources to their best use is often overridden by political intervention. Such intervention necessarily distorts the market process, which can only serve its function if producers are subject to the discipline of both profit *and* loss.

Indeed government in the United States massively intervenes in the market process. It attempts to control the direction of resources not by outright abolition or confiscation of private property but rather tax and regulatory policy and other forms of legislation. It encourages the production of certain goods and services by means of subsidies, bailouts, and tax credits and discourages other types of production by imposing taxes or regulations on the industry in question. Firms regard both taxes and regulatory mandates as a cost of production. An increase in tax rates and regulation thus raises costs of production, costs which firms attempt to pass on to the consumer in the form of higher prices. *Ceteris paribus*, the higher the price, the lower the demand. By raising costs of production, taxes and regulation discourage both production and consumption. Such is yet another reason for the existence of Washington lobbyists. Even firms and industries that do not attempt to gain special privileges realize that they must be either represented in the federal legislative process or its victims—the lambs slaughtered by voracious taxes on the goods and services they produce or draconian regulation of their production. For such reasons, many corporations, in mere self-defense, contribute significantly to candidates of both major political parties. By so doing, they hope to win favor with the powers-that-be, of whichever party happens to win an election.

Political privilege and favoritism toward special-interests are routinely bought and sold in the "market" of contemporary American politics. The result is a most uneven "playing field," where organized and politically influential interests gain economic advantage over their unorganized and less-influential competitors. Unorganized interests, including those which are generally impossible to organize—small businesses, individual entrepreneurs, taxpayers, and consumers—pay the costs of such cronyism. Woodrow Wilson once remarked, "I have always in my own thought summed up individual liberty, and business liberty, and every other kind of liberty, in the phrase that is common in the sporting world, "A free field and no favor."[45] The "special-interest liberalism" embodied in the contemporary American corporate-welfare state bears little resemblance to the constitutional political order and free-market economic order characteristic of traditional American ideals.

In conclusion, political intervention in the market process suffers from the same flaw that proves fatal to any form of planned or command economy—the fact that government officials in any complex society do not and cannot know how resources "should" be utilized any better than central planners in the former Soviet Union. The only way such knowledge can be gained is by reading the language of relative prices and acquiescing to their guidance. Economic intervention by government, however, generally consists precisely in overriding or ignoring market-generated prices, that is, substituting political will for a rational allocation of scarce resources in the production of items most valued by consumers. Political actors intervene in the market process for various, and related, reasons—to reward political supporters; gain votes by providing economic benefits to particular groups; gain control over the direction of resources through tax and regulatory policy; protect certain politically influential industries (often major donors to electoral campaigns) from competition; ensure that certain favored groups maintain their historical standard of living; redistribute income and wealth from one group to another; and so on. In all cases of political intervention in the price system, however, politicians substitute their own will or the will of their contributors or constituents for the facts of

---

[45] Woodrow Wilson (1856-1924), U. S. President, Speech 1915.

reality. To disregard or override a price signal, whether by subsidy, legislative enactment of price and wage controls, manipulative tax policy, regulatory edict, or other such devices, is to defy the actual conditions of existence. Freely forming market prices embody truth, that is, the actual conditions of supply and demand that exist at a given time. To willfully override such facts is to misallocate scarce resources. Crony capitalism or political privilege is wasteful and wrong from any economic point of view beyond those of its direct beneficiaries.

Economic intervention by political authority, moreover, violates not only economic rationality but also the traditional American sense of justice. Justice within the Western and Anglo-American tradition, as we have seen, has long been bound to the moral demand for equality under law or equal treatment under the law. Economic privileges, however, cannot uniformly be provided to every individual and every profession, firm, or industry in society. Obviously only some individuals or groups can be granted "privileges"—special advantages or immunities.[46] It would clearly be impossible to subsidize every failing individual, firm, and industry with taxpayer funds. Some individuals, firms, and industries must be earning sufficient profit to pay the taxes necessary to subsidize their failing counterparts; the former must pay the cost while the latter receive the benefits. Crony capitalism and other forms of political intervention in a market economy always involve winners and losers; one person or group gains at the expense of others. Such is to violate the principle of equality under law and the rights of the "losers." "Justice," said James Madison, "is the end of government." Political intervention in the price system necessarily violates that end.

---

[46] A privilege may be formally defined as a special right, advantage, or immunity granted or available only to a particular person or group of people.

114

NINE

THE MARXIST CRITIQUE OF CAPITALISM

. . . [M]odern bourgeois private property is the final and most complete expression of the system of producing and appropriating products, that is based on class antagonisms, on the exploitation of the many by the few.

—Karl Marx

The theory of Communists may be summed up in the single sentence: Abolition of private property.   —Karl Marx

Previous chapters examined the essential differences between capitalism and socialism principally from an economic point of view. Both theory and historical experience clearly demonstrate the superiority of the market process with respect to both the allocation of scarce resources and fulfillment of subjective human values. The free-enterprise system has resulted in the greatest and most far-reaching prosperity ever achieved in human history, while the experiment in economic centralization, wherever implemented, has universally failed to produce the results anticipated by its advocates. The disparity in performance is not accidental but rather stems from the nature of things—from the fundamental fact of scarcity and the fact that no human being or select group of human beings can know more than an infinitesimal fraction of all the relevant facts that must be taken into account in solving the economic problem that arises from scarcity. Planners in a centralized economy have no means of accessing the knowledge and information that daily and spontaneously informs the market process via the price system secured by the rule of law. Both reason and experience, theory and history, conclusively establish the inherent superiority of the market solution to the economic problem that confronts every human society.

Neither the demonstrations of reason nor the evidence of history, however, have led to the abandonment of socialist aspirations. It is true that pure communism—total government ownership of the means of production and other resources—has been rejected in all but a few nations, such as North Korea. But to the astonishment of those familiar with the catastrophic history of the twentieth century—the Age of Totalitarianism—significant portions of the contemporary American electorate, as well as their political leaders, seem oblivious to such experience. A growing number of Americans, like the millions who pursued a similar dream in the previous century, seem enchanted by the siren song of socialism. In recent years the United States has adopted policy after policy—health-insurance legislation; nationalization of student loans; governmental direction of private industries and financial institutions; so-called "economic stimulus" plans; massive regulatory and other interventionist policies—more typical of a socialized than a free economy. Indeed in 2016 a self-avowed Socialist achieved considerable success in presidential primary elections.[47]

One would expect heirs of the twentieth century to know better, having gained knowledge and experience unavailable to the initial champions of economic socialization. The results of the collectivist experiment—economic collapse, immiseration of the populace, and tragic destruction of both human life and human values—are not mere theoretical possibilities but documented historical fact. Indeed, the twentieth century was among the most barbaric in human history, if wanton destruction of human life is regarded as barbaric. By conservative estimates, more than one hundred million people were killed as a direct or indirect result of the implementation of the economic plans advanced by political leaders in the Age of Ideology.[48] Millions more experienced terror, deprivation, and hopelessness, not to mention loss of individual freedom.

Such were not the results intended by the early advocates of economic centralization and collectivization. Their aim was rather pursuit of a grand moral ideal purportedly superior to the traditional ideals embodied in liberal democracy and capitalism. The pursuit of an ideal

---

[47] Senator Bernie Sanders (Vermont).
[48] Jean-Louis Panné, Andrzej Paczkowski, *Black Book of Communism* (Cambridge: Harvard University Press, 1999).

that results in the death of millions of human beings, however, should give pause. The tragedy that ensued in the wake of the collectivist experiments suggests that their inspiration—their motivating ideal—is somehow false or illusory, in conflict with reality, the nature of things. Ideals are essential guides to human action but fruitful ideals must be inherently capable of actualization. The twentieth century has demonstrated all too clearly that the pursuit of impossible or unrealizable ideals leads not to human flourishing but rather disaster. History, said the American Founders, is the "lamp of experience." George Santayana warned that "those who cannot remember the past are condemned to repeat it."[49] The hope remains that the American people are willing to learn and remember the lessons taught by the tragic history of the recent past. The light of human experience, supported by the conclusions of reason, may yet prevent them from sharing the fate of those millions of human beings who so needlessly suffered under the great collectivist experiment that all but defined the twentieth century.

Such lessons must begin with a thorough examination of the moral ideal pursued by advocates of centralized or socialized economic organization. Social phenomena of any form—economic, political, legal, or cultural—are never self-contained, autonomous, self-generating entities but rather manifestations of the beliefs and values embraced by the individuals who constitute any given society. To paraphrase David Hume's expression of the basic insight, in the end, "opinion governs all"; as Hayek expressed a similar conception, "values generate facts." In other words, the rise of the ideological movements over the past century can only be understood in light of the values, beliefs, and ideals that inspired them. We have previously noted Marx's significant success in winning the moral high ground for the socialist ideal. He and his acolytes successfully persuaded millions of human beings that moral progress entails the replacement of capitalism with economic centralization of one form or another.

Both capitalism and socialism are generally, and rightly, regarded as economic and not moral constructs. It is impossible, however, to dissociate economic from moral considerations because human action in the face of scarcity, the subject matter of economics, cannot be

---

[49] George Santayana, *The Life of Reason* (Amherst, NY: Prometheus Books, 1998 [1905].

dissociated from moral considerations. Not only does human nature comprise an inherent moral dimension but, as Hayek suggests, strictly speaking, there are no purely "economic" ends.[50] Human pursuits are ultimately oriented toward fulfillment of abstract or immaterial value—happiness, love, justice, goodness, peace, truth, fame, security, power, and so on. Human beings do not generally desire or value material goods for their own sake but rather to fulfill such nonmaterial values, whether love for a child expressed by the gift of a gold locket or the sense of personal security anticipated by home ownership. Few people covet gold lockets or houses for the sake of mere possession; authentic misers are rare among the human community. The discipline of economics addresses the material means that human beings must necessarily employ to achieve their largely immaterial ends, means that necessarily possess a moral dimension.

Material goods and services, in other words, are instrumental and not ultimate values. Economic science, which deals with the best means (instruments) by which human beings can fulfill their subjectively valued ends or purposes, has, for that reason, been described, pointedly if unimaginatively, as a science of means and not of ends. Economic theory is not a substantive worldview, religion, or philosophy that advocates for or against the embrace of particular values; it has nothing to say about what people *should* value. The scope of economics is far more limited and humble. It deals solely with the means by which individuals may obtain the material goods necessary to fulfill their individual values, and especially with the necessity of choice in the face of scarcity. Economic theory *per se* is silent with respect to the substantive content of human choices. An economic "good" is simply an item or service that is *in fact* desired by someone, in sharp distinction to an item or service that *should* be desired, one that is morally or otherwise *desirable*. The problem to which capitalism and socialism offer divergent solutions concerns how

---

[50] "The ultimate ends of the activities of reasonable beings are never economic. Strictly speaking, there is no 'economic motive' but only economic factors conditioning our striving for other ends. What in ordinary language is misleadingly called the 'economic motive' means merely the desire for general opportunity, the desire for power to achieve unspecified ends." Hayek, *Road to Serfdom*, 125.

human beings can obtain the means to fulfill their ultimate ends or values, whatever these may be and however they are formed.

That said, however, the two rival economic systems do embody definite and competing moral ideals. Ultimately, the advocacy of socialism, like that of capitalism, is the advocacy of a particular moral vision of human existence. An exploration of the distinct moral views implicitly and explicitly informing socialist and capitalist economic constructs will bring the grounds of such a conclusion to light.

The Marxist Critique

Karl Marx may be the most well-known modern champion of communism and socialism but he was far from the first thinker to advance such views. He was preceded in the late eighteenth and early nineteenth centuries by various socialist thinkers centered largely in France. The term itself was coined by Henri de Saint-Simon (1760-1823), often regarded as the "founder of French socialism," and propagated by his followers, including the so-called St. Simonians and Auguste Comte (1798-1857), founder of the modern discipline of sociology. Marx, however, proved to be an especially powerful and prolific writer, and his particular ideological constructions would succeed in capturing mind, heart, and soul of countless contemporaries and their descendants. Few persons may actually have read Marx's extensive corpus but almost every literate person has at least passing acquaintance with *Das Kapital* or *The Communist Manifesto*.[51] Indeed, even persons who have never heard of Marx have nevertheless been influenced by his thought. Not only was Marxism explicitly adopted as the theoretical foundation of twentieth-century communist regimes and satellite states, but various Marxist tenets have been widely assimilated by mainstream Western society, including American society. Marxian assumptions and beliefs permeate the consciousness of modern man, informing language, politics, formal education, media, and other forms of cultural expression.

---

[51] Karl Marx, *Das Kapital*, in three volumes (London: Penguin Classics, 1992 reprint ed, [1861-1894]). The *Communist Manifesto* is the most frequently assigned reading in American universities at the present time.

Marx's fame undoubtedly rests upon his radical critique of the capitalist order. His economic analysis, however, does not stand in isolation but is rather embedded in a wider critique of Western liberal society, one that involves a sweeping rejection of its fundamental premises, including and especially its self-characterization as a "free society." Marx's milieu was of course nineteenth-century Europe—the so-called "Age of Liberalism" marked by widespread embrace of classical liberal values and principles. Classical liberalism, as we have seen, represents a systematic or principled defense of the free society and its constituent elements—limited government, private property and the rule of law, traditional Judeo-Christian moral values, and capitalism, regarded as the only economic system compatible with the preservation of individual liberty and related liberal values. The free society so conceived is an integrated or coherent whole whose social institutions and customs (political, legal, moral, and economic) implicitly and explicitly embody a consistent set of abstract values and principles, including the core value of individual liberty. Marx well understood that fact. He understood that capitalism stands or falls with the values, beliefs, social institutions and practices requisite to its sustenance; no form of economic arrangement does or can exist in a social vacuum. His critique of capitalism thus necessarily involved a critique of the comprehensive moral and institutional structure of Western society developed over centuries if not millennia of experience.

*

We begin with Marx's assault on the self-characterization of Western liberal society as the free society. Classical liberal society entails, above all, limits on the coercive power of government. In the American case, such limits are established by the terms of a more or less Lockean social compact. On such a view, as we recall, the principal purpose of government is to secure the rule of law, which itself aims to protect the natural and negative rights to life, liberty, and property possessed by each and every individual. Such a society neither recognizes "positive" rights nor maintains a politically organized "safety net" such as exists in contemporary American society—welfare, food stamps, public housing, Medicaid, and other material entitlements provided by government at taxpayers' expense.

According to Marx, the free society so conceived is an illusion, a lie and a sham; no individual, he suggests, is actually free within such a regime. Consider, for instance, the fate of an individual in liberal capitalist society who for one reason or another voluntarily chooses not to work. For the sake of argument, assume that such an individual is without financial savings or support from friends or family. Under such circumstances, an individual who remains unemployed for any length of time, without income or material resources, will not only find his opportunities for achieving personal goals severely circumscribed but, indeed, will probably perish. To put it bluntly, individuals who choose not to work in a putatively free society ordered by market exchange will die. If freedom means the absence of coercion, then it is obvious to Marx that no one in such a society is free. Every member of liberal society, on the contrary, exists under the continual and ominous threat of coercion that, like all coercion, reduces their options to two undesirables, in this case, work or die. Every person is forced or compelled to work, whether he will or not, on penalty of death. Such "choice" as he or she can exercise is not free or voluntary but rather coerced. Marx concludes that true freedom does not and cannot exist within liberal capitalist society.

Marx's judgment, if true, must call into question the legitimacy not only of capitalism but modern Western order in general, which largely justifies itself on the very grounds of individual freedom. The seriousness of his allegation thus demands an equally serious inquiry into its validity. Is it true that individual freedom in liberal capitalist society is mere illusion or delusion? Is it true that relentless coercive pressure forces upon every individual the involuntary servitude of a slave, that is, compulsory labor, performed without volition or choice?

The attempt to answer such questions must begin with restatement of the definitions of freedom and coercion that historically informed the development of Western political and economic order, particularly its Anglo-American expression. Freedom, as we have seen, involves the ability to act in the absence of coercion. Coercion exists whenever one human being attempts to determine the consequences of another human being's choice in such a way that the victim will act as the coercer desires rather than as the victim himself desires. Any act of coercion (and thus any violation of freedom) necessarily involves the existence of at least two conscious and willing human beings—the coercer and the coerced. The exercise of coercion further entails intentionality, that is, the coercer must *deliberately* aim to induce another person to act, not as he himself wills, but rather as the coercer wills.

Marx's critique of freedom fails to meet such conditions. Such failure is immediately apparent upon posing the relevant question: *Who* in the Marxian scenario is exercising coercion, that is, is deliberately forcing upon the individual the awful choice of work or die? *Who* is the identifiable human actor who holds both the intention and power to determine the consequences of another individual's choice—either work and survive or do not work and die—such that the latter will choose to act as the former wishes (work) rather than as he himself wishes (not to work)? A moment's reflection reveals that no such person exists in a free society. No human being possesses either the intention or the power to force another human being to work if he does not voluntarily choose to do so. Slavery is legally prohibited in modern liberal society, and capitalism, as we have seen, legally prohibits the use of force in market exchange.

We recall that freedom in the Anglo-American tradition is a specific and qualified kind of freedom, namely, the ability to act in a voluntary manner. A person is free provided that no other human being possesses both the intention and power to prevent his voluntary choice of belief or action. Such freedom does not involve the ability of the person to do whatever he desires, such as live without working. Individual freedom, as we have seen, is rather conceived as a negative value secured by the absence of a particular condition, namely, intentional coercive action on the part of another human being. The fact that human beings must work to survive does not violate human freedom so conceived. Such violation would require the existence of an identifiable human being deliberately exerting coercive pressure on another human being toward a specified end. Such a condition, as said, is absent in the Marxian critique. No one is coerced to work in a free society because there is no identifiable, or even conceivable, human coercer.

Marx's critique is plausible but fallacious. His reasoning, like that involved in most fallacious conclusions, does embody an element of truth, namely, in a free society, a person who voluntarily chooses not to work will eventually perish (assuming, again, no other source of support). His conclusion—the denial of the reality of freedom in liberal capitalist society—however, is false, because such a consequence does not result from human intentionality and power, a necessary condition for the violation of freedom. Existence in a free society does make stringent demands on every individual, even to the extent of Marx's "work or die." Such demands, however, derive not from morally or politically meaningful human coercion but rather from the nature of things. They derive, that is, from the *kind* of world inhabited by human beings, a world characterized by the fundamental fact of scarcity. The human necessity to work is "caused," so to speak, by the fact that the goods required for human survival and flourishing do not exist in unlimited supply.

In such a world, the only conceivable agent that could be charged with coercion—intentionally forcing individuals to work on pain of death—is the agent responsible for creating the *kind* of world in which such a choice is necessary. In the minds of most members of Western society, that agent could only be the transcendent God of the Judeo-Christian tradition, the maker of heaven and earth. Such was undoubtedly the view held by the majority of Marx's nineteenth-century contemporaries. God, the omnipotent creator of the world *ex nihilo*, is ultimately responsible for the nature of things, for creating the kind of world in which man is forced to work in order to survive ("By the sweat of your brow you will eat your food . . . " [Genesis 3:19]).[52] The necessity to choose between work and death cannot be attributed to human design or intention; obviously no human being is or can be held responsible for the nature of things. For such reasons, the coercer implied in the Marxian critique can be none other than God, a conclusion supported by Marx himself. As he says in the well-known foreword to his doctoral thesis, "[P]hilosophy makes no secret of it. Prometheus' confession 'in a word, I hate all gods', is its own confession, its own motto against all gods in heaven and earth who do not recognize human self-consciousness as the highest divinity."[53]

Marx's critique of the free society, cast largely in economic terms, penetrates far more deeply than economics. It represents a radical

---

[52] "By the sweat of your brow you will eat your food . . . until you return to the ground, since from it you were taken; for dust you are and to dust you will return." Genesis 3:19

[53] Marx, "The Difference Between the Democritean and Epicurean Philosophies of Nature" (1839-1841), *The Collected Works of Marx and Engels*, 1835-1843, Vol. 1 (NY: International Publishers, 1975).

critique of Western civilization in general and its religious tradition in particular. Indeed Marx played a leading role in the profound existential drama enacted in Western society throughout the nineteenth century, what Albert Camus famously characterized as "metaphysical rebellion" against the God of the Bible and correlative elevation of "Humanity" ("man's self-consciousness") to godlike status.[54] The existential and metaphysical thrust of Marx's mission has been described by various scholars as the attempted "self-divinization" of man, a mission pursued not only by Marx but other major thinkers of the era as well.[55] The modern ideological movements inspired by Marx and fellow travelers cannot be comprehended apart from their profound and mutual rejection of transcendent religion, a subject extensively explored in Volume III of this study.

Dialectical Materialism and Alienation of Labor

According to Marx, then, capitalism and supporting liberal institutions do not and cannot realize freedom, which alone provides sufficient grounds for their condemnation. The failure to realize freedom, however, is not the only or even the most problematic flaw of the market system. Capitalism must be condemned not only for its alleged violation of freedom but for an even more profound moral fault: the system itself, Marx sweepingly concludes, is intrinsically and irremediably unjust. The grounds on which he bases such a devastating conclusion must be comprehended in light of his general vision of capitalism, a subject to which we now turn.

Marx clearly recognized that capitalism is dependent upon the institution of private property. Capitalists, by definition, own the means of production—the factories, tools, machines, and other material inputs into the production process—which means that they and they alone decide if and how to employ such resources. Marx sometimes refers to this group of capitalists/owners as the *bourgeoisie*, conventionally translated as the "middle class." The *bourgeoisie*, according to Marx,

---

[54] Albert Camus, *The Rebel: An Essay on Man in Revolt* (New York: Vintage, 1992 [1951]).

[55] Henri de Lubac, *The Drama of Atheist Humanism* (San Francisco: Ignatius Press, 1996). Hereinafter cited as *Drama*.

necessarily confronts a second and distinct class of human beings in liberal society, the so-called *proletariat* (from the Latin *prole*, "without issue"), conventionally translated as the "workers." The *proletariat* comprises all individuals who do not own capital, who own no factories, tools, or other material means of production. Their sole possession is their own labor. Modern society, according to Marx, is thus divided into two classes, the *bourgeoisie* and the *proletariat*—those who own capital and those who do not. The two economic classes, moreover, relate to one another not in friendship and cooperation but rather enmity and antagonism.

Such mutual hostility, however, is to be expected, for, according to Marx, struggle between contending classes ("class struggle") has not only existed in every society known to man but indeed is the driving force of history. Class struggle, he maintains, has been a constant feature of human society, merely assuming different forms in different historical eras. In the ancient world, the class struggle pitted masters against slaves; in the feudal world, overlords and nobility against serfs; in the modern era, the struggle is between capitalists and workers. As Marx put it,

> The history of all hitherto existing society is the history of class struggles. . . . Freeman and slave, patrician and plebeian, lord and serf, guildmaster and journeyman, in a word, oppressor and oppressed, stood in constant opposition to one another, carried on an uninterrupted, now hidden, now open fight, that each time ended, either in the revolutionary reconstitution of society at large, or in the common ruin of the contending classes.[56]

The movement of human history over time is driven by antagonism between the two historically pertinent classes. Tension between them generates conflict that demands resolution. When such a point is reached, the conflict is resolved by the emergence of new "relations of production"—the birth of a new structure of economic organization. Eventually each newly born economic structure will in turn generate tension and conflict, leading to its replacement by the relations of production appropriate to the movement of history. By such a

---

[56] *Communist Manifesto*, 473-474.

"dialectical" process, ancient slavery eventually transformed into feudalism, which eventually transformed into capitalism. Capitalism is similarly destined to transform into what Marx regarded as the final goal or end of the historical process, namely, communism.

Many nineteenth-century thinkers held what is called a determinist philosophy of history. The course of history is conceived as an autonomous and self-directing entity that proceeds in accord with its own laws—the so-called "laws of history"—and toward a predetermined goal established by those same laws (the "End of History"). Marx was a man of his time, a fervent champion of historical determinism in general and his own version in particular, which he called *dialectical materialism*. History, he maintained, is not only driven by class struggle but also toward achievement of its own goal or purpose, independent of the goals or purposes of individual human beings. The march of history toward its goal is ineluctable and inevitable, determined not by human subjects but objective and immutable laws indifferent to human preference. Marx, like other historical determinists of the era, claimed to know the final goal of history, that toward which it has been striving for all time. The modern struggle between capitalists and workers is simply a necessary stage in the historical process. The resolution of capitalism's internal conflicts will lead not only to resolution of its particular conflicts but indeed of class conflict itself, which, according to Marx, will be achieved by the final, once-and-for-all, establishment of communist relations of production. Individuals may be utterly unaware of the role they play in realizing the "end of history" so conceived, instead believing in their capacity for exercising voluntary choice in the face of historical circumstance. Such conviction, however, is more or less illusory. Every human being, in truth, is an instrument of history with no choice but to participate toward fulfillment of its final goal. The transformation of capitalism into communism is beyond human control because the laws of history are beyond human control.

Marx further believed that contemporary society was in the throes of the final class struggle that would culminate in communism. Such culmination, while inevitable, could nevertheless be facilitated by the so-called "vanguard of the proletariat," intellectuals such as Marx who understand the laws of history and can guide society toward its final goal, serving, one might say, as midwives to the birth of a new world order. One aspect of such a role involves raising the consciousness of the workers. The proletariat must come to realize its oppressive condition and recognize its cause—capitalism. Having gained such understanding, workers as a whole will unite against capitalists as a whole, rise up in violent revolution, throw off their chains, and seize the means of production from the *bourgeoisie*. Thus begins the process whereby the final goal of history, the establishment of communism, is realized.

One of Marx's tasks, accordingly, is to enlighten the workers regarding the injustice of the capitalist order, in which a minority of society, the capitalists, exercise exclusive control over the means of production. Workers in a capitalist society, he says, are little more than "wage slaves" controlled by the "Lords of Capital."[57] Workers are not free; they themselves own no capital and thus have no choice but to work for their capitalist masters. Those who refuse to do so, as we have seen, will die; their very existence is dependent on their capitalist oppressors. Moreover, such work as they are forced to perform not only destroys their freedom but also their humanity. According to Marx, the nature of man, his so-called "species being," demands free creative activity. Man is *homo faber*—"Man the Maker." His nature can only be fulfilled through spontaneous exercise of his abilities, acts of production that authentically express his being and his creativity. Such fulfillment, however, requires possession of the means to engage in spontaneous creativity activity, a condition that is absent under capitalism. Instead of freely pursuing the creative expression of human being, workers are forced to expend their life force on mere drudgery, producing items over which they have no creative control and which, moreover, ultimately belong not to themselves but rather the capitalist overlord.

The labor enforced by capitalism, then, does violence to man's species being. A worker in a capitalist economy only feels human, whole and free, when not working, during his few hours of leisure. His nature—his innate need to create freely and hold the fruits of creativity in his own hands—is starved of fulfillment. Such conditions produce what Marx calls the *alienation of labor*, a dreadful state of affairs in which a person's very *being*—his life force—is vitiated through employment structured by capitalist relations of production. Capitalism prevents human beings

---

[57] Robert C. Tucker, *Philosophy and Myth in Karl Marx* (Cambridge: Cambridge University Press, 1961); Linda C. Raeder, "Marxism as Psychodrama" (*Humanitas* 7:2 (1994). Hereinafter cited as "Psychodrama."

from fulfilling their nature by employing their consciousness in the creative act. It forces upon them, on the contrary, the so-called objectification, externalization, or alienation of consciousness. Capitalist economic relations necessarily render a worker's consciousness alien ("other") to himself insofar as it is objectified or externalized in the material objects he must produce for the capitalist. The alienation of the worker's life force involves its simultaneous absorption by the objects produced by his forced labor. In other words, according to Marx, laboring under capitalist relations of production entails the simultaneous and proportionate evisceration of the worker's being, life force, or consciousness. Thus the more a worker labors, the greater his alienation of being; the more he produces, the greater his loss of existence. Under capitalism, as Marx says, man experiences work not as creative fulfillment but rather as "loss of his self."[58]

Marx's Labor Theory of Value

The violation of both human nature and individual freedom that Marx regards as intrinsic to capitalism is exacerbated, as previously observed, by its intrinsic injustice. The grounds of the latter accusation may be traced to Marx's influential version of the so-called "labor theory of value." Various economists prior to Marx had attempted to identify the determinants of economic value, that is, the value of any good or service exchanged on the market. Influential thinkers such as Adam Smith and David Ricardo had concluded that such value is largely if not entirely derived from the value of the labor required for its production. Economic value, on such a view, is *objective*, that is, intrinsic to the object and unrelated to human or subjective preference. The value of any good or service can be objectively determined by calculating the objective value of the labor involved in its production. Such was more or less the conventional view that Marx inherited from the British classical school. Marx, however, moved beyond the classical economists, interpreting the labor theory of value in a way that would lead him to denounce the capitalist system root and branch.

---

[58] Marx, "Economic and Philosophic Manuscripts of 1844," in *Marx-Engels Reader*, 74.

According to Marx, the entire economic value of any good or service is attributable exclusively and solely to labor. In a capitalist order, he argues, labor is performed exclusively by workers, the proletariat who possess nothing but their labor; the capitalist class contributes no labor and thus no value to any good or service. The economic value of a final or consumer good such as a wristwatch can be objectively ascertained by calculating the value of the labor involved in producing each of the components and inputs required for its manufacture and assembly. The value of each and every input at every stage of production, from initial mining of the metals to final assembly of components, is attributable solely to the labor of the workers. The final or market value of any good is nothing more than the total value of all the labor involved in its production. Such applies not only to consumer and intermediate goods but also producer goods—the tools and machines and factories that constitute the "means of production" exclusively owned by the capitalists. In other words, the means of production, while controlled by capitalists, were actually and wholly built by the workers. Labor—the proletariat—is the sole source of the value inherent in *all* goods, including the means of production. The non-laboring class—the capitalists—contribute zero value to any good or service.

In a capitalist system, however, the proletariat, the laboring class of workers, does not receive wages or compensation equal to the value of its contribution to production but rather is subject to systematic exploitation. The capitalist, as the owner of the firm and means of production, sells the final product, distributes a portion of total revenue to the workers in the form of wages, and retains the remainder for himself. Moreover, competition among workers, who are in abundant supply and have no choice but to work for the capitalists, ensures that their wages will not rise far above subsistence level.

If Marx's argument is correct, it is difficult not to concede the injustice of capitalist economic relations. If workers exclusively produce all the value inherent in any good or service, then justice requires that they receive all the value in return—"to each his due."[59] According to Marx, however, workers receive only a fraction of the value they produce; the lion's share is retained by their capitalist masters, justified on the

---

[59] Marcus Tullius Cicero (106 BC – 43 BC): "*Iustitia suum cuique distribuit*" ("Justice renders to everyone his due.") *De Natura Deorum*, III, 38.

specious grounds of "property rights." In their failure to distribute one hundred percent of total revenue to the workers, capitalists thus violate the most elementary standard of justice. Capitalists not only exploit the workers, that is, pay them less than the value of their contribution to production, but, even more egregiously, effectively confiscate ("appropriate") what rightfully belongs to the workers. The greedy capitalists, who contribute no labor and thus no value to production, simply appropriate or steal the bulk of value created by the workers and belonging to them by right. A system that permits such monstrous wrong must be rectified. It is time, Marx suggests, to re-appropriate the appropriators. Indeed it is time for revolution: "Workers of the world unite! You have nothing to lose but your chains!"[60]

By such reasoning, Marx successfully persuaded significant numbers of people of the profound injustice of the capitalist system. One readily understands how workers might feel resentful and exploited under capitalism as portrayed by Marx and inspired to rise against such unspeakable injustice. Despite the undoubted efficacy of Marx's rhetoric and reasoning, however, the greater issue has yet to be addressed, namely, whether he accurately captured the nature of capitalism and the manner in which income is determined by the market process. The short answer is that he did not. The fundamental error in the Marxian critique of capitalism derives from its erroneous labor theory of value. Economic value is not, as Marx and the classical economists believed, an objective entity determined by the value of the labor involved in the production of a good or service. The economic value of any good or service, as we have seen, is always *subjective*, that is, based upon the personal values, beliefs, and circumstances of the individual perceiver. The value of any economic good—consumer, intermediate, or producer—is always *imputed* value, attributed to the good or service in question by its observer. Economic value never inheres in a good or service; it is never intrinsic or objective but rather subjective, as beauty is said to be, lying only and always in the mind or eyes of the beholder.

---

[60] This is a popular English paraphrase of the closing lines of the *Communist Manifesto*, where Marx says, "Working Men of All Countries, Unite!" ("*Proletarier aller Länder, vereinigt euch!*"). *Communist Manifesto, Marx-Engels Reader*, 500.

We recall in this context our previous example regarding the value of a bottle of spring water. The value that an individual attributes to the water will vary considerably depending on his particular circumstances. A person in possession of a plentiful supply of bottled water will place far less value on another bottle than the value he would perceive if dying of thirst in a desert. Moreover, the value of the labor that went into its production is irrelevant to the prospective buyer in either situation. What matters is his subjective assessment of present need or desire in light of his present circumstances. Indeed the individual rarely if ever evaluates any good or service on the basis of its cost of production, whether labor or other cost, but rather upon his particular needs, circumstances, tastes, and preferences; as these change, the value of the perceived item to the individual changes. A potential buyer does not generally base his decision to purchase or not purchase a good on the value of the labor that produced it but rather asks himself, "What is it worth to me?" Economic value is never objective.[61] Marx and the classical economists were simply wrong.

In fairness to Marx, however, it must be said that the correct theory of economic value, subjective value, was not discovered until the great bulk of his corpus had been completed. Its discovery—bound up with the so-called "marginal revolution" in economics—involves one of those remarkable coincidences in human history that thrill the imagination. Between 1871 and 1874 three economic theorists—Carl Menger in Austria, Leon Walras in France, and Stanley Jevons in England—independently and more or less simultaneously formulated the theory of subjective value that is universally accepted within the discipline of economics to the present day.

The Function of the Capitalist

---

[61] Such is true even if the buyer is altruistically aiming to raise the income of, say, impoverished women in Nepal. Such a consumer may purchase a handmade bracelet from a cooperative formed to assist such women, not because she desires the bracelet but because she deliberately aims to reward their painstaking labor and increase their income. In such a case, however, the value of the bracelet is nevertheless imputed to it by the altruistic consumer and not intrinsic to the item itself.

We have seen that, according to Marx, labor not only objectively determines the value of an economic good or service but solely determines such value. The capitalist, he maintains, contributes no value to the final product, all of which is ultimately reducible to the value of the labor involved in its production. Such a claim, like the labor theory of value more generally, is false. The source of Marx's error can be brought to light through an examination of the function of the capitalist in a market economy. We shall see that the crucial purpose he or she serves not only justifies retention of profit but also explains why a worker or employee is justly entitled only to wages or salary.

The capitalist, by definition, is the owner of the means of production—material equipment such as tools, factories, machines, and so on. Such so-called producer or capital goods cannot be consumed to satisfy immediate human needs such as food, clothing, and shelter but rather constitute the means by which such consumption (consumer) goods are brought into being. Tools and other producer goods are no more free gifts of nature than consumption goods, which means that scarce resources must deliberately be allocated to their production. The "capitalist" is the individual (like Robinson Crusoe in our previous example) who saves a portion of his personal resources and decides to invest such savings in the production of non-consumable capital goods. The ability to save, as previously discussed, depends upon fulfillment of two necessary conditions. First, a would-be capitalist must produce more than is necessary for his daily subsistence (produce more than he consumes); and, second, he must conserve the excess of production over consumption (his "surplus"), which can only be accomplished by foregoing or curtailing immediate consumption. Obviously an individual who is unable to produce more than is necessary to survive will be unable to save. An individual who chooses immediately to consume his entire productive output will similarly be incapable of saving. The capitalist can only emerge in a society if one or more of its members are simultaneously capable of producing more than necessary for daily subsistence and willing to curtail immediate personal consumption in favor of saving.[62]

---

[62] Alternatively, the individual can maintain an even level of consumption but increase his productivity, that is, produce more with the same expenditure of

A capitalist, then, is an individual who meets both necessary conditions of capital formation, as well its final or sufficient condition, namely, the decision to employ his savings ("capital") toward production of goods that cannot be immediately consumed, the producer or capital goods that constitute the means of production. The incentive to do so, as we recall, is the marked increase in the productivity of labor that arises from the use of capital goods (tools, machines, and the like). It is far more productive and efficient to build a house with a hammer than a rock found in a stream. Resources, including human labor, are scarce. A rational society aims to employ scarce resources as efficiently as possible, that is, obtain maximum production with minimum expenditure of labor and other scarce resources. A hammer or other capital good will greatly facilitate that goal. Economically under-developed societies are typically characterized by both low productivity of labor and the inability to produce much more than required for mere subsistence. Such conditions are cause and effect, respectively, of a lack of savings or capital. Low productivity means that individuals must expend the vast bulk of their labor producing items necessary for their very survival. As a result, they have limited labor resources available for the production of either higher-order consumption goods or producer goods. Low productivity prevents them from achieving the excess of production over consumption necessary for saving and thus capital formation (cause). Enhanced productivity would require the acquisition of tools and other capital goods but such is precluded by the prevailing low productivity of the populace (effect).

The ability to produce capital goods is a mark of economic development that benefits every member of society. Such goods enormously enhance the productivity of labor, which means more can be produced with less expenditure of labor. The less labor employed in the production of one good or service, the more labor is available for the production of other needed goods and services. An individual or a society, however, that spends every last penny on immediate consumption, whether due to low productivity or lavish consumption expenditure, will be unable to acquire the savings (capital) requisite to the production of non-consumable tools such as hammers. Capital

---

resources. In other words, individual savings can be achieved either by reducing personal consumption or increasing personal productivity.

formation can only be accomplished with savings—resources over and above that which are used for immediate consumption. In a market economy, such savings constitute the funding source for all "investment." "Capital," in the end, is nothing more than savings, which, in the end, is "investment." In a market economy the provision of such investment funds (savings/capital) is among the major functions of the "capitalist."

The capitalist, as we have seen, must forego immediate consumption in order to accumulate funds for saving or investment. Delaying gratification of present needs and desires is prerequisite to the accumulation of capital and production of capital goods. A person who invests $10,000 in the production of hammers cannot use that same $10,000 to satisfy immediate consumption needs or desires. In the formal language of economics, the action of the capitalist indicates a particular "time preference," more particularly, a greater preference for future than present satisfaction. By the act of saving and investing, the capitalist demonstrates his preference for foregoing present consumption in anticipation of increasing his consumption in the future. The anticipated increase in his future consumption is to be achieved by the profits he hopes to make in the production and sale of hammers. Let us assume that our capitalist plans to sell the hammers he has produced with his savings to the building trades. It would seem he has good prospects of success: the introduction of hammers to the market means that builders will be able to construct more houses, or the same number of houses with less input of labor, than prior to their production. If the capitalist does achieve success in selling his hammers, he will be rewarded for his efforts by earning profit. If total revenue from sale of the hammers is greater than total cost of production, his income after producing and selling hammers will be greater than prior to his investment in hammer production. He will thus be able to consume more in the future than would have been possible had he not chosen to invest his personal savings in the production of hammers.

Such a possibility is the motivating force driving capital formation and investment in a market economy. The actual achievement of profitable investment, however, depends on many factors, including the capitalist's initial ability to produce more than required for subsistence, his willingness to curtail immediate consumption, and, equally important, the extent of actual demand for his product. The final condition of success—the existence of demand—means that the capitalist must be willing to assume *risk*. The producer in our example has invested his personal savings in the production of hammers, anticipating that such investment will lead to future profit. As we have seen, however, the market is a process that unfolds over time. Human existence is not static, and the future, including the actions of other human beings, is difficult to predict with certainty. With respect to the present example, such uncertainty means that the hammer producer may have to contend with various unanticipated events that may significantly affect the outcome of his business venture. To take just one possibility, perhaps our producer will be challenged by other investors and entrepreneurs pursuing plans of their own. It is possible, for instance, that during the period required for production of the hammers, another entrepreneur invents an even better tool, one that will render the building of houses even more efficient than a simple hammer. If such should occur, our producer's hammers may be obsolete by the time they come to market and thus impossible to sell. Such of course may not occur, but it is clear that our capitalist runs the risk of losing his entire investment in hammer production.

He is not the only producer to face such a possibility. All capitalists assume unavoidable risk when making investment decisions, risk that involves the possible loss of their personal savings or resources. A rational society will nevertheless encourage potential investors to assume such risk; if they are successful, their actions benefit society as a whole. Everyone is better off if more houses can be built with fewer resources; resources are scarce and should be used as efficiently as possible. The less labor required for building houses, the more is available to produce other needed or desired goods and services. The essential activity of saving and risk-taking ("investment") is thus encouraged in a market economy by permitting the capitalist/investor to reap the potential rewards of his actions, rewards that constitute "profit." Imprudent or thoughtless risk-taking, which would needlessly waste scarce resources in the production of unneeded or unwanted items, is simultaneously discouraged by penalizing reckless or incompetent capitalists with the risk of punishment, punishment embodied in "loss." As previously discussed, *both* profits and losses of capitalists or investors are essential guides to production in a market economy.

Marx not only mischaracterized the nature of capitalism in general but the "capitalist" in particular. Contrary to Marx, capitalists not only contribute to the value of goods and services exchanged in a market economy but make an indispensable contribution to market-based production. Moreover, the Marxian vision, as we recall, perceives inherent and perpetual antagonism between "capitalists" and "workers," the two classes said to constitute modern society. The capitalists, on such a view, gain only at the workers' expense.

No such antagonism, however, exists in a market economy, which rather ensures a pronounced harmony of interest among all members of society, capitalist, worker, or other. Indeed among the greatest beneficiaries of capitalism are workers themselves: in the absence of capitalists, they would have no machines or other tools to assist their labor. Tools, as we have seen, dramatically increase the productivity of labor. In a capitalist economy, wage rates are a function of the productivity of labor. *Ceteris paribus*, the higher a worker's productivity, the higher his wage rate; the lower a worker's productivity, the lower his wage rate. Consider the difference between typical wage rates of workers in the automobile industry and workers who wash dishes at the local restaurant. The former employ highly complex and sophisticated capital equipment, while the latter employ relatively simple capital equipment, perhaps running water and a dishwashing machine. (Of course even a simple dishwashing machine greatly enhances the productivity of labor: compare washing dishes by hand with washing them in a machine.) The disparity in the income of autoworkers and dishwashers does not entirely stem from differences in the intrinsic abilities of workers in the two industries; many dishwashers could probably learn the skills needed to operate the sophisticated equipment at Ford Motors. The wage disparity largely stems from the great advantage the automobile workers derive from enormous capital investment in their industry, an investment funded in a market economy by capitalists motivated by anticipated profit. Profit is not stolen from workers but is rather the incentive and reward to the capitalist for saving and risking personal savings in the act of production.

Marx's general critique of capitalism, like his labor theory of value, is simply false. Capitalists are not monstrous exploiters who steal what rightly belongs to workers but, on the contrary, the great benefactors of workers. The capital goods they provide through their saving and investment in so-called means of production enormously heighten the productivity and thus wages of labor. Laborers in less developed economies, those with minimal capital formation, uniformly receive significantly lower wages than their counterparts in developed capitalist economies. Such, however, is not a matter of justice or injustice—the result of just or unjust human action—but of economic reality, that is, the low productivity invariably linked to inadequate capital formation.

Despite both the theoretical refutation of Marxian economics masterfully accomplished by various twentieth-century economists and the massive historical evidence of its catastrophic consequences throughout the same era, Marx's caricature of capitalism continues to captivate the imagination of many members of contemporary society.[63] Its enduring popularity no doubt stems from its appeal to the "lower angels" of human nature. The characterization of workers as oppressed victims of exploitative and greedy capitalists resonates with the human propensity to feel undervalued and unappreciated; few people feel their personal worth is sufficiently reflected in their paychecks. Marxian victimization also feeds on what Friedrich Nietzsche (1844-1900) famously termed *ressentiment*—the low-level and chronic anger many individuals feel toward their general lot in life. Individuals prone to such resentment may feel that life itself is unfair. They may experience themselves as powerless, victims of forces over which they have no control, including the overarching economic order of society. Others succumb to simple envy of the more successful. Marx provided an easy target for resentment, envy, and other forms of chronic existential dissatisfaction in the symbol of the capitalist "Lord of Labor." Capitalists or the capitalist system itself is to blame for one's personally unsatisfactory economic circumstances or those of one's fellows, in particular, those workers who possess relatively less material wealth.

Indeed, Marxists and fellow travelers regard the great disparity of wealth produced by putative capitalist exploitation as not only intrinsically wrong but the very height of injustice. The intrinsic evil of material inequality follows from the distinctive definition of right and wrong implicit in Marxist thought. Marxism involves a revolution not only in economic organization but also morality, in particular, its

---

[63] Including Hayek, Mises, Friedman, Roepke, Boehm-Bawerk, Thomas Sowell, and others.

redefinition along materialist and consequentialist lines. The radical materialism of Marxism involves the attribution of causality to material factors and reduction of human experience to exclusively immanent or intra-worldly dimensions. The consequentialism of Marxist moral constructs involves the attribution of good and evil, right and wrong, not to individual action-in-itself but rather the results or consequences of human action. The conjunction of radical materialism and moral consequentialism leads to a redefinition of good or right as that which results in a relatively equal distribution of material resources, evil or wrong as that which results in an unequal or widely disparate distribution of such resources. Communism and other forms of collectivist economic organization that aim result in a greater equalization of wealth are therefore good; capitalism, which results in an unequal distribution of wealth, is therefore evil. The validity of such judgments will be further examined in a following chapter.

The Marxist moral vision may further be characterized as a variant of the so-called "politics of projection" widely associated with certain influential forms of modern political ideology.[64] Western civilization traditionally conceives the battle between good and evil as occurring not in the external social or economic order but rather *within* the individual human breast. Good and evil are traditionally regarded as attributes of individual intention and action, not attributes of the abstract order of society as a whole. Such reflects the moral realism characteristic of traditional Judeo-Christian ethics. As has been discussed, moral realism involves the recognition that only human beings bear moral agency; a social or economic order is not a conscious, thinking, willing entity capable of intention or action, moral or immoral. Over the course of modernity, however, various philosophies have emerged that project the battleground between good and evil from the interiority of individual conscience onto the external social order, especially its political and economic dimensions. The source of evil is typically linked not to individual choice and action but rather a particular political or economic system. Jean-Jacque Rousseau (1712-1778), the eighteenth-century writer who profoundly influenced French thought in the decades preceding the French Revolution, pointedly expressed the leading idea: ". . . [M]an is naturally good . . . it is by their institutions alone that men

---

[64] See Raeder, "Marxism as Psychodrama."

become wicked."[65] Rousseau, however, was not the only modern thinker to engage in psychological projection of this nature. Marx and his descendants similarly regard evil as an attribute of the overarching social order and not the individual. Insofar as man "becomes bad" by virtue of existing "institutions," the eradication of evil requires the eradication of such institutions, including the economic, political, and legal institutions comprised by liberal-capitalist order.

Selfishness, Greed, Materialism

We previously observed that the widespread if implicit embrace of the socialist vision in modern society stems in large part from the conviction that socialism embodies a morality superior to that of capitalism. The essence of the socialist ideal is greater equalization of material wealth among members of society. Such a goal is portrayed as an unequivocal moral advance over the individualism and alleged selfishness of both capitalism and the traditional Judeo-Christian ethics implicit in its operation. Marxists and fellow travelers subject capitalism to intense and unremitting moral criticism. As discussed, it is depicted as intrinsically evil and radically unjust, a system in which the "rich get richer and the poor get poorer." Capitalism is said to benefit only the privileged few, the capitalists; the vast majority, the workers, are exploited and oppressed. It is further charged with promoting vulgar greed, selfishness, and materialism, fostering a society whose members care for little more than mere accumulation of personal possessions. Advertisers and marketing experts are said to encourage a "false consciousness," persuading the people, among other untruths, that material possessions will lead to happiness. Not only are higher, nonmaterial, values neglected or despised but the impersonal "cash nexus" of the market demeans the value of human being. Human personality counts for nothing to capitalist employers, whose only concern is the hard "bottom line"— increasing their profits. Nor is individual personhood valued by buyers in the marketplace, whose only concern is to pay as little as possible for producers' wares. Human beings in a capitalist economy are dehumanized, treated as replaceable cogs in the grinding wheel of "buy

---

[65] Jean-Jacques Rousseau, cited in Cranston and Peters, eds, *Hobbes and Rousseau* (New York: Doubleday, 1972), 297.

and sell." Indeed, as we have seen, Marx maintains that the very essence of human being—man's species being—is systematically violated by capitalist relations of production.

Economic socialization will rectify all such evils. Communist relations of production will establish a more just society concerned with the good of all its members, not merely the dominant class of capitalists. Socialized economic organization will not only achieve justice but also diminish and perhaps eliminate the greed, selfishness, and materialism wrought by capitalism. It will do so by removing the cause of all such evils at their very root, namely, the institution of private property that gives rise to the nefarious motive of profit. Moreover, the dehumanizing impersonalism of competitive capitalist economic relations will be replaced by a system of social cooperation that permits each individual the full realization of human nature. Socialist men, unlike their capitalist counterparts, will care for one another: "From each according to his ability, to each according to his need." Selfishness, materialism, and possessiveness will eventually recede from human experience as new socialist relations of production transform human values and beliefs.[66] Class status itself will disappear, as will the class struggle that has heretofore plagued every society in human history. Every person will be equally valued, the needy and poor, the sick and homeless, as well as the productive and the strong. All members of society will be sustained by the collective efforts of the whole. No person will live in want; every human being can realize his potential. History itself has been aiming for such a glorious and inevitable end—the establishment of a truly just society—throughout the long and tortuous experience of humanity in time.

*

Few people dispute the fact that capitalism produces a material prosperity unparalleled in human history. From the perspective of morality, however, such material success does not decisively establish the superiority of capitalist economic relations. If capitalist prosperity can only be achieved by the institutionalization of immorality, greed, selfishness, and injustice, by dehumanization and violation of human nature, capitalism must of course be rejected despite its proven material benefits. For such reasons, the morality of the market order must be

---

[66] Raeder, "Psychodrama," 12.

scrutinized and appraised, as must the competing morality and moral claims of socialism and other forms of economic centralization.

The typical moral charges leveled against capitalism, as we have seen, include selfishness, greed, materialism, callous indifference to human welfare, and injustice. We begin with selfishness, previously touched upon in discussing Smith's metaphor of the "Invisible Hand." We observed in that context the irony of the modern criticism of the market as inducing selfishness, a view in contradiction to that of Smith and other classical economists. Early proponents of the market economy lauded capitalism precisely for its propensity to mitigate, not encourage, the moral flaw of selfishness. It does so, as we recall, by institutionally and spontaneously channeling self-interested and even selfish desires into actions beneficial to other human beings. Such follows from the fact that the material goals of any individual, whether selfish or altruistic, can only be realized in a market economy by serving other people, the consumers. A selfish monster who greedily aims to amass wealth merely to gratify his own pleasure must, at least for a time, set aside his own desires and consider the needs and desires of others. There is no other way to achieve financial success, and thus obtain the means necessary to gratify personal or selfish desires, in a capitalist economy.

The market's propensity to mitigate selfishness in this manner may be further elucidated by a concrete illustration. To that end, imagine the existence of two hypothetical groups of people in a society ordered by market exchange, whom we shall call the "selfish" and the "selfless." The first group is composed of narcissists and sociopaths, persons so consumed with unspeakable selfishness as to *never* consider anything beyond their personal gratification. The second group represents the moral opposite, a group, one might say, composed of Mother Teresa's. Such individuals are genuinely selfless, caring nothing for themselves but only the welfare of others; their consuming life-purpose is to relieve human suffering to the extent of their ability. We assume that members of the disparate groups live one among the other in a free society ordered by market exchange and satisfying its preconditions (private property, the rule of law, and mutual trust). The government is classically liberal, limited and concerned with securing to every individual his natural rights to life, liberty, and property. There is neither a governmental "safety net" that secures to individuals the necessities of life nor corporate welfare that subsidizes business with taxpayer funds.

Our interest concerns the manner in which the constituent members of the two opposing groups, the selfish and the selfless, can achieve their widely divergent goals in a free society so conceived. The selfish egoists aim only to gratify themselves; the altruists aim only to alleviate suffering in this world. How may such opposing goals be realized? The first point to emphasize is that members of both groups require material goods and services to achieve their goals. The selfish materialists need gold or automobiles or mansions or whatever—the more the better—to gratify their desires. The selfless altruists have no desire for such goods; they care nothing for their own material well-being. These too, however, require material goods, although of a very different kind: they need food and clothing, medicine and housing, and all the complementary goods required to relieve human suffering. However angelic the selfless servants, such material goods do not fall from clouds.

The second point, indeed the crucial point, is that members of the two groups, despite their radically different goals, must, in a capitalist economy, employ identical means to achieve them. A market economy, as we recall, provides one way, and only one way, to acquire income or wealth, which of course is necessary for the acquisition of any material good or service.[67] Both the selfish and the selfless must generate the income needed to obtain the material goods essential to fulfilling their respective goals, whether luxury automobiles or medicine for a sick child. As we have seen, the only means by which this can be accomplished in a market economy is by producing a good or service that other persons, customers or consumers, will voluntarily purchase.

We recall in this context that economic theory does not address the ends or goals that people *should* value, whether these *should* be selfish or selfless. "Economics is a science of means, not of ends"; it is neutral with respect to the substantive content of human ends and discloses only the means necessary to realize them. An individual's values or purposes are not determined by the economic arrangements of a society but rather by

---

[67] We are again excluding the possibility of inheritance or gift. These are of course means of obtaining resources but they are not the general method of so doing in a market economy; they are the exception rather than the rule. Moreover, a person who inherits wealth simply benefits from the fact that his ancestors produced something of value to other people (provided they earned such wealth fairly, that is, through market exchange).

his character, shaped by his philosophy, religion, and beliefs—his worldview. A spiritual or morally sensitive person may share the values of Mother Teresa; insensitive and vulgar brutes will pursue values of quite another sort. Whatever an individual's personal values, however, the only way to realize them in a society ordered by market exchange is to obtain the means (income) required to do so by producing a good or service subjectively valued by other people. The vulgar brutes can only gratify their selfish desire for material possessions by first producing something that other people will voluntarily purchase from them, and to do so they must consider the needs and desires of other people. The brutes can then use any profits so gained to acquire self-gratifying possessions (or perhaps spend their evenings counting their gold). The Mother Teresa's of this world can only obtain the funds they need to alleviate suffering in the same manner; they too, like the brutes, must produce some good or service that other people will voluntarily purchase. They can then use any profits so gained not to gratify themselves but rather to help those in need, to buy and provide food, medicine, and so on.

Selfless altruists do have the further option of soliciting donations for their humanitarian mission ("charitable contributions") and using such contributions in turn to purchase the goods they distribute to those in need. This latter method, however, does not change the nature of things. Those persons who donate to charity must first obtain the resources to do so, and this, again, can only be achieved by producing something of value to other people. In a capitalist economy the dramatically opposing ends of the selfish and the selfless must be realized by identical means. The divergent ends of the respective groups are not determined by the economic system but rather chosen by the individuals themselves. Capitalism no more forces selfishness than selflessness upon individuals; it no more produces the selfish monster than the Mother Teresa. Capitalism, contrary to its critics, cannot be blamed for human selfishness.

It is as false to blame capitalism for materialism and greed as for human selfishness. There is nothing intrinsic to a market economy that compels people to be materialistic, greedy, or selfish. Such vices are potentialities of human nature wherever and whenever found, personal values informed by extra-economic factors and prevalent in every society and every form of economic organization known to man. Indeed, capitalism may serve to mitigate not only selfishness but greedy materialism as well. Individuals fortunate enough to live in a prosperous capitalist economy have the added luxury of potentially raising their sights beyond materialistic concerns and pursuing values higher than material satisfaction. The prerequisite for such moral and cultural advance—the prior satisfaction of fundamental material needs—is far more likely to be realized in a capitalist order than any form of socialized economy. Capitalism, as repeatedly noted, not only facilitates satisfaction of material needs but has produced the highest standard of living for the largest number of people in the course of human history. Such material prosperity, in turn, has created conditions conducive to cultural development and pursuit of spiritual, intellectual, and artistic values.

Moreover, an individual can live quite well on relatively limited income in a market-based society, if content with basic necessities. It is true that writers, painters, musicians, and other creative individuals may fail to find a wide market for their art in a capitalist economy, but such is a more or less inevitable outcome of a system tailored to satisfy consumer tastes and values. The tastes of the masses are generally more pedestrian than *avant-garde*. Those artists, however, who decide that pursuit of their art is of greater importance than personal development of more marketable skills can nevertheless live comfortably if not luxuriously in a competitive market order, which tends to drive costs of living to a minimum. Moreover, wealthy individuals in capitalist society often employ their wealth not solely for personal gratification but also to help others, including starving artists. Philanthropic or charitable giving in the United States has traditionally played an important role in American society.[68] Americans are among the most generous people on earth by any objective measure of philanthropic activity, a fact no doubt related not only to their spiritual heritage but also the material success of a capitalist economy.

Both theory and history demonstrate that a centrally organized economy cannot provide a standard of living for the masses equal to that achieved by capitalism, a fact clearly relevant to issues of materialism and

---

[68] The most recent studies indicate that the historical generosity of the American people may be declining. In 2013 the United States ranked thirteenth among the nations of the world in terms of charitable contributions; in 2010, it ranked in sixth place.

greed. Persons who are chronically dependent on political power, and not their own efforts, for the satisfaction of their most basic needs must live in a perpetual state of economic insecurity that readily encourages preoccupation with material concerns. It is difficult to study Shakespeare if one is hungry; it is difficult to care about the starving children in India if one's own children are starving. Consider the experience of Communist China in the 1960s under the totalitarian dictator Mao Tse-tung. The communist government devised and implemented widespread centralized economic planning, including a plan for rice production; individual production was outlawed. The failure of the central plan resulted in death through starvation for millions upon millions of Chinese people, who were utterly dependent on government-provided rice for their survival.[69] Moreover, governments that exercise command-and-control over basic resources are tempted to employ such power to suppress resistance to their rule, as occurred in the Ukraine under Josef Stalin; it is estimated that 35 million Ukrainians starved to death as a result of the forced imposition of collectivized agriculture.[70] The tragic experience of the people of communist North Korea further demonstrates the devastating consequences of centralized economic control. The infamous North Korean famine of 1994-1998 resulted in death from starvation or hunger-related illnesses of somewhere between 240,000 and 3,500,000 North Koreans, from a total population of approximately 22 million people.[71] In 2011 it was anticipated that one to six million North Koreans would starve in the following year if international aid were not forthcoming.[72] In every instance, the implementation of a centralized command-and-control economy has been disastrous for the people at large. Such systems readily reduce human existence to a sheer struggle for material survival, which

---

[69] Jung Chang and Jan Halliday, *Mao: The Unknown Story* (Norwell, MA: Anchor, 2006).

[70] Panné, and Paczkowski, *Black Book of Communism*.

[71] Steve Coll, "North Korea's Hunger," *The New Yorker*, Dec. 21, 2011, One study shows that the average North Korean solider is 10 inches shorter than those in the South Korean military—a sign of chronic acute malnutrition affecting an entire generation of young North Koreans.

[72] Jordan Weissman, "How Kim Jong Il Starved North Korea," *The Atlantic*, Dec. 20, 2011.

obviously must take precedence over preoccupation with "higher" values. For such reasons, a centrally organized economy is far more conducive to engendering materialism than its capitalist counterpart, and understandably so. Indeed, as previously observed, communism and related constructs are fundamentally materialist ideologies. Marx named his philosophy of history dialectical materialism and implicitly defined morality in material terms. There is simply no basis for the charge that individuals who order their affairs by market exchange are more materialistic than their counterparts in a centralized or socialized economy. Indeed the opposite may be closer to the truth.

Nor are they more greedy. Greed is yet another propensity of human nature found in every economic order known to man, capitalist, socialist, or mixed, ancient, feudal, or modern. The classical Greek philosophers were among the first to highlight and condemn insatiable desire, the immoderate appetite they termed *pleonexia*.[73] Capitalism does not cause human beings to develop an insatiable appetite for ever-greater material possession, and socialism does not transform human beings into selfless altruists. Such qualities, again, are a function of personal or individual character and values, not the prevailing economic system. Moreover, greed can be expressed in many forms, not all of which are economic. Greed can and does manifest itself not only in the drive to accumulate material wealth but also in the drive to accumulate political power, which can provide to its holders a non-economic means of accumulating wealth and privilege. Political elites in communist, socialist, quasi-socialist, fascist, and mixed economies such as the contemporary United States can gratify their greed not, as must the capitalists, by producing items of value to the consumer but rather by appropriating the resources of other persons through taxation or direct confiscation or otherwise using political influence to gain personal wealth. Luxury trips to Spain and Martha's Vineyard, like villas on the Black Sea, can be acquired by political as well as economic means.

---

[73] *pleonexia* (πλεονεξια), is a philosophical concept which roughly corresponds to greed, covetousness, or avarice. The term has been formally defined as "the insatiable desire to have what rightfully belongs to others" and otherwise described as "ruthless self-seeking and an arrogant assumption that others and things exist for one's own benefit." John W. Ritenbaugh, "The Tenth Commandment," *Forerunner* (January 1998).

TEN

JUSTICE VS. SOCIAL JUSTICE

We have rights as individuals to give as much of our own money as we please to charity; but as members of Congress we have no right so to appropriate a dollar of public money.   —Congressman Davy Crockett

The most damaging moral charge leveled against the market order, indeed the centerpiece of the Marxian critique, is the characterization of capitalism as inherently unjust. Such a serious allegation demands an equally serious response. If capitalism truly is unjust and socialism truly does secure a higher justice, as Marxists and fellow travelers claim, then regardless of the material prosperity generated by capitalism, it cannot be supported by decent people. Indeed the question of the justice and morality of the two competing paradigms may rightfully be regarded as paramount to all other considerations.

What is justice? The question is as old as political philosophy itself, the central inquiry of Plato's *Republic,* widely regarded as the first formal contribution to that uniquely Western discipline. Political philosophy, as we recall, is a specialized branch of moral philosophy. Moral or ethical philosophy deals with the substance of morality in general and the requisites of a personally ethical existence. Political philosophy focuses on a related but narrower issue: the moral rules that one human being should observe in his treatment of other human beings. Such an inquiry, as previously observed, is not optional for human beings but rather springs from the nature of things, from the fact that "no man is an island." Human existence is invariably existence within community, an association referred to by the Greeks as the *polis.* From birth to death every person (assuming he is "neither a beast nor a god," as Aristotle remarked) is necessarily in relation with other persons. Political philosophy deals precisely with such relations, that is, the question of how human beings *should* treat one another given the fact that human existence is social existence. It deals, in other words, with the question of justice.[74] Indeed, the relation between political philosophy and justice is so close as to border on identity, sharing as they do the identical moral concern, namely, the rules of just conduct that individuals should observe in their treatment of fellow human beings, in other words, the rules that *ought* to govern human relations in society. The question of justice, then, like political philosophy more generally, arises from the social nature of human existence; indeed, it is the "social" virtue" *par excellence*. Robinson Crusoe has many concerns but justice is not among them. Alone on his island, he does not confront the question of how he should treat other persons or how they should treat him—the question of political philosophy in general and justice in particular.

Deontological and Consequentialist Morality

The broad discipline of moral philosophy conventionally comprises two main categories or schools of thought—so called *deontological* morality and *consequentialist* morality. Deontological morality is correlative to the philosophical discipline of ontology, which is concerned with the nature of Being, the kinds of things that have existence—what *is*. The deontological school conceives morality—what *is* right and what *is* wrong—as deriving from Being itself, from what *exists*. Particular actions are regarded as right-in-themselves or wrong-in-themselves depending on their alignment with what *is* intrinsically right or intrinsically wrong. The deontological school thus regards morality as objective, that is, independent of subjective human preference. Traditional Western or Judeo-Christian morality falls within the deontological category. Right and wrong are thought to be rooted in *what is*, more particularly, in what God *is*, in the very Being or nature of God. Actions are regarded as right- or wrong-in-themselves if in accord with or in violation of the substance of morality-in-itself. It is right-in-itself, for instance, to be truthful and honest because truth and honesty are inseparable from the substance,

---

[74] Plato himself held a different view, identifying justice as a virtue to be applied to government of the individual psyche or soul. Indeed Plato employs the term justice in such a way that it becomes synonymous with virtue or morality itself. This is different from the manner in which justice is generally conceived throughout the later development of Western civilization.

nature, or Being of God. Similarly, it is wrong-in-itself to murder an innocent person or steal because such actions violate the nature of morality itself; they are inherently wrong. Deontological or in-itself morality, moreover, is pursued or avoided for its own sake, that is, regardless of consequences that may ensue ("virtue is its own reward"; "the ends do not justify the means"). The deontological school conceives consequences as more or less irrelevant to morality. What matters is doing what is right for its own sake and avoiding what is wrong for its own sake. Such a conception of morality tends toward moral absolutism. Being (*what is*), the root of morality, does not change and thus morality does not change, consisting rather of rules valid for all times and all places, regardless of circumstances or consequences. As we shall see, such is the kind of morality implicit in the so-called "procedural justice" that sustains both the capitalist economic order and the limited constitutional government of the American Founders.

The second chief school of moral philosophy is generally referred to as ethical or moral consequentialism, briefly discussed in a previous context. Consequentialism, in contrast to deontological ethics, regards right and wrong not as intrinsic qualities of action-in-itself but rather as contingent on the consequence of action. What is right is that which produces right consequences; what is wrong, is that which produces wrong consequences. For that reason, ethical consequentialism is sometimes referred to as "outcome-based" morality. Standards of right and wrong are said to derive from the outcome or consequence produced by human action, not qualities intrinsic to an action itself. One of the more influential forms of ethical consequentialism in the modern period is the so-called Utilitarianism commonly associated with the teaching of Jeremy Bentham (1748-1832) and his most celebrated descendent, John Stuart Mill (1806-1873). According to Benthamite Utilitarianism, the end or goal of all human action is happiness, and the supreme end of human action, the *summum bonum*, is the "Greatest Happiness of the Greatest Number."[75] The right or the good is defined as that which

---

[75] In the spring of 1776, in his first substantial (though anonymous) publication, *A Fragment on Government*, Jeremy Bentham invoked what he described as a "fundamental axiom: it is the greatest happiness of the greatest number that is the measure of right and wrong." *Summum bonum* is a Latin expression meaning "the highest good," introduced by Cicero to correspond to the Idea of the Good in ancient Greek philosophy. The *summum bonum* is

produces such a consequence—the "Greatest Happiness of the Greatest Number"—and wrong as that which does not. Standards of right and wrong are determined not by what is right-in-itself or wrong-in-itself, as claimed by the deontological school. Such conceptions, on the utilitarian view, have no meaning or reality. Moral standards are determined not by a nebulous and perhaps illusory "Being" but rather the consequences of human action in this world. Marxist morality, as previously mentioned, represents a second form of ethical consequentialism that has achieved prominence in the modern era. Consequentialism of any form tends toward moral relativism. The standard of right and wrong may depend on outcomes whose desirability fluctuates over time and place. The Greatest Happiness for one group of people may differ from the Greatest Happiness for a group situated in different historic or cultural circumstances. The particular moral outcome aimed for by Marxism—greater equalization of wealth—does not itself fluctuate but the means necessary to achieve that end may be relative to particular historical circumstance. The moral demands embodied in the socialist conception of justice, as we shall see, represent a classic instance of "outcome-based" justice informed by ethical consequentialism.

Justice and Capitalism

Having discussed the two chief schools of morality in modern Western society, we are now prepared to explore the question of justice. We begin with an examination of justice as traditionally conceived within American society, that is, within a capitalist order governed by the rule of law. As we recall from previous discussion, the traditional American sense of justice is unambiguously represented by its traditional national pastime, baseball. Justice, as we have seen, involves playing by the established rules of the game (the "procedure"), and the umpire's role is to ensure the players do so. The outcome of a baseball game does not determine the rules of fair play but rather the opposite: the rules of fair play determine the justice of the game's outcome. The outcome of a baseball game is considered fair or just *if and only if* the winning team scores the highest number of runs *and* the team members play in accord

---

generally regarded as both an end in itself and, at the same time, an end that encompasses all other goods.

with the rules. Although it is common to speak of a game that meets both criteria as "fair" or "just," strictly speaking, there is no such entity as a "fair game." We again recall that only human agents, in this case the individual players and the umpire, are capable of acting fairly or justly. Only persons are capable of honoring or violating the rules of the game because only persons possess conscious minds and capacity for moral choice. A "game" of course cannot "act," justly or otherwise. It can only metaphorically be described as "fair" or "unfair," a metaphor that indicates whether the team members and umpire adhered to or violated the rules of the game.

We further recall the analogy between the role of the umpire in a baseball game and the role of government in a free society. The function of both entities is to secure the rule of law, that is, ensure that the established rules of just conduct, whether the rules of baseball or the wider "game of life," are observed by all parties. Such a function is particularly relevant to the sphere of economic life. Capitalism, as has been discussed, is not an autonomous process but rather dependent upon a particular framework of law and morality. A functioning market economy depends upon observance and enforcement of certain rules of just conduct, such as prohibition of theft, fraud, and arbitrary coercion. Neither stealing nor misrepresentation of goods and services nor coercive force in the act of market exchange can be permitted. We have also seen that the market process is further dependent upon a widespread if tacit moral consensus that permits a requisite measure of trust among market participants. Members of society are expected to behave in accord with certain moral rules, whether implicitly embodied in custom or explicitly enforced by law. Employers are expected to pay their employees the salaries they have earned and customers to pay their bills on time. Drivers are expected to follow the rules of the road whether a police officer is nearby or not. Everyone relies upon the observance of such rules in their daily interactions with other persons. The tacit moral consensus prevailing in every society enables its members to predict the behavior of their fellows with some confidence, and social life would be impossible in its absence.

The market order, then, is dependent upon an abstract framework of rules of just conduct, including both explicit, legal, and enforceable rules (laws and legislation) and implicit, tacit, or customary rules (practice, convention). Justice in a market economy, like justice in a baseball game, involves adherence to such an established framework, the rules of the game of life that constitute the prevailing sense of justice. Such rules embody mutual social expectations—how the individual expects to be treated and how he is expected to treat other individuals. They are expected to govern all social interaction among individuals, including business or economic interaction. The rules of just conduct require that a person who signs a contract fulfill the terms of that contract. Justice requires that a producer who advertises a product actually supply the product as described in the advertisement. Justice requires that an employee who performs his job as expected actually receive the salary initially negotiated with the employer. Justice requires that a business owner who employs his own resources to produce a good or service that is voluntarily purchased by consumers be permitted to retain the fruits of his investment, his profit. Justice requires that a person who desires a wristwatch owned by another person either persuade the owner to sell it or otherwise engage in voluntary exchange; he is not permitted to snatch the watch from the owner's wrist. The traditional sense of justice tacitly informing the market process is eloquently summarized in Cicero's celebrated definition—*Iustitia suum cuique distribuit* ("Justice renders to everyone his due")."[76]

Justice, again, is a social virtue that can only be exercised in dealing with other human beings. Every rule of just conduct involves a relation between *persons*—the person or moral agent who acts, either justly or unjustly, and another person who is the object of such action. It must again be emphasized that, strictly speaking, only a person can be just or unjust; only a person can bear moral agency. With respect to economics, people commonly speak of a "fair transaction," as they do of a "fair baseball game." Indeed Marx and fellow travelers, as we have seen, condemn capitalism as a whole as "unjust." Such judgments, however, can never be more than metaphor or rhetoric; there is no such entity as either a "fair transaction" or a "just" economic system. A transaction is simply a relation between persons; like a game, it does not and cannot possess a conscious mind and thus capacity for moral choice. Similarly, an economic "system" is nothing more than a set of abstract relations, an institutionalized or formalized set of arrangements that guide transactions between and among *persons*. Capitalism or the market

---

[76] Cicero, *De Natura Deorum*, III, 38.

system is precisely such a set of abstract relations among individual market participants, not an autonomous entity capable of choice or action. The capitalist system as a whole is no more capable of bearing moral agency than the game of baseball. A set of abstract relations cannot act, justly or unjustly. Capitalism, like a baseball game or like "society," can only be considered "just" or "unjust" in a loose or metaphorical sense. In all cases, such a description can only refer to the actions of the individuals participating in the order, whether the order of the market, the order of a baseball game, or the order of society as a whole. Only human beings are moral agents capable of acting justly or unjustly. An abstract name for an impersonal set of economic arrangements, transactions, or relations—capitalism—is not and cannot be a moral agent and thus is not and cannot be termed just or unjust in any literal or meaningful sense.

Equally important, traditional justice, like law in general, is not concerned with the *outcome* of interpersonal transactions but rather with the *means* individuals employ when interacting with their fellow human beings. Justice is not concerned with an individual's ends or goals, for instance, whether he aims to possess another person's watch, but rather the *means* he employs to possess the watch (e.g., voluntary exchange, theft, or fraud). Traditional justice so conceived and as mentioned is formally classified as procedural or rule-based justice. Whether or not the acquisition of a watch is just or unjust depends on the procedures employed by the parties to the transaction, for instance, voluntary trade or violence. Such is identical to the sense of justice embodied in the game of baseball and other traditional American sports: "it's not whether you win or lose (the outcome), but how you play the game" (the procedure). Justice so conceived applies to all human interaction within traditional American society, whether winning means scoring the highest number of runs for the team or earning the highest income in a competitive market economy. Justice is served for the losing team, as for the relatively less economically successful members of society, so long as everyone involved has observed the rules of the games in their respective spheres (baseball and economic activity). The outcome of their various activities is irrelevant to justice.

On the traditional Anglo-American view, then, justice is achieved when individual members of society act justly toward one another, that is, when they treat one another according to the established rules of just conduct, both legal and customary. Justice, like law and like economic theory, is not concerned with the concrete substance of individual goals (that for which a person aims) but with the means employed to achieve them. Nor is justice concerned with the outcome of the individual's endeavors, whether or not he succeeds in realizing his goals. Traditional justice is exclusively concerned with the procedures or means individuals employ to pursue their self-chosen goals. Those responsible for enforcing the rules of justice are to be as indifferent to the outcome of individual rule-governed behavior as the umpire to the outcome of a baseball game. Their only concern is to ensure that established procedural rules have been observed. Applied to the capitalist economic system, justice is achieved whenever individuals pursue their economic goals within the established framework of morality and law. Justice is indifferent to the outcome of their economic pursuits, whether acquisition of wealth or suffering of economic loss; such outcomes are as irrelevant to economic activity as to baseball. Whether a person wins or loses the economic "game," achieves or does not achieve prosperity or wealth, is not a matter of justice. What matters with respect to justice is whether an economic actor has played the game fairly, that is, observed the established rules of just conduct in his treatment of other market participants. In the economic dimension of human action as in sports, what matters on the traditional American sense of justice is "not whether you win or lose, but how you play the game."

Justice and Equality

Perhaps the most unacceptable moral feature of the market order, from the Marxian perspective, is the fact that capitalism results in a wide disparity of income and wealth. It is undeniable that some persons in a capitalist economy become wealthier, perhaps much wealthier, than others. We have seen, however, that the American people have traditionally regarded such unequal "outcomes" of the game of economic life as just or fair, in accord with the prevailing sense of justice. Indeed, inequality of material outcome has long been recognized as a necessary consequence of the consistent application of justice. Traditional justice requires strict adherence to the rule of law, which involves, among other elements, equal treatment under the law. Equality under law, as we have seen, means that that the same rules apply to every individual, regardless of status or group affiliation; the garbage collector is governed by the same rules as the president of the United States. Justice is blind. We have previously noted the ancient lineage of such a conception of justice, to which the early Greeks applied the term *isonomia*. Justice so conceived and applied will inevitably produce an economically diverse society encompassing a wide array of material outcomes. Human beings are distinctive individuals with distinctive propensities, talents, and values, as well as varying levels of education, ambition, perseverance, self-discipline, creativity, and other personal qualities. Individuals are also members of diverse family structures that transmit diverse cultural values and aspirations, as well as financial means, to their children. No two snowflakes are identical, and no two human beings are identical. Indeed Western civilization would come to treasure that fact, glorying in the uniqueness of the human person, the uniqueness of the individual.[77]

The central point with respect to justice, however, is that the universal application of identical laws to unique individuals who possess widely varying skills, abilities, and values *must* result in unequal economic or material outcomes, in an unequal distribution of wealth across society. If unique individuals are governed by identical rules, the outcome of their individual endeavors will never be uniform or equal by any material measure. In a market economy, some individuals—those will skills more highly valued by other members of society—will become relatively wealthier than others. The economic inequality that prevails in a market order is an inevitable consequence, not of injustice but, on the contrary, the consistent application of justice as traditionally conceived. Equal justice under law and economic inequality are two sides of the same coin.

The relation between traditional justice and economic inequality may be further brought to light by recalling the profound American conviction that every individual is endowed with certain natural and unalienable rights, the classic Lockean trilogy of life, liberty, and property. Justice and the rule of law secure to each individual not only life and liberty but also property, which of course includes income in the form of wages and profit earned from personal economic activity. We further recall the manner in which income is determined in a market economy. The income of any individual is ultimately determined by the

---

[77] Larry Siedentop, *Inventing the Individual: The Origins of Western Liberalism* (Cambridge, MA: The Belknap Press of Harvard University Press),2014.

subjective value that consumers place on his particular skills and abilities, a value that varies not only from consumer to consumer but also skill to skill. Consumers are typically willing to pay more for the skills involved in brain surgery than those involved in washing dishes because they value the former skills more highly than the latter. Moreover, the possession of particular skills varies greatly among individuals—not everyone can paint like Van Gogh, play baseball like Babe Ruth, or perform brain surgery. Individual income in a market economy is determined by an *impersonal* process ultimately dependent on the subjective value imputed to various goods and services by the consumer.

In a capitalist economy, the security of individual property rights conjoined with the subjective evaluation of consumers thus ensures that individuals whose skills are perceived as more valuable by their fellows will earn a higher income than those whose skills are perceived as less valuable. Such is the inevitable result of market exchange. Individuals who possess skills of relatively greater value to other members of society will be voluntarily offered more in exchange for such skills, while those individuals who possess less valuable skills will be offered less. The strict application of justice in a regime that honors universal individual rights to property requires that each individual be secured in the possession of any income so acquired, however great or meager. The simultaneous achievement of justice (equality under law) and income equality could only occur if every individual were to possess identical market skills that were identically valued by consumers. Such is obviously impossible, in violation of the nature of things.

Consequently, the only way to achieve an equal distribution of income among unique individuals, as socialist morality demands, is to violate justice as traditionally conceived. As previously discussed in the context of positive rights, attempts to achieve a greater equalization of wealth in a market economy invariably involve the political redistribution of wealth. Such necessarily involves violation not only of individual property rights (of those persons or groups whose wealth is involuntarily taxed for purposes of redistribution) but also the ancient ideal of equality under law. Individuals must be treated very differently if the goal is economic or material equality among persons of widely varying abilities and skills. Those with more valuable market skills and talents must be penalized and those with less valuable skills and talents must be subsidized or otherwise rewarded. Traditional justice and equality of economic outcome are intrinsically in conflict, and there is no way around this fact. Accordingly, socialists and fellow travelers uniformly reject the traditional conception of justice in favor of a competing conception—so-called "social justice"—a concept to which we return in a following section.

The Demand for a Desert-based Justice

We have seen that the sense of justice informing capitalist economic arrangements is intimately related to certain profound moral convictions implicit in the Western political tradition and particularly its American expression. First and foremost among these is the inherent value of the individual. Every person, as we have seen, is regarded as unique, inviolable, and "endowed by their Creator" with certain unalienable rights. Every person is entitled to a particular kind of moral treatment simply by virtue of his status as a human being. The free society, said the philosopher Immanuel Kant, is a "kingdom of ends, not of means."[78] Each person is regarded as an end-in-himself, which means he may not be regarded as mere means—a mere tool—to be used in fulfillment of another person's goals, including persons organized as government. The equality of individual worth—the inherent and uniform substantive value of every person—further demands that every person be governed by the same laws, a demand embodied in the Anglo-American ideal of equality under law. We have seen that application of identical laws to persons of varying talents and skills inevitably produces unequal economic outcomes. Economic success or failure in a market economy is determined not by the intrinsic worth of the individual, which is equal across all human beings, but rather by the value that other persons subjectively impute to his or her marketable skills, an entirely different criterion. The economic position of any individual does not reflect his inherent worth as a human being. The market does not reward inherent personal worth but merely the ability to produce goods and services of instrumental value to other individuals. The rich are not rich because they are superior persons, morally or otherwise, and the poor are not poor because they are inferior persons. Persons are richer or poorer

---

[78] Immanuel Kant, *Groundwork of the Metaphysic of Morals* (Cambridge: Cambridge University Press, 2012 [1785]).

depending upon their ability to produce goods or services that other members of society will voluntarily purchase. There is little or no relation between such economic outcomes and personal or moral merit. Wicked people can and do prosper, while saints can and do starve. The market does not reward objective moral worth but rather the subjective and utilitarian worth of particular skills to market participants.

The absence of intrinsic connection between personal moral worth and economic status, however, seems a hard lesson to grasp. Human history has been marked by a persistent and recurring yearning for so-called "desert-based justice," a state of affairs wherein the economic status of every individual directly and transparently corresponds to his moral status. It would undoubtedly be gratifying to witness universal material prosperity among good human beings and universal poverty and want among the wicked: people should get what they "deserve." Such a moral yearning, however, while understandable, cannot be fulfilled by a market economy, or, indeed, by any form of economic arrangement. An individual who purchases an automobile in the free market is not thereby rewarding the seller for being a good person nor is the seller rewarding the buyer for being a good person. The buyer values what the seller has produced, not his personal moral qualities, and the seller values the money the buyer offers in exchange for the automobile, not the personal moral qualities of the buyer. An individual who applies for a job expects that the potential employer will evaluate the skills he brings to the firm, not his personal moral worth. No applicant for employment wants to stand in moral judgment before the potential employer as if the latter were God.

Not only is such the common practice and expectation in a market economy, but personal moral merit *cannot* be rewarded in a modern capitalist economy, however much participants might yearn to do so. As has been discussed, contemporary market relations constitute an "extended order of human cooperation" that encompasses the globe; income or economic outcome is determined by an impersonal process that involves millions and millions of persons largely unknown to one another.[79] As we have seen, an individual who purchases a can of cat food

---

[79] F.A. Hayek, "The Errors of Constructivism," *New Studies in Philosophy, Politics, Economics, and the History of Idea* (Chicago: The University of Chicago Press, 1978), 21. Within such a spatially extensive order, it is highly unlikely

is partially if unwittingly determining the income of every person directly or indirectly involved in its production. Buyers in a modern market economy generally have no way of knowing the identity of such persons, let alone whether they are good or bad people from a moral point of view. Nor do sellers generally have any way of knowing either the identity or the personal moral merit of those to whom they sell their goods or services. It is impossible to consciously "distribute" income in a developed market economy, according to personal merit or any other criteria. Any individual's income represents the value of his particular contribution to the production of a final good or service, a value impersonally and subjectively imputed by buyers, most of whom do not and cannot know the individual's personal identity, let alone his personal circumstances or moral merit. Such qualities are, and must be, largely unknown to both buyers and sellers in a spatially extended market order such as contemporary American society.

For such reasons, the yearning for a desert-based justice cannot be fulfilled in a market economy. Such a conclusion, however, is not unique to capitalism but applies with equal force to any form of collectivized, socialized, or command economy. Desert-based justice, again, involves the correspondence of economic success to personal moral goodness and economic failure or poverty to moral wickedness. The only means of approaching such a goal in a centralized economy, wherein resources are controlled by government, is to allow political authority to distribute material resources based on a standard of desert. That is, public officials would have to evaluate the personal moral merit of each and every individual and decide whether or not the individual is deserving of material reward. It is difficult to conceive an arrangement more disastrous to human wellbeing. Each individual would literally have to stand before their political superiors as if before God, proving his or her moral worth, merely to obtain the basic means of subsistence. Government officials would literally possess power of life and death over every individual in society, whose very existence would depend on his ability to convince the powers-that-be of his moral worth. No human being, however, whatever their political power or status, possesses either the right or competence morally to judge other human beings in such a

---

that either buyer or seller will possess any knowledge of his trading partner's identity, let alone his moral qualities.

fashion. Desert-based justice cannot be realized on earth unless and until government officials become God. Needless to say, such is unlikely to occur.

*

The justice intrinsic to capitalism, then, like the justice implicit in the game of baseball, is not an outcome- or desert-based justice but rather a procedural or rule-based justice. It is "blind" in the sense that every individual, regardless of personal circumstance, is to be governed by the same law. Traditional justice entails both universal enforcement of established rules of just conduct and indifference to the consequences or outcomes produced by observance of such rules. Justice, like law and economic theory, concerns not the goals of human action but rather the means by which they may be pursued. Economic outcomes, like the outcomes of baseball games, are thus regarded as fair or just so long as they are achieved by fair or just means. Only persons bear moral agency, which means that justice is always and everywhere an attribute of individual human behavior within a context of human relations; it can be attributed to an "outcome" only in a loose or metaphorical sense. Justice is achieved, whatever the material consequences, so long as people treat one another fairly in their mutual relations, and fairly means in accordance with the prevailing legal and moral rules, explicit and tacit, of a given society.

In American society, and Western society more generally, the prevailing rules of justice and morality have traditionally been conceived as objective rules of right and wrong, deriving from a source independent of human preference—deontological rules deriving from what *is*, from what is right-in-itself and what is wrong-in-itself. It is intrinsically right, right-in-itself, that human life be preserved; it is intrinsically wrong, wrong-in-itself, to murder an innocent person. On such a traditional view, government does not "make" the rules of justice but rather enforces a pre-existing order of right and wrong—the "Laws of Nature and of Nature's God" championed by Locke and his American counterparts and discussed in a previous volume. Such is the tacit conception of justice informing Madison's resolute conviction that "justice is the end of government; it is the end of civil society."

The Morality of Private Property

We have seen that capitalism, as Marx correctly perceived, is inseparable from the institution of private property. The morality of the market system thus stands or falls, to a large extent, on the morality of private property. The word property derives from the Latin *proper*— "characteristically belonging to the being or thing in question."[80] With respect to the institution of private property, the being in question is of course a human being; "property" is that which "characteristically belongs to" a human being. Property—what one owns—represents an extension of a human being's selfhood, personhood, or individuality. Indeed it is difficult to conceive of a human being without property of some kind, something he considers his own, even if simply his personal identity and physical body.

The concept of property, then, relates to the nature of things, more particularly, the characteristics of human being or personhood. Human beings universally share the same nature, which means that human beings universally possess property (that which "characteristically belongs to" a human being). The legitimacy of private property has nevertheless long been a matter of controversy, and the protection actually afforded individual property has varied considerably throughout history. The main concern of the present discussion, however, is not the particular protection afforded property in various societies over time but rather the general *moral* justification for the institution of private property. The short defense of the morality of private property is simply to invoke the near-universal condemnation of theft. In almost every society known to man, stealing is condemned as immoral and prohibited in one way or another.[81] The prohibition of theft presupposes the legitimacy of private property: theft can only be morally wrong if private

---

[80] Property comes into English from Anglo-Norman *properté* and Middle French *propreté*, with their own antecedents in Latin *proprius* and *proprietas*. . . . Adjectival *proprius* meant "particular" or "peculiar" and conveyed distinctiveness of the self, in contrast with *alienus*, meaning "other" or "foreign" (cf. English alienation), and with *communis*, "common" or "shared." The noun *proprietas* conveyed an analogous sense of "characteristic" and was often combined with *rerum* (of things). But *proprietas* is also cited with an overt "ownership" sense and also commonly used to convey aptness or suitability (reflected in English proper and propriety).

[81] One possible exception is ancient Sparta. It has often been observed that even thieves do not want the goods they steal stolen from themselves.

property is morally right. The universal moral and legal injunction against taking a person's property without his consent implies that the person is morally entitled to regard his possessions—his property—as his own. Indeed, even human infants and children display evidence of holding such an assumption. A young child who bursts into tears when his toy is rudely ripped from his hands seems to express a sense of violation even if yet unable to articulate the experience.

A more elaborate defense of private property, one that would become central to American political thought, was provided by John Locke. We recall that, according to Locke, the primary reason people leave the state of nature by compacting to form and live under civil government is precisely the "preservation of [their] property." Locke, as we have seen, employed the term property in both the broad and classic sense of "life, liberty, and estate" and the narrow contemporary sense of material possessions. The right to private property, he argues, is derived from the individual's prior right of self-possession. Every individual, Locke says, "has a *property* in his own *person*" (on loan, so to speak, from God, its ultimate possessor) and thus in his own body and labor.[82] The right of private property is established, he concludes, when an individual "mixes" his labor, which he owns by the natural right of self-possession, with the resources of the earth.

Locke acknowledges that God originally gave the earth and all its resources to mankind in common. Property is originally communal, not individual, property. He attempts, however, to explain how originally communal property eventually comes to be held by the individual by right. Imagine, he says, an individual in the state of nature who exerts himself to pluck an apple from a tree and then eats the apple to allay his hunger. What, Locke asks, gives the individual the right to engage in such actions, that is, to pluck and eat an apple that does not belong to him personally but rather to all men in common? He answers that such a right is established by the individual's initial exertion of labor, established at the moment he plucks the apple from the tree. Locke recognizes that some persons may regard such an act as a violation; the individual has taken the resource given to all men in common without

---

[82] ". . . [M]en being all the workmanship of one omnipotent, and infinitely wise maker . . . sent into the world by his order, and about his business; they are his property, whose workmanship they are. . . ." *Second Treatise*, 19, 9.

the consent of its rightful owners—all mankind. On such a view, the individual's appropriation of the apple is, in effect, mere theft. Locke, however, denies such a claim and rather asserts the legitimacy of the individual's actions. Yes, he acknowledges, God did give the earth to mankind as their common possession. He further argues, however, that God is a rational Being who also desires mankind to flourish and multiply. Accordingly, He could not have intended that each individual obtain prior permission from all other persons on earth before legitimately using or appropriating any common resource. If such were morally obligatory, all men would perish: it is clearly impossible to obtain the unanimous permission of all mankind. God, then, could not have intended such prior permission because he did not intend the destruction of mankind. Furthermore, Locke continues, the resources of this earth were intended for employment by the "industrious and rational," not the "quarrelsome and contentious."[83] For such reasons, he concludes, property by right belongs to the individual who possesses the drive, energy, and rationality to exert his labor in employing the resources of the earth for his own benefit or benefit of others.[84]

Locke's defense of private property carried forward a longstanding tradition of Christian reflection on the institution of private property. Among his predecessors was the celebrated Christian philosopher Thomas Aquinas (1224-1274), who, like Locke, provided a common-sense defense of the institution. Aquinas defends the necessity of private property on three grounds. First, human nature is self-interested: it is such that "every man is more careful to procure what is for himself alone than that which is common to many or to all, since each one would shirk the labor and leave to another that which concerns the community." Second, private property enables a more "orderly" conduct of human

---

[83] Locke, *Second Treatise*, 21-22.

[84] Locke does initially limit the extent of private property by the provision that no individual may accumulate more than he can use without waste. Such a qualification, however, is overcome, he says, by the invention of money. The use of a durable medium of exchange, one that will not rot or otherwise deteriorate over time, means that those who produce more than they themselves can personally consume can exchange their surplus for money, which in turn can be used to purchase the goods and services of others. The invention of money, then, removes the initial limit to individual accumulation established by the prohibition of waste.

affairs because it allows each person to "take care of some particular things himself; whereas there would be confusion if everyone had to look after any one thing indeterminately." Third, private property minimizes conflict within society, that is, "a more peaceful state is ensured to man if each one is content with his own. Hence it is to be observed that quarrels arise more frequently where there is no division of the things possessed."[85] Aquinas shares Locke's concern with the "quarrelsome and contentious."

The institution of private property has existed in some form or another in every developed or civilized society known to man. Communal or collective property, on the other hand, is characteristic of relatively primitive societies in early stages of cultural development.[86] Advanced civilization is inconceivable in the absence of private property. As has been discussed, a property right, in effect, is a decision right. The complexity of any developed society in a spatially extensive territory requires that individuals have both the right to make decisions regarding the direction of resources and the incentive to do so. Such a conclusion follows from the epistemological facts discussed in previous chapters. Only individuals possess the requisite knowledge—tacit and fleeting knowledge of time, place, and circumstance—to ensure an efficient utilization of scarce resources directed to the production of goods and services that people actually need and want. The right to direct such resources is guaranteed by the right to private property. The incentive to act on that knowledge is provided by the possibility of profit, secured to risk-takers by the enforcement of individual rights to property. We have also seen that the formation of an accurate structure of relative prices is similarly dependent on the institution of private property. Marx was correct: private property is indeed the linchpin of a capitalist economic order. The success or failure of a market economy, more precisely, the success or failure of the individuals who order their activities through

---

[85] Thomas Aquinas, *On Law, Morality, and Politics*, ed with intro by William P. Baumgarth and Richard J. Regan, S.J. (Hackett Publishing Company: Indianapolis, 1988). Question 66, Second Article, "Is It Lawful for a Man to Possess a Thing as His Own?" 178-179. Hereinafter cited as *Law, Morality, and Politics*.
[86] F.A. Hayek, *The Fatal Conceit: The Errors of Socialism*, ed, W.W. Bartley III (Chicago: University of Chicago Press, 1988).

market exchange, hinges on the scrupulous protection of the individual's right to decide, that is, his right to private property.

Justice and Socialism: Social or Distributive Justice

We have seen that the overarching moral goal of Marxism and its variants is greater equalization of material wealth among members of society. Toward that end, collectivist ideology not only proposes fundamental institutional change but also a redefinition of morality. Morality, as discussed, is implicitly redefined in material terms and along consequentialist lines congruent with the central collectivist end: good or right is identified with greater equality of material outcome and bad or wrong with inequality of material outcome. We have further seen that the equalization of material outcome valorized by collectivist ideology intrinsically conflicts with traditional justice, particularly its principle of equality under law and protection of universal, individual, negative rights to property. Economic centralization or collectivization of any kind is irreconcilable with traditional justice. Accordingly, advocates of economic socialization reject traditional justice in favor of a competing conception of justice, variously termed "social," "distributive," or "economic" justice or, more recently, "global," "racial," or "environmental" justice. All such terms are more or less synonymous. They all represent the demand for greater equality of economic or material outcome, to be achieved by the political distribution and/or redistribution of wealth.[87]

---

[87] The term "social justice'" is also used, vaguely and without clear definition, to connote various moral demands within certain Christian religious traditions, including the Roman Catholic Church, Methodism, and others. The term emerged in nineteenth-century Europe along with the widespread embrace of the "social" values championed by Marx and fellow travelers. Not all religious demands for social justice always and necessarily involve the forceful redistribution of wealth but the use of the term evidences once again the tremendous influence of socialist ideals on modern Western society. Moreover, its use to express moral demands apart from wealth distribution is unfortunate, obscuring rather than clarifying the meaning of justice. The very term "social justice" makes little sense, considering that justice is a virtue only applicable within the context of social (human) relations.

The attempt to achieve "social" or distributive justice—greater equalization of wealth—can be approached in various ways, just as the attempt to achieve governmental control of resources can be approached in various ways. Classic communism, as we have seen, demanded outright governmental confiscation and exclusive ownership of the means of production and subsequent distribution of wealth according to the dictates of political elites. As we recall, however, various fellow travelers and sympathizers quickly realized that the Marxist vision can be brought to fruition by means far less drastic than those envisioned by Marx himself. They realized, in particular, that democratic legislative action—the careful crafting of tax and regulatory policy—can also bring resources under control and direction of government and effectuate redistribution of wealth, with the great advantage of simultaneously permitting nominal preservation of private property. Similarly, the realization of social or distributive justice can be attempted in one of two ways. It can of course proceed along the lines of classic communism— outright governmental ownership of resources and industry (and subsequent material distribution by government). It can also be attempted by maintaining nominal private property but taxing and spending taxpayers' resources in such a manner as to achieve greater equalization of wealth across society (governmental redistribution of wealth). The collectivist moral ideal can be pursued through either political distribution or redistribution of resources.

We have previously touched upon the ideal of social or distributive justice as conceived by classic Marxism. Marx, as we have seen, condemned capitalism as profoundly unjust. Capitalists, he claimed, appropriate or steal what rightfully belongs to the workers—the entire value of the goods and services produced by their labor, staking their claim to exclusive possession of profits on the ground of individual rights to property. The *Communist Manifesto* aims straight at the heart of such injustice—the chronic and massive legal theft enabled by the institution of private property. It straightforwardly demands "the abolition of private property . . . [especially] *bourgeois* private property."[88] The Marxist vision, as discussed, involves direct governmental ownership and control of all resources in a manner that aims, in principle, to benefit every member of society, not merely the privileged capitalist class.

---

[88] *Communist Manifesto*, 484.

Government planners devise and implement production plans and distribute their fruits equitably across society. Each individual worker contributes to fulfillment of the central plans in accord with his unique abilities. Political authority assesses the relative needs of members of society and meet such needs by distribution from the common pool—the fruits of production jointly generated by all individual workers: "From each according to his ability, to each according to his need."

The end and purpose of all such procedures is justice—social or distributive justice, a more equal distribution of the material goods of this world. Workers, the source of all value, will finally receive their due, their fair share of the value they produce. Society will no longer be plagued by the obscene spectacle of extravagant luxury juxtaposed to grinding poverty, as under capitalism. Every member of society will be provided with decent food, housing, medical care, educational and cultural opportunities, and so on. Every member of society will be provided with the material means necessary to fulfill their lives and realize their potential. The class conflict that has plagued mankind throughout all previous stages of history will disappear. The "haves" and "have-nots" will be supplanted by the universal class of "Socialist Man," each member of which is equipped with the necessities of life and selflessly motivated to promote the common good. Justice will be realized at long last—social justice, an equitable distribution of material goods across all members of society.

Indeed, socialized economic relations will achieve not only justice but also freedom, not the sham "freedom" of capitalist society but rather true freedom—freedom from necessity. No longer will human beings be forced to work against their will, on pain of death. Instead government, the state, will "regulate the general production" and administer its distribution to ensure the material wellbeing of all persons. Human beings will finally achieve the freedom requisite to fulfillment of their nature, the spontaneous creative activity their species being demands. Indeed, the communist horizon beckons with the promise of untold joys, including release from the dreary tedium and monotony putatively intrinsic to capitalist relations of production. The specialization and division of labor demanded by capitalism will disappear under socialist relations of production, permitting the individual simultaneously to pursue his myriad inclinations and develop his myriad abilities. As Marx depicts the dream:

> In communist society, where nobody has one exclusive sphere of activity but each can become accomplished in any branch he wishes, society regulates the general production and thus makes it possible for me to do one thing today and another tomorrow, to hunt in the morning, fish in the afternoon, rear cattle in the evening, criticise [*sic*] after dinner, just as I have a mind, without ever becoming hunter, fisherman, herdsman or critic.[89]

Human beings will never again have to suffer the deadening pain of *boredom* in their working hours or sacrifice development of their various abilities for exclusive development of one. Socialism, unlike capitalism, will require no such painful trade-off.

Such is the essence of the ideal that drives the socialist aspiration in its myriad forms. It should again be emphasized that the collectivist ideal, cast in economic terms, is fundamentally a *moral* ideal. Equality of material distribution is portrayed as the highest moral good; inequality of material distribution as the epitome of injustice, immorality, and selfishness. Socialism thus asserts itself, as previously observed, as a decided moral advance over capitalism, which is said to be concerned not with the good of the whole of society but merely the rights and interests of the individual or a privileged group of individuals, the capitalists. On the Marxist view, the individual property rights that sustain capitalist exploitation have value only to this privileged group; they have no value to those who own no property but their labor, the workers. As Marx says in the *Communist Manifesto*,

> You are horrified at our intending to do away with private property. But in your existing society private property is already done away with for nine-tenths of the population; its existence for the few is solely due to its non-existence in the hands of those nine-tenths. You reproach us, therefore, with intending to do away with a form of property, the necessary condition for whose existence is the non-existence of any property for the immense majority of society.

---

[89] Marx, *The German Ideology* (1845), in *Marx-Engels Reader*, 160.

> In one word, you reproach us with intending to do away with your property. Precisely so: that is just what we intend.[90]

Capitalism only benefits the select few, the *bourgeoisie*, and this at the expense of the many, the *proletariat*. The superior morality of socialism, by contrast, is concerned not with the mere individual or one class of individuals but the good of all. The word "socialism" itself points to the elevation of the collective whole over the individual or the minority. As Adolph Hitler, leader of the German National Socialists, pointedly remarked, ". . . the state must act as the guardian of a . . . future in the face of which the wishes and the selfishness of the individual must appear as nothing and submit."[91] Such sentiments underlie not only Nazi socialism but all the various forms of modern collectivist ideology.

Marx and fellow travelers are correct to identify capitalism with individualism. As we have seen, the market order, along with the moral, legal, and political framework that sustains it, presupposes the value of the individual human person. The purpose of law in a free society, as well as the limited government established to declare, enforce, and adjudicate the law, is precisely to protect *individual* rights to life, liberty, and property. The elevation of the collective or the "social" over the individual is alien to the American political tradition, as is the corresponding conception of "group," "collective," or "social" rights.

The American commitment to individual rights developed upon the foundation of the Western tradition more broadly conceived. One of the distinctive characteristics of that tradition is the profound value it places upon the individual person. Such a value, as we shall see, largely derives from the particular religious influences that shaped the development of Western civilization, in particular, Christianity, the religion of the individual *par excellence*. The relation between Christianity and individualism was well understood by enemies of liberal-capitalist society. Thus it is not surprising that carriers of the modern ideological impulse would condemn Christianity as fervently as capitalism, and on similar grounds. Capitalism, as we have seen, was denounced by

---

[90] Karl Marx and Friedrich Engels, *Manifesto of the Communist Party,* Robert C. Tucker, ed, *The Marx-Engels Reader,* 2nd ed (New York: W.W. Norton & Company, 1978 [1848], 486). Hereinafter cited as *Communist Manifesto* and *Marx-Engels Reader.*

[91] Adolph Hitler, *Mein Kampf* (Boston: Houghton Mifflin, 1998), vol 2, Ch. 2.

collectivist ideologues as fostering selfishness and other moral vices. Nineteenth-century critics of capitalism had no difficulty relating that propensity to the religious milieu that fostered its rise: Christianity, proclaimed John Stuart Mill, is the Religion of the Selfish.[92] In the eyes of its adherents, socialism and the social ethics it advances are morally superior to both capitalism and Christianity, both of which are said to elevate selfish individualism over selfless concern for all members of society.

Consciousness as "Epiphenomenon"

The free society, as previously mentioned, is an integrated whole whose flourishing depends upon the existence of harmonious and complementary moral, legal, political, and economic institutions. Its economic dimension, capitalism, cannot be isolated from the more comprehensive social or cultural environment requisite to its operation. Marx well understood this fact, and his condemnation of Western liberal capitalism thus extended to a thoroughgoing condemnation of the moral, legal, and political institutions with which it is inextricably linked. Constitutional government is a case in point. Champions of limited government, he suggests, invariably portray its virtues in the most high-minded and noble light, as the quintessence of freedom, justice, and morality. According to Marx, however, such a depiction is false and contrived, a veil of illusion that obscures the truth of liberal constitutionalism, namely, the role it plays in safeguarding the selfish interests of the ruling class, the capitalists. As he says in the *Communist Manifesto*, "The executive of the modern state is but a committee for managing the common affairs of the whole bourgeoisie. In other words: the State is the executive committee of the ruling bourgeois class. . . ."[93]

Marx castigates not only liberal constitutionalism but every moral, political, and religious ideal characteristic of the Western tradition. He scorns and ridicules traditional notions of freedom, justice, law, morality, religion, rights, and familial bonds. Such alleged "ideals," he

---

[92] J. S. Mill, *On Liberty, Utility of Religion*, in *Collected Works of John Stuart Mill* (Toronto: University of Toronto Press, 1963) Vol 10: 51, 422. Hereinafter cited as *CW*.
[93] *Communist Manifesto*, 475.

suggests, are little more than propaganda, manipulative rationalizations or lies whose purpose is to camouflage the reality of capitalist exploitation, to confuse the workers by masking the brutal fact of class struggle. Liberal ideals are mere inventions of the ruling *bourgeoisie,* beautiful words that signify nothing, and their purpose is to preserve the power of that class. As Marx says,

> The ideas of the ruling class are in every epoch the ruling ideas, i.e. the class which is the ruling material force of society, is at the same time its ruling intellectual force. The class which has the means of material production at its disposal, has control at the same time over the means of mental production, so that thereby, generally speaking, the ideas of those who lack the means of mental production are subject to it. The ruling ideas are nothing more than the ideal expression of the dominant material relationships, the dominant material relationships grasped as ideas.[94]

Marx's critique of traditional moral and political ideas and ideals is related to his general theory of consciousness, which must therefore be briefly considered. The question at issue concerns the status of ideas and values in history. The philosophical response to such a question is conventionally divided into two chief categories, so-called philosophical idealism and philosophical materialism. "Idealist" philosophers such G. W. F. Hegel (1770-1831) and others regard abstract ideas and the values they represent as the driving force of human history. Society, to paraphrase the idealist Plato, is man writ large. The character of any society derives from the character of its members, which itself is shaped by the ideas they hold and the values they pursue. Human existence is inescapably oriented toward fulfillment of value. The abstract values held by individual members of any society inform the ideas, beliefs, customs, institutions, and other cultural expressions characteristic of that society. A people who value individual freedom, for instance, will seek to devise institutions that protect and preserve that value; a people who value justice will seek to devise rules and laws that serve that value, and so on. The essence of such philosophical idealism may be summarized

---

[94] Marx, *The German Ideology,* in *Marx-Engels Reader,* 172.

by Hayek's observation, previously mentioned in another context, that "values generate facts."

Philosophical materialism, such as advocated by Marx, rejects the primacy of abstract ideas and values and posits instead that concrete or material factors of one kind or another ultimately determine human experience. The young Marx was greatly influenced by Hegel, particularly his dialectic view of historical process. He came to believe, however, that Hegel's work was flawed by a fundamental error—philosophic idealism. To assume the primacy of ideas, Marx believed, is to put the cart before the horse, as the saying goes. In Marx's own metaphor, Hegel had it "upside down"; Marx would correct his error, as he said, by turning Hegel "right side up."[95] Hegel had rooted experience in ideas. The truth of reality, according to Marx, is that personal and social experience is rooted not in "abstractions" such as ideas, ideals, and values but rather concrete material forces.

Marx's revision of Hegelianism is embodied in his materialist philosophy of history, the dialectical materialism discussed in a previous chapter. Marxist materialism teaches that particular material facts prevailing in any epoch, namely, the existing status of so-called "productive forces" (technological development), conjoined with existing "relations of production" (freeman/slave; guildmaster/journeyman; capitalist/worker, and so on) are the primary and ultimate determinants of human experience. Human consciousness—abstract ideas, ideals, and values—is a mere "epiphenomenon," that is, a byproduct of the concrete relations of production prevailing in any given society. As Marx put the leading idea, "[i]t is not the consciousness of men that determines their being, but, on the contrary, their social being that determines their consciousness."[96]

> Morality, religion, metaphysics, all the rest of ideology and their corresponding forms of consciousness, thus no longer retain the semblance of independence. They have no history,

---

[95] "My dialectic method is not only different from the Hegelian, but is its direct opposite. . . . With him it is standing on its head. It must be turned right side up again, if you would discover the rational kernel within the mystical shell." Marx, Afterword, *Das Kapital,* Second German Edition (1873).

[96] Karl Marx, *A Contribution to the Critique of Political Economy* (Moscow: Progress Publishers, 1977 [1859]).

no development; but men, developing their material production and their material intercourse, alter, along with this their real existence, their thinking and the products of their thinking. Life is not determined by consciousness, but consciousness by life.[97]

Marxist materialism is a species of philosophical determinism, a general class of philosophical viewpoints united by a common conviction that human experience is "determined" by one or another force or forces beyond human control, that is, by something other than individual choice. In the case of Marx, the force in question is economic. Marxism is based upon a thoroughgoing economic determinism: the economic relations and productive forces prevailing within society are said to "determine" (cause) not only the general course of history (dialectical materialism) but also the particular beliefs and values held by members of a particular society. Members of Western society may imagine that they autonomously value individualism, freedom, justice, the rule of law, peace, God, family, and so on, in-themselves and for-their-own-sake. According to Marx, however, this is an illusion. Such ideas and values, he claims, are actually determined or caused by prevailing economic (capitalist) relations and forces of production, by economic status and class interest. The capitalist ruling class, he further maintains, is the actual ruling power in Western liberal society; it thus possesses the power to form its prevailing ideas and values. The dominant ideas and ideals of liberal society, such as individual freedom and individual rights, have actually been devised and propagated by the capitalist ruling class to further its own interests, interests that conflict with those of the workers, the great majority of the populace. Marx recognizes, however, that the capitalists themselves are not fully responsible for the ideas and values they promote; they too are pawns of history, and their views too are determined by prevailing economic relations. Capitalists hold the particular beliefs and values they hold *because* of their class position, a position which itself is determined by the objective laws impelling history towards its final goal, the establishment of communism. The values of the capitalists, then, are as much the byproduct of their historical class position as those of the hapless workers. All ideas and

---

[97] Marx, *German Ideology*, in *Marx-Engles Reader*, 154-155.

values, including and especially the ideological propaganda of the capitalist class, can ultimately be traced to the economic forces and relations of production prevailing in a society or epoch.

Marx's theory regarding the causal relation between material forces and abstract ideas is related to another well-known Marxian concept—so-called "false consciousness." False consciousness is a consequence of economic determinism. An individual's ideas and values are determined by his historical position in a particular economic class within a society characterized by a particular set of productive or technological forces and particular relations of production. Capitalist relations of production, for instance, will lead many individuals raised within a capitalist economy to embrace the value of private property. Indeed they may cling to such a value even though Marx believes he has demonstrated its immorality as well as its transitory or provisional nature in the movement of history. The stubborn refusal to abandon one's attachment to private property, indeed to claim such property as a natural and unalienable right, is a classic instance of Marxian false consciousness. On the Marxist view, there is no such entity as a trans-historical or natural right to private property. The concept bears no substance but is rather a mere epiphenomenon, a byproduct of prevailing capitalist relations of production, an ideological construct designed to protect the interests of the ruling class. It is mere propaganda.

False consciousness arises from regarding such capitalist propaganda as truth. The reality, according to Marx, is that concepts such as natural rights are illusions deriving ultimately from the prevailing economic forces and relations that determine ideas and values. Accordingly, the only way to pierce the illusions and delusions of false consciousness is to change the prevailing economic forces and relations that gave rise to them in the first place. The communist revolution will accomplish precisely the needed change. In particular, it will abolish capitalist relations of production, which not only cause false consciousness but, according to Marx, have been rendered historically obsolete by the massive growth in productive forces unleashed by capitalism itself. Because human consciousness is a byproduct of prevailing economic relations, a change in such relations will change human consciousness, will change the way people think, their beliefs, values, philosophy, religion, and so on. The replacement of capitalist with socialist relations of production will not only eliminate all class distinctions, capitalists and workers, *bourgeoisie* and *proletariat*, but liberal and capitalist ideas and ideals as well. The causal force of economic relations means that newly established socialized relations of production will ultimately transform the ideas, beliefs, and values of the populace in the direction of socialist ideas and ideals.

Marx thus anticipates a dramatic and beneficial change in human being. Socialism will produce not only more equal material conditions and a new ideology for the masses but also a new kind of human being. As previously mentioned, "capitalist" man will be superseded by "socialist man"—unselfish, unattached to possessions, willing to employ his unique abilities for the general good. The joint contributions of such newly born men will form a pool of resources unhesitatingly shared among all members of society, according to their need. Human behavior under capitalism—selfishness, possessiveness, individualism, greed, materialism, and so on—is not natural or inevitable but rather a result of capitalist economic relations and ideological indoctrination. Only individuals who cling to the false consciousness developed by their experience under capitalism will have difficulty imagining the glorious future of the human race under socialism. Indeed such individuals may experience not only a dearth of imagination but a variety of other difficulties in adjusting to the new socialist order; in such cases, "reeducation" may prove of value. If educational efforts should fail to transform hearts and minds, those who insist on obstructing progress toward History's final and inevitable goal may have to be dealt with in other ways.

The Redistribution of Wealth

We have seen that many persons persuaded of the moral superiority of the socialist ideal came to realize that collectivist goals could be achieved not only by revolutionary violence and abolition of private property but also peacefully, especially by a widening of democracy. The central element of the socialist ideal—greater equalization of wealth and material resources—could also be achieved by democratically supported tax and regulatory policy within a framework of nominal private property. Classic communism envisioned exclusive governmental production and distribution of material resources as the best means to realize that ideal. Fabians, Progressives, and fellow travelers came to realize that redistribution of privately produced wealth by a democratically elected government can achieve the same end. The command-and-control procedures of classic economic centralization could be jettisoned in favor of progressive taxation, appropriate regulatory controls on economic activity, and legislative enactment of various entitlement programs.

Contrary to Marx, then, the attempt to achieve greater equalization of wealth across society does not require the utter abolition of private property and exclusive governmental *distribution* of resources. A politics of wealth *redistribution* in the context of nominal private property can also serve that end, at least in the short run. The crucial issue is not the nominal ownership of property—whether assigned to the individual or the state—but rather who actually and ultimately controls the direction and use of resources. Individuals may retain legal rights to their property but have little say in how it is actually employed. In the United States, for instance, elected officials determine tax and regulatory policy and also enact programs that provide material benefits (entitlements) to certain citizens. Government determines not only the amount of income citizens are permitted to retain (tax policy) but also how taxed wealth will be spent (government spending) and perhaps even how retained income must be employed (regulation and other legislative mandates). Despite retaining nominal ownership of the resources affected by such governmental policies, the individuals who produced them no longer have actual control over their allocation or use. Such decision rights have rather been transferred to government. We have previously noted the inadequacy of the textbook definition of socialism—"public ownership of the means of production." Socialism exists, in practice if not in name, whenever government, and not private individuals, controls the direction of resources within society. The fact that private individuals may retain nominal ownership of such resources is irrelevant. The great insight of the English Fabians, American Progressives, and their modern-liberal descendants was to recognize that socialism by any other name is still socialism.

Redistribution may be formally defined as the transfer of wealth from *net* taxpayers to *net* tax beneficiaries by means of the political process. Net taxpayers are those who pay more in taxes than they receive in government benefits; net tax beneficiaries, conversely, receive more in government benefits than they pay in taxes. Contemporary governments in the United States and many Western democracies are essentially huge machines of redistribution so defined. Governments, federal, state, and local, collect enormous amounts of taxes, micromanage economic activity through tax and regulatory policy, and devise myriad entitlement programs. So-called "entitlements" are more or less equivalent to positive rights to various material goods and services, for instance, welfare, food stamps, Medicaid, public housing, Aid to Families with Dependent Children, and so on. Such programs are financed by transferring revenue obtained from taxpayers to those persons eligible for the government benefits. The two groups may, in principle, coincide, that is, it is theoretically possible that every taxpayer receives as much in government benefits as he contributes in taxes. Such coincidence, however, is highly improbable and thus the definition of redistribution previously stated, that is, legal transfer of wealth from *net* taxpayers to *net* tax beneficiaries. Some people pay more in taxes than they receive in benefits, and vice versa. The former group materially supports the latter; the latter benefits at the expense of the former, receiving the fruits of the net taxpayers' productive activity in the form of legislated entitlements, subsidies, bail-outs, and so on. As previously remarked, there are winners and losers in a politics of redistribution. The ascendancy of such a politics over the course of the twentieth century has thus created a "class struggle" in American society but not the kind envisioned by Marx. The relevant class struggle in contemporary society is not between capitalists and workers but rather net taxpayers and net tax beneficiaries.

The United States, like most other Western democracies, employs a system of progressive taxation, which involves taxing relatively higher income at a higher rate than the rate applied to relatively lower income. The political redistribution of wealth is generally thought to involve a transfer of resources from more affluent to less affluent members of society, accomplished, in part, by progressive taxation. In 2012, for instance, the top one percent of all income earners in the United States paid about forty percent of all federal income taxes; it is unlikely that this one percent received forty percent of the benefits distributed by the federal government. The top five percent of all income earners paid about seventy percent of all federal income taxes; it is again doubtful that this five percent received seventy percent of federal benefits. Almost fifty percent of all Americans pay no federal income taxes at all yet many persons within this group probably receive federal entitlements of one form or another. Those with relatively lower income also receive additional federal subsidies in the form of the so-called "Earned-Income Tax Credit" and similar devices. Such are the results of a progressive federal income tax and a democratic legislative process. By such means wealth is routinely transferred from one group to another by both federal and state governments (insofar as the latter also engage in a politics of redistribution). Political redistribution of wealth is an effective tool, at least in the short run, for advancing the classic socialist goal—greater equalization of material wealth—or, as one high official in the American government recently expressed it, "spreading the wealth around."[98]

The public generally believes that the political transfer of wealth flows from the "richer" to the "poorer," a belief often encouraged by the rhetoric of politicians and political parties. Such, however, is not necessarily the case. Wealth can be politically redistributed to any group designated by the government, whatever its economic status. Such can be achieved not only by tax and entitlement policies but other governmental measures as well, including direct legislative subsidy, awarding of government contracts, expansion of the federal work force, foreign aid, and many others. The redistributive apparatus of government is not confined to transferring income from the relatively wealthy to the relatively poor but also transfers wealth from relatively poorer to relatively wealthier citizens. We previously discussed the so-called "corporate-welfare state" in the context of crony capitalism. Certain major industries receive enormous governmental subsidies and bailouts, funded by taxpayers, many of whom possess relatively limited income. Massive amounts of taxpayer funds, for instance, are redistributed from taxpayers to politically influential corporations, campaign donors, and special-interest groups (e.g., Solyndra, AIG, General Motors, Fiskars, private military contractors, agribusiness, and similar beneficiaries of governmental largess). Organized or "Big Labor" is yet another major beneficiary of political redistribution. Labor unions are comprised not only of industrial and service workers but also increasingly of governmental workers such as employees of federal, state, and local governments, teachers unions, police unions, and the like, all of whose income is paid for by taxpayers, many of whom earn far less

---

[98] ". . . I think when you spread the wealth around, it's good for everybody." Presidential candidate Barack Obama, Oct. 12, 2008, outside Toledo, Ohio.

than those on governmental payrolls. The relatively poor, like all other members of society, also pay state sales taxes, which are generally regressive, that is, represent a larger percentage of a poorer person's income than a wealthier person's income.[99]

The essential point is that redistribution of wealth in the United States, commonly thought to involve a transfer of wealth from "rich" to "poor," is not in fact confined to that result. Tax revenue is also used to send well-compensated IRS agents on lavish taxpayer-funded jaunts to exotic places, to bail out wealthy corporate giants like AIG, and subsidize the risky ventures of a Solyndra and other politically privileged corporate interests. Hence the importance of differentiating *net* taxpayers from *net* tax beneficiaries. A working mother of limited income may conceivably be subsidizing the activities of mega-corporations controlling multibillion dollars of assets.

The Funding of Government

To further understand how redistribution of wealth is achieved in a liberal-democratic political order such as the United States, it is necessary to discuss the means by which the activities of government are funded. All government programs and policies, from salaries of Supreme Court justices to government-funded research on the alcohol consumption of Argentinian homosexuals, must somehow be financed.[100] Government is neither a god who creates *ex nihilo* nor a magician who waves a magic wand and creates resources out of thin air. If government is to provide entitlements or other material assistance it must obtain the financial means to do so. If government is to engage in "public works" such as building bridges and repairing highways, it must obtain the material resources needed to build a bridge, repair a highway, and so on. Resources, as has been extensively discussed, do not grow on trees. The fact of scarcity or limited resources applies to government or public

---

[99] Regressive taxation is defined as a tax on income in which the proportion of tax paid relative to income decreases as income increases.
[100] "International Differences in Alcohol Use According to Sexual Orientation." NIH study published in *Substance Abuse* 2011 Oct (32: (4): 210-219.

resources as well as private resources; as the popular expression has it, "there is no such thing as a free lunch."[101]

The discipline of public finance explores the various means by which government at all levels obtains the resources required to fulfill its constitutional responsibilities and execute its programs and policies. The simplest way to understand government funding, however, is to realize that there are basically three ways in which government in a free society can obtain funding for its activities—taxation, borrowing, and implementation of monetary policy. In the United States, the federal government possesses constitutional authority to employ the first two methods and legislative authority to employ the third. State and local governments are more limited in that they do not possess the third option, the authority to create money. American government possesses few if any resources of its own, perhaps revenue from the postal service, various licensing and service fees, the collection of fines, and so on. The vast bulk of the funds it requires must be obtained in one of the three ways indicated.

To illustrate the funding process, we shall use a familiar entitlement program such as food stamps, which of course aims to provide nutritional support to relatively low-income persons. If government is to provide food stamps to certain individuals, the money needed to do so must be obtained either by taxation, borrowing, or the creation of money, all of which funds are ultimately provided by taxpayers. The provision of food stamps entails the transfer of resources from those who must pay for the stamps to those who receive them. Resources to effect such a transfer can be obtained directly from the taxpayer in two ways— taxation and borrowing. We first discuss the means of taxation. Money obtained by taxation reduces the resources available to the taxpayer by the amount of the tax. Present taxpayers' wealth decreases as the present food stamp recipients' wealth increases; the latter's gain is the former's loss. We next consider the means of borrowing. Funds obtained by

---

[101] Uses of the phrase dating back to the 1930s and 1940s have been found, but its first appearance is unknown. The "free lunch" in the saying refers to the nineteenth-century practice of offering a "free lunch" in American bars as a way to entice drinking customers. The phrase and the acronym were popularized by Robert Heinlein's 1966 science-fiction novel *The Moon is a Harsh Mistress* and its later use as the title of a 1975 book by free-market economist Milton Friedman.

borrowing have the same consequences as those obtained by taxation; the only difference is that such consequences are projected into the future. Money borrowed today to fund the current food stamp program must be paid back at some point in the future, with interest. Current food stamps that are financed by governmental borrowing must be paid for not by present taxpayers but rather *future* taxpayers; the present food-stamp recipients' gain is the future taxpayers' loss. Future taxpayers must either repay the money borrowed for the present food-stamp program (with interest) or the government must declare bankruptcy, that is, default on its debt obligations. The latter of course would be disastrous for the American economy and American standing in the world.

The third possible means by which the federal government can obtain the funds needed to pay for its food-stamp program is the printing of money. Since the creation of the Federal Reserve System in 1913, the United States operates what is called a *fiat* monetary system. A *fiat* is a command. Every unit of paper currency in the United States unequivocally states that "This note is legal tender for all debts, public and private." In other words, no one may legally refuse a dollar offered in payment for any kind of economic transaction. A dollar bill is legal tender by *fiat*, which means that a dollar bill is valid currency because the government says it is. The federal government possesses a monopoly on the production of the money supply. States are prohibited by the Constitution from coining money, and no form of money but paper currency printed by the federal government is considered legal tender.

Government officials are always short of money to pay for the many activities and programs they champion. Moreover, individual citizens may support certain governmental programs and entitlements but not personally want to pay the taxes necessary to fund them. Such individuals will be tempted to support methods of finance that require other persons to bear the cost of such programs. Political campaigns are saturated with promises of benefits to come, but politicians seeking election are loath to mention that such benefits must be paid for either by current or future taxpayers. Immediate taxation is obviously unpopular; politicians who suggest they will raise taxes are vulnerable to losing the next election. Borrowing ("deficit spending") is usually less unpopular mainly because the tax burden is not immediate but projected into the future. Voters may think that they themselves will not have to repay the borrowed funds; taxpayers of the future, perhaps their children or grandchildren or other people's children or grandchildren, will bear that burden. Nevertheless, both immediate tax increases and wanton deficit spending bear political risk for politicians. The temptation is thus great for elected federal officials to employ the third means of raising funds available to the federal government—the printing press.

Monetary policy is a complex subject that cannot be explored at depth in the present work, but several elemental principles must be briefly discussed. A concrete example may most readily highlight the issues relevant to our topic. Assume a hypothetical scenario in which the federal government decides to finance the food-stamp program by borrowing the requisite funds. It does so by issuing (selling) Treasury bonds on the capital market. Bond dealers buy and hold these government bonds in their portfolios or sell them to other investors. The issuing of government bonds increases the debt of the federal government, that is, increases the so-called "budget deficit" (federal spending minus federal revenue). The dramatic rise in the federal budget deficit over recent decades, however, has rendered such federal borrowing increasingly unpopular with the American public. Citizens are coming to recognize the implications of a massive federal debt for the long-term wellbeing of the American people.

The Federal Reserve can help politicians bypass such a political obstacle. Instead of requiring the federal Treasury to issue bonds on the open market to obtain the desired funds and thus openly increase the federal budget deficit, the Fed can choose to "monetize the debt." Federal Reserve officials possess the legal authority to create new currency by engaging in so-called "open-market operations." The Fed purchases assets, usually Treasury bonds previously issued by the federal government, from bond dealers who, as said, typically hold such assets in their portfolios. It pays for the bonds with money the Fed itself creates, thereby injecting additional currency into the monetary system. Such action reduces the appearance of federal government debt—the outstanding bonds owned by the dealers are now retired—but this is mere illusion. Government has actually obtained the needed funds by borrowing (selling Treasury bonds to the dealers) but this is disguised by the Fed's purchase of the very same bonds, paid for by newly printed currency. The bond dealers are merely middlemen. They purchase the Treasury bonds issued by the government (and government receives the funds to pay for its programs), but the bonds are repurchased from them by the Federal Reserve with newly issued currency. The bond dealers could be eliminated with no effect. The Federal Reserve could simply purchase the bonds directly from the Treasury and pay for them with newly created money. The result is the same in either case: government funding by means of money creation. The advantage of such a procedure to the federal government is the nominal reduction or stability of the national debt.

By such means current government programs can be funded, not through politically unpopular taxation or deficit spending, but rather by creation of money *ex nihilo*. Such policy, however, does carry certain widely recognized dangers, for instance, potential destabilization of the value of the dollar. Excess currency injected into the economic system will lead over time to *inflation*—an increase in the money supply that leads to a rise in the price level. We have discussed the all-important guiding function of prices in a market economy. Inflation—the increase in prices that results from an increase in the money supply—distorts the relative price structure in a society and thus leads to misallocation of resources. During the initial period of monetary stimulus (the "boom"), the Federal Reserve buys massive quantities of Treasury bonds financed by money creation; the injection of additional currency into the market leads over time to a rise in various prices. Firms and investors will tend to interpret the rise in prices as either an increase in demand or decrease in supply, in any event, as a signal to increase production. Rational economic decisions, however, depend upon accurate relative prices—prices that reflect *actual* conditions of demand and supply. Increased prices signal producers to increase production, which would be appropriate if the rise in prices were caused by actual increase in demand or decrease in supply. Increased production is not appropriate, however, if the price rise is due to inflation, a mere increase in the quantity of money in circulation. In such a case, conditions of demand and supply have not actually changed; the only change is the increase in the quantity of circulating currency, newly created by the monetary authority.

Producers will eventually discover that they have been misled by false signals. When they bring to market the goods produced in response to the price-rise effected by monetary stimulus, they will discover that demand (supply) has not actually increased (decreased) and will be unable to sell such products. The errors they made will be exposed, errors that resulted from acting upon false information—the distortion in relative prices caused by increase in the money supply. What they anticipated to be profitable turns out not to be profitable after all. Firms that cannot sell their products will decrease production; employees are laid off, unemployment rises, and "recession" ensues. Inflation leads to recession—"boom" leads to "bust"—as surely as night follows day.[102] Such is the high cost of "monetizing the debt" and other feckless manipulations of the money supply.

The federal government may also simply borrow funds from the capital markets without assistance from the Federal Reserve. In such a case, the federal deficit will increase but there is no inflation or distortion of relative price signals. There is nevertheless a cost to such policy. We know that all resources are limited or scarce, financial as well as material resources. The supply of funds available for borrowing, by government or anyone else, is not unlimited. Accordingly, the more funds borrowed by government, the fewer funds available for borrowing by private firms and investors. Governmental borrowing is said to "crowd out" private borrowing, which leads over time to reduction in economic growth. Government spending, unlike authentic capital investment made by private individuals and firms, is not generally productive or investment spending but rather spending for immediate consumption. The individuals in our example who receive the food stamps financed by governmental borrowing spend that resource for personal consumption, not investment in means of production such as tools, machines, and other capital equipment. As has been discussed, however, such capital investment is crucial to the development and vitality of a market economy, enormously enhancing productivity and thus wages and income. Governmental borrowing depletes the supply of investment funds and thus reduces future economic growth or development.

In conclusion, an unwarranted increase in the money supply leads to inflation—a rise in prices—which in turn leads to distortion of the relative price structure upon which a market economy crucially depends. Such distortion of the information conveyed by prices leads to investment and production errors that can only be corrected or liquidated by economic recession—curtailing production (and thus employment) that has proved to be uneconomic. Monetization of the

---

[102] Ludwig von Mises, Murray Rothbard, F.A. Hayek, *Austrian Theory of the Trade Cycle and other Essays* (Auburn, AL: Ludwig von Mises Institute, 2009.

debt is a precarious strategy that can destabilize an economy in the long run. Nevertheless, such a strategy is often appealing to government officials concerned more with short-run election considerations than the long-run economic wellbeing of society. Inflationary monetary policy is politically appealing in the short run—the boom period when prices first begin to rise and production and employment increase; the long-run consequences—the inevitable bust or recession—are readily ignored or minimized. The time horizon of most politicians is notoriously short. What matters in many cases is simply the next election cycle, not the long-term stability and flourishing of the economy. For such reasons, the boom-and-bust cycle engendered by politically motivated monetary (and fiscal) policy is sometimes referred to as the "political business cycle."

The Ethics of Redistribution

The widespread embrace of socialist aspirations in many Western democracies, including the United States, has led such governments to adopt tax, regulatory, and spending policies that result in significant redistribution of wealth. As has been discussed, the purpose of such redistribution in many instances is to achieve a greater equalization of wealth and income than would be achieved in a market economy. Such is represented not only as fair but indeed as a higher form of justice than the justice of capitalism, which necessarily results in inequality of material outcome. Marx and fellow travelers not only condemn capitalism as unjust but vigorously assert the moral superiority of economic socialization. Both the gravity of such moral claims and their widespread currency within contemporary society call for scrupulous inquiry into their legitimacy.

The rhetoric of socialism is undeniably appealing. Socialism, as we have seen, is said to care about the good of the whole, not merely a certain historically privileged class. Socialism is portrayed as "altruistic"—concerned with the welfare of "others"—in contrast to the selfishness and egoism allegedly intrinsic to capitalism. Socialism claims to be the special champion of the poor, the downtrodden, the oppressed, the have-nots, the "marginalized." It promises a society in which every human being can realize his or her potential, regardless of economic position. It further promises the elimination of drudgery and coerced labor, providing every person with opportunity for creative and fulfilling work. It promises to achieve what Franklin Delano Roosevelt proclaimed as one of four essential freedoms—"freedom from want."[103] Economic socialization will eradicate hunger and need, providing every person with life's material necessities, cradle to grave. It will eliminate gross inequality and every sort of class distinction. Rich and poor, black and white, high and low, all such classes will be supplanted by the socialist brotherhood of man. Indeed socialism will not only rectify the human condition but transform human nature itself. We have seen that establishment of socialist relations of production, in line with Marxist determinism, promises the emergence of Socialist Man—compassionate, cooperative, generous with his abilities, concerned with the good of all. Individual selfishness will be transformed into universal selflessness. Even the desire for private possessions, a byproduct of capitalist relations of production, will eventually disappear. Liberated from the greed for possession, every person will learn to enjoy and appreciate the objects of this world as the artist enjoys them, contemplatively, for-their-own sake.[104] It is difficult to imagine the indifference of any human being to the promised bliss of such a moral and material paradise.

Champions of socialism and champions of capitalism share many ultimate goals. It seems fair to say that advocates of both forms of economic arrangement would prefer a society that allows for maximum flourishing of human potential, one in which every person has opportunity to fulfill his abilities and realize his life-purpose. Undoubtedly most people would also prefer universal material prosperity; no one wants some children to starve while others are indulged in extravagant and superfluous luxury. Most people would prefer to live in a cooperative society whose members are concerned with one another's welfare. Of course differences between the two schools exist as well. Advocates of capitalism, for instance, do not equate the good with equality of material distribution nor envision an ultimate

---

[103] The Four Freedoms were goals articulated by United States President Franklin D. Roosevelt on January 6, 1941. In an address known as the Four Freedoms speech (technically the 1941 State of the Union address), he proposed four fundamental freedoms that people "everywhere in the world" ought to enjoy: 1. Freedom of speech; 2. Freedom of worship; 3. Freedom from want; and, 4. Freedom from fear.

[104] Raeder, "Psychodrama."

transformation of human nature. The decisive difference between the two schools of thought, however, relates not to ultimate ends but rather the *means* required to achieve them. Socialism, as we have seen, aims to achieve its goals through governmental direction or outright control of resources, whereas capitalism aims to achieve them through private direction of resources. Such a difference not only has far-reaching practical consequences—the relative ability of the two competing systems to solve the economic problem—but profound moral consequences as well.

We have extensively discussed the strictly economic objections to economic socialization: central or governmental planners simply cannot acquire the knowledge and information requisite to efficient employment of scarce resources in production of goods and services most urgently needed or wanted by consumers. There is no question of the strictly economic superiority of capitalism to socialism in this regard. As previously observed, however, the relative economic efficiency of capitalism and socialism is not the only, or even the chief, consideration. It is equally if not more important to evaluate the morality that implicitly informs the two competing systems, that is, the morality of private and public direction of resources.

Both socialism and capitalism are intimately wedded to particular but distinct sets of moral values. Capitalism presupposes the deontological morality that definitively informed the development of Western civilization over the centuries, namely, Judeo-Christian or biblical morality. Socialism presupposes a novel and putatively superior consequentialist morality, the naturalistic humanism constructed and intended to supplant such traditional morality. As we shall see, the two moralities, including their respective conceptions of justice, conflict in decisive ways. Socialist aspirations embody various moral constructs that raise serious concerns from the perspective of traditional morality. The problem is that the means requisite to all forms of economic socialization—governmental control or direction of resources—necessarily violate certain moral and political principles implicit not only in capitalist economic arrangements but Western order more generally. Socialism necessarily violates several fundamental American rights, such as freedom and property, as well as various moral principles central to both the traditional American sense of justice and Judeo-Christian morality more generally. Indeed socialism, raising as it does the fearsome specter of unlimited political power, inevitably threatens the central value of American constitutionalism, namely, limited government. In economics, as in other spheres of human action, it is thus necessary to inquire whether the ends justify the means.

Altruism

We have seen that both distribution and redistribution of material resources in society entail governmental control and direction of resources, that is, government, and not private individuals, possesses ultimate decision rights over the resources under its control. We have also seen that government in a free society possesses few if any resources of its own, which means that funding for its activity must be obtained from private citizens in one manner or another. In a pure communist society, government simply abolishes private property and appropriates all the citizens' resources to itself. In both socialized and mixed-economies such as the United States government typically acquires resources by taxation, borrowing, and/or money creation. In all cases government obtains the bulk of the resources under its control from private citizens, either directly or indirectly, whether through outright confiscation or the other methods previously discussed.[105] Pure communism, as we have seen, involves the distribution of such acquired resources by a central political authority; socialism and mixed economy involve the redistribution of such resources from one group of citizens to another via the political process. Our present concern is the morality of redistribution in a mixed economy, by far the most prevalent means of realizing socialist or quasi-socialist aspirations in modern Western society, including the United States. Few contemporary persons, as noted, openly advocate pure communism on the Soviet or North Korean model.

The morality of socialism is often cast as a morality of altruism, a term coined by Auguste Comte, previously encountered in our discussion of early socialism.[106] Altruism ("of or to others") was a central element of

---

[105] Certain economists regard inflation, which decreases the value of money, as a form of taxation.

[106] Altruism, from French *altruisme*, coined by Auguste Comte in 1830, from *autrui* ("of or to others") + *-isme*, from Old French, Latin *alteri*, dative of *alter* ("other"), from which also English alter. Apparently inspired by French Latin

the novel morality constructed by Comte and other ideologues of the era as a substitute or replacement for traditional Judeo-Christian ethics. Morality in the West is of course traditionally conceived as originating in the God of the Bible. Comte and fellow travelers relentlessly castigated such theologically based morality as selfish and egoistic, morally suspect and base, springing not from purity of heart but rather venal expectation of heavenly reward. The novel morality of altruism, by contrast, was portrayed as sublime and unselfish, concerned not with the individual's personal welfare but rather the welfare of "others." The putatively selfless morality of altruism was sometimes referred to as "social" morality and aligned with a correlative novelty of the era—the so-called Religion of Humanity, the "social" or "Positive" Religion also constructed by Comte and whose adherents were exhorted to "Live for Others."[107] The moral and religious aspirations embodied in altruistic Humanism achieved wide currency throughout the course of the nineteenth century. Indeed, over time, the concept of the "moral" came more or less to be identified with or supplanted by the concept of the "social." Such is evident, for instance, in the decline of what the nineteenth century called the "moral sciences" (economics, political economy, and related disciplines) and correlative rise of the so-called "social sciences" of the twentieth century and beyond. The triumph of "social" over traditional (personal) morality in Western society is further evidenced by contemporary usage, which often employs the term social to convey implicit moral praise. Individuals who are "socially responsible," guided by a "social conscience" and concerned with "social" problems are typically held in high esteem, associated with noble and high-minded purpose, indeed with the pursuit of "social justice."

The majority of persons who champion contemporary "social" values, however, are probably unaware of their origin, namely, as deliberate moral constructions intended to replace traditional Judeo-Christian ethics. The new virtue of altruism and related moral obligation to "live for others" arose as rivals to and substitutes for traditional Western morality, historically grounded in the transcendent God of the Bible.

---

legal phrase *l'autrui, from le bien, le droit d'autrui* ("the good, the right of the other").

[107] Linda C. Raeder, *John Stuart Mill and the Religion of Humanity* (Columbia, MO: University of Missouri Press, 2002). Hereinafter cited as *Religion of Humanity*.

Altruism and related virtues were intended to form the basis of a naturalistic morality—non-theological, "terrestrial," or "strictly human"—that was henceforth to serve, as J.S. Mill explained, as "the law of our lives." The social morality crafted by Comte and disciples, like the ethics of socialism proper, was portrayed as a decided moral advance over the purportedly selfish and individualistic personal morality associated with the Judeo-Christian tradition. Marx's assertion of the moral superiority of socialism would prove enormously influential, but he was neither the first nor the only advocate of the social morality that captured minds and hearts of the era. The ground for the Marxian evangel was well prepared by the St. Simonian and Comtean prophets of altruism and Humanity, among others.

Socialist aspirations of all kinds, Marxist or otherwise, are not only wedded to the notion of a superior social morality but also imbued with profound moral expectations. The replacement of Judeo-Christian with social ethics will replace selfish concern for the mere individual with altruistic concern for the good of the whole. They further involve profound political consequences. It seemed apparent to carriers of such aspirations that their social goal—selfless concern for the welfare of society as a whole—could only be realized by means of expanded and activist government. Such was certainly the conclusion drawn by Comte and Marx, as well as American champions of the novel social ethos, in particular, the so-called Social Gospelers and Progressives of the era who will be extensively discussed in Volume III. Both groups were important carriers of naturalistic social morality in the American context, and both assumed that only government possesses the broad perspective and necessary means to ensure the social good, that is, to ensure social justice.

Justice of course is a prime moral virtue. Thus it is not surprising that the concept of justice, like morality more generally, would undergo transformation under dispensation of the Religion of Humanity and the social morality it embodied. Traditional justice—capitalist justice—and especially its valorization of individual rights to life, liberty, and property, was denigrated as a relic of the selfish and individualistic Judeo-Christian worldview, in particular, Christianity, the very Religion of the Selfish. [108] The moral advance putatively represented by social

---

[108] The system of bribes to the selfish, according to J.S. Mill, "Utility of Religion," *CW* 10:422-423).

morality and justice would transcend the egoism regarded as intrinsic to the biblical worldview, especially its specifically Christian dimension. Justice would no longer serve mere self-regarding interests—individual property and profits—but rather secure an altruistic sharing among the whole. Justice, in other words, was transformed into social justice. The term was (and is) rarely defined with precision but, as we shall see, the demand for social justice invariably involves the demand for greater equalization of material wealth across members of society, to be achieved by means of expanded government. The market process, as we have seen, inevitably results in an unequal pattern of material distribution, and only government possesses the means—the coercive sanction of law—to override such results. Only government, therefore, is capable of rectifying the social injustice allegedly intrinsic to capitalism. Such a conclusion leads back to the central moral question raised by any ethic of redistribution: Does the end—greater equalization of wealth, whether in pursuit of the communist paradise or an altruistic social justice—justify the means?

The Demand for Social Justice

The demand for social justice, however vaguely conceived or articulated, is invariably a demand for a fair or just distribution of material wealth or resources across society. Any such demand, whatever its particular form, stems from the belief that the existing distribution of income or wealth in a given society is unfair, unjust, wrong from a moral point of view. The first problem that arises from any demand for social justice is the difficulty of determining the constitution of a "fair" or "just" distribution of wealth. According to philosopher Immanuel Kant (1724-1804), such a problem is insoluble. "Welfare," he observed, "has no principle," in other words, there is no objective standard by which to determine the substantive content of a "just" distribution of material resources ("welfare"). Every individual will hold a subjective view of what might constitute a "fair" pattern of material distribution. One person may believe that fairness demands radical material equality; everyone should be provided with identical amounts of rice, milk, oil, shoes, electricity, and so on. Another person may think it "fair" that individuals who have earned doctoral degrees be provided with greater resources than individuals with a grade-school education. Yet another person may think the opposite—fairness demands that the less educated be provided with more than the better educated. A person who loves animals may think it "fair" that he be provided with a hundred cans of cat food and two hundred pounds of birdseed each month to feed his beloved cats and ducks. Who is to say that he or any of the others are wrong? By what objective measure can such competing conceptions of fairness be evaluated? The simple but decisive answer is that no such measure exists—"welfare has no principle." Human beings possess no means of objectively determining which of competing conceptions of material distribution better serves "social" fairness or justice. Such a conclusion follows from the fact previously discussed in another context: economic value, the value of material goods and services, is always, like beauty, *subjective* value; the value of any economic good is never inherent to that good but always imputed by a human perceiver. Every demand for social justice is thus ultimately and inescapably subjective, that is, a demand for the particular distribution of material goods and services favored by the person making the demand.

Nevertheless, all demands for social justice, however substantively particular or unique, do share a universal attribute, namely, the aforementioned demand for a pre-determined concrete pattern of resource distribution. Moreover, while such patterns will vary according to personal subjective preference, their achievement can be accomplished in one and only one way—governmental control of resources. The market, ordered through voluntary exchange, does not and cannot produce a pre-conceived pattern of material distribution, whatever its particular substantive content. For that reason, whether apprehended by its advocates or not, the demand for social justice is always and inevitably a simultaneous demand for governmental direction of resources, whether achieved by outright command-and-control or taxation, regulation, or other forms of legislative enactment. Social justice and political distribution or redistribution of material resources are two sides of the same coin.

We have discussed the problems that plague every form of centralized economic decision-making, in particular, the fact that government officials or planners have no means of acquiring the knowledge that would be necessary to meet the subjective needs and desires of millions of people in the absence of the information embodied in a prevailing structure of relative prices. Central planners must work in the dark, merely guessing or, worse, imposing their personal subjective preferences on society as a whole. Such, however, is precisely what is demanded by advocates of social justice, however well their subjective preferences are veiled behind the cloak of "justice" and however unaware they may be of the implications of their demands. If successful, that is, if certain individuals or groups obtain political power sufficient to impose their subjective conception of social justice on their fellow men, then all persons who hold different conceptions of justice, traditional or social, will find their individual freedom curtailed or even eliminated. They will be forced to implement the vision of the politically successful advocates of social justice, which means they will be required to serve, not their own values and purposes, but rather values and purposes chosen and imposed upon them by others. The advocacy of social justice thus raises a profound moral concern. The question is whether individuals are morally obligated to obey the commands of a political authority intent on imposing a particular vision of social justice, a vision that can never be more than merely subjective or arbitrary preference.

Social Justice in Practice

A concrete example may further clarify the moral issues involved in the pursuit of social justice. Let us assume the existence of an individual, say, a professor of political philosophy, who is fervently committed to the realization of social justice. The professor, like most other people, is fully aware that basketball players in the United States earn much higher salaries than scholars who write philosophical treatises on freedom. The professor is firmly convinced that such a situation is unjust. Philosophy, he maintains, is far more important to society than basketball, and the enormous disparity of income between scholars and basketball players is wrong; it is unfair. The scholar devotes decades of his life to the pursuit of learning, years of sacrificial solitude spent in study and writing, contributing his abilities to society at great personal and financial cost. The income he earns for such prodigious effort, however, barely enables him to pay the rent.

Basketball players, by contrast, generally have little education; indeed many have simply been born with a talent that others, such as scholars, do not possess, but for which they earn many millions of dollars in the market. Is it fair than an accident of birth (genetic endowment) should provide such enormous material advantages to some persons, advantages denied to others? Indeed, is it fair that basketball, a mere recreational activity, should be financially rewarded so much more highly than scholarship, the discovery of knowledge? The professor does not think so. He demands that justice be served—social justice. The achievement of social justice, in this case, will require redistribution of wealth according to the professor's preferred pattern of distribution: scholars should receive more, basketball players less. The fairest way to achieve such an outcome, the professor believes, is to transfer a portion of the players' income to scholars. The scholars deserve it, considering not only their hard work but also the value of their contribution to society, which, the professor maintains, is far greater than the value of mere basketball. Such is the professor's vision of social justice, and it is impossible to convince him otherwise.

Further suppose that the professor's passion for social justice inspires him to make common cause with a charismatic politician who also believes the prevailing pattern of material distribution is unfair. The politician campaigns on a platform of social justice and manages to persuade a majority of voters of the justice of redistribution as proposed by the professor. He wins the election and is instrumental in the passage of legislation that limits the maximum salary of any basketball player to, say, $200,000 a year. The legislation further establishes a maximum price ("price ceiling") that may be charged for admission to any basketball game. Such a provision aims to prevent the organizers of such games from making "excessive" (unfair) profits or perhaps to make basketball affordable for lower-income people. Finally, the legislation also increases tax rates on income earned through basketball and creates a new entitlement program for scholars and professors; the tax revenue so obtained will be transferred, redistributed, from basketball players to scholars and professors. The professor and politician can claim a moral victory; they believe social justice has been achieved, as does the majority who supported the legislation. The basketball players and organizers may have a different view.

Every act of political redistribution of wealth raises issues concerning both justice and freedom. Such is more clearly perceived by recalling the manner in which income is determined in a market economy. It is true that successful basketball players in a capitalist economy typically earn higher income than scholars or philosophers. As we recall, however, the income of both groups is determined not by the personal decision of any human authority but rather impersonal market forces, that is, the voluntary choices of consumers of the two goods—basketball games and scholarly treatises. The fact that basketball players earn more than scholars results from the fact that many market participants place a higher value on basketball than philosophy or scholarship. More buyers voluntarily choose to spend their income on basketball games than philosophical expositions. This and this alone—the difference in the value subjectively imputed by the consumers to the two goods—is the "cause" of the disparity in income between basketball players and scholars. No human authority decided that basketball players should earn a greater income than scholars. The consumers of basketball games merely aim to enjoy the performance, not determine the players' income. Consumers who shun the professor's books and lectures do so for lack of interest, not to determine his income. The income disparity between basketball players and scholars is an impersonal and unintended consequence of the simple fact that many Americans prefer basketball to philosophy.

The professor's demand for greater equalization of wealth between basketball players and scholars, then, is a demand that the voluntary choices of consumers be overridden by political power. It is implicitly to assert that consumers are wrong to prefer basketball to philosophy. The professor obviously believes that their consumption choices are in error, that consumers *should* value philosophy more than basketball, as he himself does. But he obviously does not believe in individual liberty. His action—his pursuit of social justice—demonstrates his willingness to use the force of law to coerce other people to adopt his values and purposes rather than allowing them to pursue their own. Those who do not value scholarship over basketball will be forced to do so by the political transfer of wealth from basketball players to scholars. Part of the income that would accrue to basketball players in a free market will be taken from them and redistributed to the professor and his colleagues.

Demands for redistribution of wealth always involve the presumption that some people *know* what a proper or moral distribution of wealth in society *should* be. We previously noted the similarity between such an assumption and that implicit in central economic planning. In a communist society, government planners decide what will be produced and who will receive it, plans that embody the planners' subjective vision ("knowledge") of the proper pattern of material distribution. In a mixed economy such as the United States, policies of redistribution embody a similarly subjective vision. In either case, comprehensive central planning or a more limited redistribution of wealth, the voluntary choices of consumers are overridden by political will, a will that embodies the planners' or legislators' vision ("knowledge") of what material distribution *should* be, that is, their subjective and arbitrary vision of social justice.

Social Justice and Freedom

A politics of redistribution has significant implications for the exercise and preservation of individual freedom. Such implications may be brought to light by exploring the consequences of the politically mandated "wage and price controls" enacted in our hypothetical case involving the professor and basketball. A price control is a legislative or regulatory act that legally establishes the price at which an item must be bought or sold in the market. (A wage is of course a price—the price of labor.) A price control may exist in one of two forms, a so-called "price ceiling" or "price floor." Price ceilings and price floors legally prohibit prices from rising above or below some politically determined level, respectively. Price controls may be enacted for various reasons, including pursuit of social justice. Some persons, for instance, may regard the relatively low salary earned by a cashier at Walmart as unfair or unjust. They may demand, in the name of social justice, that such low-income workers be guaranteed a so-called "living wage"—a wage rate sufficient to support the worker's existence. If politicians heed their demand, a price floor may be established by law, more particularly, enactment of so-called "minimum-wage" legislation that prohibits employers from paying any worker less than the legislatively mandated wage. Our example concerning basketball and scholarship entails the imposition of the second form of price control, price ceilings: employers are legally prohibited from paying any basketball player more than the legislatively mandated salary, and consumers are legally prohibited from paying more for a game ticket than the legislatively mandated price.

All price controls, ceilings or floors, not only impair the functioning of the market process but curtail the exercise of individual freedom. The first violation of freedom in our hypothetical case involves the basketball players, in particular, their so-called freedom of contract. Freedom of contract refers to the ability of individuals to voluntarily negotiate the price at which they are willing to buy or sell a good or service, in this case basketball skills and tickets to basketball games. The legislative cap on basketball salaries restricts such freedom by forcing players to accept less for their skills than they might receive in a voluntary market transaction. The freedom of the organizers of basketball games—their ability to voluntarily purchase such skills at a price they consider worthwhile—is similarly violated; they are prohibited by law from paying more than the legislated price. The cap on basketball salaries is a price control that infringes the freedom of both parties to an employment contract.

The consumers of basketball also experience a loss of freedom as a consequence of the price ceiling imposed on basketball tickets. No consumer is permitted to pay more for a ticket than the politically mandated price. Such a restriction on price levels may seem advantageous to consumers, preventing ticket prices from rising to exorbitant levels. Such seeming advantage, however, is bought at a high price, the price of freedom. To see this, imagine that a celebrated basketball player comes to town and fans are eager to watch him perform. In a free market, the limited number of available seats (supply) means that the price of available tickets will rise in proportion to consumer demand. The limited supply of tickets will be allocated by the consumers themselves, that is, according to the subjective value each of them imputes to the basketball game. Those who value a ticket more highly will be willing to offer a higher price and will thus receive a ticket; those who place less value on a ticket will not be willing to pay a higher price and withdraw themselves from the market. Supply will equal demand; everyone who wants a ticket and is willing to pay the market price will receive one. In our example, however, the mandated price control legally prohibits ticket prices from rising in accord with consumer demand; the market is not permitted to function. The result is a politically created "shortage" of tickets. Because they must by law be sold at a fixed (below market) price, the tickets quickly sell out; many fans, some of whom may strongly desire to attend the game, will be disappointed. The existing ticket supply is distributed not to those fans who value them most highly but rather those with the good fortune to be first in line ("first come, first served"). The two groups may, but need not, coincide.

We have seen that the subjective value imputed to a good by a potential buyer is indicated by the price the buyer is willing to pay. In the case under discussion, fans who are willing to pay more to see the celebrated player are forbidden by law to do so, which means that their freedom, their ability voluntarily to act in pursuit of their own values and purposes, is violated. The politically mandated price control narrows the choices available to passionate fans to two undesirables: either buy the ticket at the mandated price or not buy a ticket. Neither option would voluntarily be pursued by fans who intensely desire to see the game. For one thing, their ability to buy the ticket at the controlled price is far from certain; supply is limited and many other fans will have the same objective. The passionate fan is left with no choice but either to stand at the head of the ticket line or do without. The achievement of such a favored position, however, may be difficult or impossible; at the very least, it will be inordinately time-consuming. The die-hard fan does not want to be so inconvenienced nor does he want to do without a ticket. He wants to obtain a ticket quickly and with certainty; in a free market he could achieve that aim by offering more for it than other potential buyers. Such an option, however, is foreclosed by the mandated price controls. The fan is unable to exercise his voluntary choice in pursuit of his personal goals, that is, he is unable to exercise his right to liberty.

Wage and price controls not only violate the freedom of market participants to buy and sell in accord with their personal values but, as noted, seriously impair the operation of a market economy. First, such controls prohibit the transmission of knowledge to producers regarding actual consumer demand, in this case the demand of basketball fans to players and organizers. The price of a ticket, which in a free market would reflect the true level of demand, is prohibited by law from rising above the mandated price. Thus neither basketball players nor organizers of basketball games have any way of knowing the actual demand for their services. They cannot perform their function—meeting such demand with appropriate supply—with precision because the absence of a freely formed market price prevents them from acquiring the knowledge or information necessary to do so. Second, price controls reduce the incentives required to bring adequate supply to the market. The value that consumers in a market economy place on basketball skills will be reflected in the price they are willing to pay to witness such skills. *Ceteris paribus*, the higher such subjective value, the higher the ticket price of basketball games; the higher the ticket price, the higher the salary of the basketball players and organizers; the higher the salary, the more incentive individuals have to develop basketball skills and organize basketball games. In a market economy, the supply of basketball players and organizers will thus tend to match demand for their skills. Wage and price controls, however, prevent the price system from fulfilling its essential function—transmitting knowledge of demand and supply spontaneously throughout society. If the salaries of basketball players and the price of basketball tickets are kept by law below the market price, the supply of basketball players and games will eventually decrease; the lower profitability of such enterprises means that fewer individuals will be drawn into their production.

Advocates of social justice, such as the professor who believes that American consumers place too great a value on basketball, may regard the contraction of the basketball industry as a moral advance. Consumers and producers of basketball may have a very different opinion. Who is right? Who is entitled or competent to decide whether basketball is a worthy activity—the political advocates of social justice who would impose price controls and thus violate the freedom of players, organizers, and consumers of basketball or those members of the general public who enjoy and value basketball? *Whose* values are to be honored? This is the central question raised by every proposal for social justice.

Social Justice versus Justice

The violation of liberty is not the only moral problem that arises from pursuit of social or distributive justice. Such a pursuit raises the further and equally serious problem of the violation of justice as traditionally conceived in Anglo-American society. We have seen that government in a free society possesses few resources of its own; thus redistribution of wealth can only be achieved by transferring the resources of one person or group to another person or group. The morality or justice of redistribution, then, stands or falls on the morality of such action. The issue is again most readily explored by consideration of a concrete example. We begin by assuming the existence of majority political support for a government program to help the "homeless." The majority of voters regard themselves as altruists who want to help such unfortunate members of society. Legislators respond by proposing a new entitlement program, perhaps proclaiming a positive "right to affordable housing." The funds to implement the program are to be obtained by raising taxes on individuals whose income is greater than, say, $500,000, a group that is certainly a minority of all taxpayers. Further assume that congressional representatives of this minority group vote against the proposed spending for the homeless, knowing that their constituents will bear the burden of its cost. Assume that the majority, who earn less than $500,000 and will pay no additional taxes, nevertheless carries the day; the program and tax policy become "law." The moral issue is whether such well-intentioned policy can be squared with justice and morality. The issue, once again, is whether the ends justify the means.

Proponents of social justice have no difficulty in this regard; they consider such redistribution of wealth the very essence of morality and justice. Such a conclusion rests on several assumptions, implicit and explicit, widely shared by such proponents. They tend to believe, as mentioned, that the existing distribution of wealth and income in society is somehow unjust (recall Marx's condemnation of the inherent injustice of capitalist distribution). They further tend to believe that wealthier members of society bear special moral obligations to less fortunate members of society. Public policy, they argue, should be concerned with the good of the whole, which includes the homeless. The "wealthy," who not only can afford increased taxes but also owe a debt to society, should be required to contribute to the common good. The "rich" earned their wealth by means of the established economic system, capitalism, and thus are morally obliged to "give back" to the society that enabled accumulation of their riches. No man is an island. The wealthy capitalists did not "get rich on their own" but were assisted and supported by the wider institutional structure of American society.[109] Thus it is only right that they be made to share their gains, to "share the wealth."

---

[109] "There is nobody in this country who got rich on his own. . . nobody." Elizabeth Warren, speech in Andover, Mass, Aug 11, 2011; "If you've got a business — you didn't build that. Somebody else made that happen." Barack Obama, Campaign speech, Roanoke, VA, July 13, 2012.

Such views are largely of Marxist inspiration, however little contemporary advocates of social justice may recognize that fact. They presuppose the Marxian notion that capitalists (the "wealthy") have won their profit at the expense of the workers or the poor. The "rich" thus bear a moral duty to restore some of their unjust gains to their rightful owners, the workers whom they have putatively exploited. Such assumptions are rarely explicitly acknowledged but held as more or less self-evident truth by many of Marx's descendants and fellow travelers. Whether recognized or not, however, they implicitly inform the argument that wealthier members of society bear a unique moral obligation to assist the less fortunate.

Indeed, proponents of social justice not only imply that the "rich" should fulfill a legislated duty to pay higher taxes without complaint but also in a spirit of love and generosity; they should not only help their fellows in need but *want* to do so. Those who begrudge such assistance are, quite simply, bad people. Such an assumption, which ignores the crucial moral distinction between *coerced* legal obligation and *voluntary* charity, is wedded to the altruistic social morality embraced by socialists and quasi-socialists of all stripes: all good people are altruists and not selfish egoists. To balk at the obligation of helping the homeless by legislative mandate is to display an inferior morality of selfishness and greed, long associated with capitalism by the collectivist Left. The incompatibility of such views with traditional American political morality is clear from the following remark of Thomas Jefferson: "To take from one, because it is thought his own industry and that of his fathers has acquired too much, in order to spare to others, who, or whose fathers, have not exercised equal industry and skill, is to violate arbitrarily the first principle of association, the guarantee to everyone the free exercise of his industry and the fruits acquired by it."[110]

From the socialist perspective, the perspective of social morality, on the contrary, redistribution of wealth in service of the homeless and similarly disadvantaged groups is perfectly moral, indeed, a requirement of justice itself—social or distributive justice. The successful propagation of socialistic views over the course of the past century means that many individuals in contemporary society, even those who regard themselves

---

[110] Thomas Jefferson, letter to Joseph Milligan, April 6, 1816, *Founders' Constitution*, Vol. 1: 573.

as apolitical, will agree with such a perspective. The homeless themselves will tend to agree that justice is on their side. Proponents of social justice have repeatedly and emphatically demanded legislative enactment of various positive rights or material entitlements over the past century, including the putative "right" to affordable housing. The homeless and beneficiaries of other government entitlements can hardly be blamed for believing they are due such benefits by right. Political leaders, university professors, media pundits, public school teachers, and others have campaigned for decades to convince the American people of their moral entitlement to certain material support by government; to deny them that to which they are morally entitled would be unjust. Moreover, the altruistic majority, who voted for the program but do not themselves bear its cost, will also tend to regard the entitlement program and taxation of the "wealthy" as just. Indeed they can congratulate themselves on their fine moral sensibilities, their acute "social conscience" and concern for the dispossessed, all of which are proven by their electoral support for a program to help the homeless.

It should be noted that every group supporting social or distributive justice—the activists, politicians, homeless and altruists—assumes the perspective of moral consequentialism. All of them regard justice as determined by the consequences or outcome of action, in this case, better housing for the homeless and more even distribution of wealth. The noble end of better housing for the least among us is believed to justify the means—the extraction of resources from the "wealthy" by means of coercive taxation. Every variant of social or distributive justice is a species of ethical consequentialism.

*

The inherent conflict between modern social justice and traditional Anglo-American justice is most clearly perceived by examining the same hypothetical case from the perspective of traditional justice. Traditional justice, as we recall, is a form of deontological, "in-itself," or procedural morality. Justice is determined not by the consequences of an act but rather the intrinsic quality of an act itself. Traditional justice is concerned not with the outcome or ends of human action but rather the means employed in pursuit of human goals. In the American context, traditional justice is informed by certain profound and "self-evident" moral convictions: first, individuals possess unalienable (negative) rights to life, liberty, and property, derived from a "Creator" superior to man;

202

second, all individuals should be governed by identical rules (equality under law); and, third, the longstanding conviction, restated by Jefferson in the Declaration of Independence, that just or legitimate government is founded on "consent of the governed." Redistribution of wealth in the name of social justice (or for any other reason) violates every one of these traditional American moral convictions. On the traditional standard of justice, the taxation of individuals with relatively higher income and the transfer of that income to a third party (the homeless) by means of the political process can only be regarded as unjust, a violation of morality in general and individual rights in particular. However desirable the end (housing for the homeless), traditional justice denies that it can ever justify the means of political redistribution.

We have discussed the nature of individual rights as embodied in American founding documents and ideals. Traditional American rights are largely negative rights that prohibit both private citizens and public officials from engaging in certain actions toward the individual right-bearer. As we have seen, for instance, the individual's right to property morally and legally prohibits all other persons, including persons organized as government, to take the individual's property without his consent. To do otherwise is theft, universally regarded as morally wrong and also prohibited by law. In the American understanding, such rights are equally the possession of every individual and each individual is to be treated in accordance with the same rules.

We now apply these criteria of traditional justice to the case under discussion: political redistribution in favor of the homeless. The redistribution of resources from the "wealthy" to the "homeless" involves taking the property of the former group and transferring it to the second. One group is taxed and the other is not; one receives benefits and the other does not. It is clear that the individuals who constitute the respective groups are governed by different rules. Wealthier individuals are treated differently than individuals who find themselves homeless; the former are penalized and the latter rewarded. Such tax and legislative policy clearly violates the traditional principle of equality under law.

Other fundamental elements of traditional American justice—individual property rights and consent of the governed—are similarly violated by a policy of redistribution. Both morality and justice forbid property to be taken from an individual without his consent. In a representative democracy such as the United States, relevant consent is thought to be conveyed through the citizens' elected representatives in Congress (or state legislatures, as the case may be). Every schoolchild is familiar with the celebrated slogan of the American revolutionaries, "no taxation without representation." Such was a simple restatement of a longstanding principle of Anglo-American justice—no individual's property may be taken ("taxation") without his consent (conveyed through his elected representatives). In the present example, the higher-income voters who rejected the proposed entitlement for the homeless were overridden by the majority who voted in its favor. Those individuals ultimately taxed did not consent to such taxation but were nevertheless taxed. Taxation in this instance thus violates both the principle of consent of the governed and the individual right to property (which obliges others to refrain from taking property without the owner's consent). A policy of redistribution to benefit the homeless that is not achieved by unanimous consent of the taxpayers who fund it thus violates three central criteria of traditional Anglo-American justice—equality under law, consent of the governed, and individual property rights. From the perspective of traditional justice, such policy can only be regarded as unjust.

One conceivable way to avoid such a conclusion is to argue that citizens in a representative democracy such as the United States agree to be bound by the decisions of the majority as reached by deliberation of their representatives in Congress. Since unanimity is all-but-impossible, it is said, all citizens, both potential majorities and potential minorities, agree to adopt the convention of abiding by majority decision. Accordingly, it may be argued, the relevant consent was given by the majority who approved the entitlement program through their representatives. Such a view, however plausible, fails to represent the nature of American constitutional order. It misrepresents the meaning of American liberal democracy in general and the meaning of unalienable rights and consent of the governed in particular. It further fails to recognize the fundamental (Lockean) principle of constitutional or limited government, namely, government is intrinsically limited by the ends for which it is created.

The justice of political redistribution of wealth hinges crucially on the issue of consent. Property cannot be taken without an individual's consent, and legitimate government is based on consent of the governed. We have seen that the majority in our example—the altruists, social activists, and beneficiaries of the new entitlement program—have indeed given their consent to taxing the "wealthy" for purposes of redistribution. Theirs, however, is not the consent relevant to American constitutionalism. The relevant consent implied in the principle of "consent of the governed" is the consent of those individuals whose income is to be taken in the form of taxation. The individual right to property and the grounding of legitimacy in consent of the governed forbid the property of any individual to be taken without his *own* consent (expressed indirectly through his elected representatives). We have seen, moreover, that the individual right to property, like other natural rights, is regarded as unalienable and derived from a source higher than government. Such a right protects the security of an individual's possessions, whether threatened by one individual or a group that constitutes a majority. The consent given by the majority to take property from a minority (the "wealthy") is meaningless and irrelevant. It is not majority consent that matters but rather consent of the person or persons whose property is to be taxed.

The consent of a majority to redistribute wealth by taxing a minority is further meaningless for the following reason. No private individual possesses the moral right to take another individual's property without his consent, even for a noble purpose. Such is the definition of theft since time immemorial. Mother Teresa herself was morally required to solicit voluntary donations to fulfill her goal of alleviating the suffering of children. She was not permitted to appropriate the resources of the wealthy or anyone else to realize her selfless mission. Private individuals are forbidden, by both law and morality, to take others' property without their consent.

Contemporary governments, by contrast, routinely engage in such activity by means of legislative and tax policy that results in the redistribution of wealth, such as the case under discussion. Public officials (legislators), in contrast to private citizens, are legally permitted to take the property of certain individuals without their consent, such as the "wealthy" in our example. We are seeking the moral justification for such governmental action. The argument that relevant consent for such action has been given by the majority of voters (through their elected representatives) who approve of the redistributive policy must be dismissed, for reasons discussed; the relevant consent is not of those who tax but rather those taxed. Moreover, no private individual or majority of private individuals is entitled to authorize another party, such as elected representatives in Congress, to take another's property without his consent. Such a prohibition follows from that fact that no individual is himself permitted to engage in such action. The only "powers," Locke says, that may rightfully be delegated to another person or persons are powers or rights that an individual himself actually possesses. Persons cannot give away or delegate something they themselves do not possess, such as a right to take another's property without his consent.

Locke and the Founders, as we have seen, did acknowledge the right of individuals to delegate the protection of their natural rights to another party (the executive authority established by the social compact). The compacting individuals in the state of nature delegate their natural right of self-defense to the executive, thereby conveying moral legitimacy to its employment of coercive force in the protection of their rights. Such delegation is legitimate, however, only because individuals actually possess the right of self-defense in the first place. No one can delegate or transfer a "right" to take another's property without his consent because no one possesses such a right in the first place. Contemporary elected officials may possess the *legal* authority to engage in political redistribution but mere legality does not establish morality. The unavoidable conclusion is that the redistributive policies of contemporary Western democracies cannot be justified on traditional moral grounds. A politics of redistribution necessarily and invariably violates traditional principles of morality and justice. Congressman Davy Crockett implicitly invoked such principles when reminding his constituents that "[w]e have rights as individuals to give as much of our own money as we please to charity; but as members of Congress we have no right so to appropriate a dollar of public money."[111]

A second and related argument occasionally employed in defense of redistribution in a representative democracy acknowledges that consent of the majority cannot and does not justify such policy. It maintains, however, that the relevant consent—consent of the taxed minority—is implied by the minority's general acceptance of that form of government. Everyone understands, as previously observed, that unanimity is impossible in a representative democracy and that its

---

[111] Attributed to Davy Crockett, "Not Yours to Give," speech in Congress, James J. Bethune, *Harper's Magazine*, 1867.

operation therefore depends on the willingness to be bound by decisions of the majority. Universal recognition of such a fact, it is said, means that the minority who agree to participate in the political process, by that very participation, implicitly grant their consent to electoral outcomes, with respect to both officeholders and legislative decision-making. If the minority does not approve of a particular legislative outcome, the proper recourse is said to be further engagement in the political process—the election of future representatives who will better protect the interests of the minority. The losing minority must gracefully accept the outcomes of the legislative process unless and until it succeeds in gaining majority status in the next election. The proper way to meet legislative defeat in a representative democracy is through future electoral victory. In the meantime, everyone is bound by the decisions of the majority of the people's representatives. If a bill passes both House and Senate, is signed into law by the president and passes constitutional muster under judicial review, the disapproving minority has no other recourse but future elections.

Such an argument, again, is plausible on its face. It overlooks, however, several crucial moral and political considerations and, as mentioned, involves a fundamental misunderstanding of constitutional government as conceived by the American founders. To perceive the grounds of such misunderstanding, we revisit John Locke. We recall that, according to Locke, the chief reason individuals agree to leave the state of nature and establish civil government is the "preservation of their property," broadly conceived as encompassing an individual's life, liberty, and estate. The individual's natural rights to life, liberty, and property are relatively insecure in the state of nature. Thus, as Jefferson restated the Lockean view, "to secure such rights, governments are instituted among men, deriving their just powers from the consent of the governed." Jefferson elaborated this conviction in a letter of 1816:

> Our legislators are not sufficiently appraised of the rightful limits of their power; that their true office is to declare and enforce our natural rights and duties, and to take none of them from us. No man has a natural right to commit aggression on the equal rights of another; and this is all from which the laws ought to restrain him; every man is under the natural duty of contributing to the necessities of the society; and this is all the

laws should enforce on him; and, no man having the right to be the judge between himself and another, it is his natural duty to submit to the umpirage of an impartial third [party]. When the laws have declared and enforced all this, they have fulfilled their functions; and the idea is quite unfounded, that on entering into society we give up any natural right.[112]

The purpose of government is clear—to secure the individual's natural and unalienable rights. Such is the reason individuals agree to form a government in the first place and, most important, *the government thus established is intrinsically limited by the ends or purpose for which it is created.* Such an inherent limitation on the power of government is both explicit and implicit in American founding documents. Explicit limitations are enumerated in the U.S. Constitution, including the Bill of Rights. Such an enumeration, however, as indicated by the Ninth and Tenth Amendments, was not intended as exhaustive. American constitutional order presupposes the general terms of the Lockean social compact, which means that government is implicitly limited by the purpose for which it was created. We recall that government, on the Lockean/American view, is regarded as a "trustee" charged with a precise moral obligation—to secure the unalienable rights of each and every individual. A government that violates that purpose, that fails to secure such rights or, worse yet, itself violates those rights, is, quite simply, illegitimate. Such is the case even in the unlikely event that its actions are supported by universal consent of the citizenry. There can be no possibility of "consenting" to a violation of unalienable rights not only because they are unalienable but because their protection is the very reason government is established in the first place. Individuals would be better off in the state of nature than to endure a government that itself violates their natural rights. An individual's rights to life, liberty, and property may be relatively insecure in the state of nature but at least he is entitled to personally defend them—to "execute" the law of nature on his own behalf.

---

[112] Thomas Jefferson, Letter to Francis W. Gilmer, 7 June 1816. Published in "Jefferson Quotes & Family Letters," Thomas Jefferson Foundation, Inc. http://tjrs.monticello.org, 2016.

On the Lockean and American view, then, legislation that violates the unalienable rights of the individual can never be legitimate or morally obligatory. A government that enacts such legislation, even on the basis of majority support, has violated its trust. It has violated both the explicit and implicit terms of the social contract and overreached the bounds of its rightful authority. The people are thus dissolved of all obligations to such a government and possess the right, indeed, says Jefferson, the "duty," to abolish that government and create another better designed to secure the safety of their rights. As we have seen, the American Revolution was understood to have resulted from precisely such a violation of the social compact between the American colonists and British government of the day.

The moral problem, then, that arises from political redistribution of wealth is identical to the moral problem that arises from the attempt to secure positive rights within the American constitutional framework, discussed in Volume I. Both a politics of redistribution and a regime of positive rights are incompatible with American constitutional order because both such objectives inevitably violate the unalienable rights of certain individuals—those whose income is taken without their consent. Social or distributive justice and traditional justice can never be squared; they are inherently in opposition. Regardless of the nobility of the particular purpose—everyone wishes to house the homeless—policies of redistribution cannot be enacted without injustice to certain individuals, without violating their individual rights to liberty and property and the principle of consent.

Such violation is morally impermissible on the traditional American view, which conceives the individual and his unalienable rights as the locus of moral concern. Moreover, traditional justice comprises deontological rules of conduct, that is, certain actions, certain means of realizing one's purposes, are regarded as right- or wrong in-themselves. If it is intrinsically wrong to steal, to take a person's property without his consent, then it is wrong for anyone, an individual or a political majority, to do so. Moreover, conduct that is wrong-in-itself cannot be justified by any ends, however desirable. If it is intrinsically wrong to take a person's property without his consent, then it is wrong to do so whether such action is taken to feed a narcotic habit or house the homeless. In the present case, the means employed to house the homeless—political redistribution of wealth—necessarily violate the natural rights of those individuals taxed without their consent to fund the program. To violate the rights of such individuals not only violates justice as traditionally conceived but is wrong-in-itself. No ends, however virtuous, can justify immoral means.

For such reasons, as has been observed, proponents of social justice must and do reject the traditional American conception of justice. They must and do reject the notion of natural and unalienable rights to life, liberty, and property, which Jeremy Bentham called "nonsense on stilts" and quasi-Marxist college professors dismiss as "American propaganda."[113] Natural rights are further denigrated as mere "negative rights" and the U.S. Constitution as a mere "charter of negative liberties." Proponents of social justice resist the limits placed on the power of the American federal government, both those implicit in the traditional social contract and those explicitly enumerated in the U.S. Constitution. Throughout the course of the past century, the pursuit of social justice has significantly contributed to the ongoing expansion of the federal government, which routinely wields powers far wider than those intended by the Founders.

*

Before concluding the discussion of the morality of social justice, several additional issues deserve brief consideration. We have seen that many voters will support policies cloaked in terms of social justice, appealing as it does to the putative superiority of an altruistic ethic. Many well-meaning people *are* concerned with the welfare of others—the poor, the homeless, the less fortunate, and so on—and redistributive policies in service of such groups often achieve substantial popular support. This is especially true under present forms of public finance, which generally make it difficult or impossible for individuals precisely to identify the total amount of taxes they pay over any determinate period. Individuals may know their federal and state income taxes with some precision, but it is more difficult to calculate the total amount of taxes they pay in other forms, such as sales and excise taxes, taxes passed on by producers in the former of higher prices for goods and services, and so on. Moreover, redistributive policies are often funded by general taxes, direct and indirect, not specific taxes on identifiable individuals or groups. Modern

---

[113] Ross Harrison, "Jeremy Bentham," in Ted Honderich, ed, *The Oxford Companion to Philosophy* (Oxford: Oxford University Press, 1995), 85-88.

methods of public finance may thus readily lead individuals to believe that someone other than they themselves, the "average voters," will bear the financial burden of providing governmental assistance to others.

Taxes targeted on the "wealthy" or "millionaires," as well as businesses and corporations, are especially popular with the electorate, partly due to the success of Marxist and other anti-market propaganda over the past century. Few voters, however, seem to understand that taxes levied on businesses or corporations are ultimately paid not by fat-cat capitalists but rather consumers of the goods and services produced by the taxed firms, many of whom may possess relatively little income or wealth. Business firms regard taxes as a cost of business. They will attempt to pass on the additional cost of increased taxes to the consumer, in the form of higher prices for the final good or service. To the extent they are successful, consumers, not "corporations," pay the additional tax. If firms cannot pass on such costs to their customers, perhaps due to a highly competitive market, workers employed by the firms will suffer the burden, either through a reduction in salary or benefits or even loss of their jobs.

Policies of redistribution, then, are often promoted to the electorate in terms that suggest that someone other than the voter himself will have to pay for the program. Some such transfer of cost often does occur. As previously mentioned, in 2012 the financial situation of approximately 47% of American citizens earned them total exemption from the federal income tax.[114] Such persons have every incentive to vote for federal policies that benefit themselves in the short run. They will personally bear little if any of the tax burden, which is disproportionately placed on higher-income earners. Moreover, the fact that the tax burden arising from redistributive policies largely falls on those with relatively higher income means that even voters who do not personally benefit from such policies may find it easy to "do good," to express their virtuous altruism, by supporting redistributive policies intended to help the less fortunate. It is easy to step into a voting booth, pull the curtain, and direct money to the homeless, money that will come, or that one thinks will come, from someone else's pocket. The altruistic voter for social justice does not *personally* have to help those in need but can simply vote to compel others to do so.

---

[114] Tax Policy Center, Urban Institute – Brookings Institution.

Indeed such a voter may obtain personal psychic benefits from pursuit of social justice. For instance, regardless of personal character, he can consider himself morally superior to his fellows insofar as he, the social justice advocate, supports the "right" social policies, policies that help the disadvantaged, overlooking the fact that such compassion comes at the expense of other people. Such self-styled virtue cannot be accepted at face value. The altruistic political activist, the "social justice warrior" who militantly advocates for governmental programs to help the homeless and other "victims" of society certainly has no claim to inherent moral superiority. Such a role can be played by persons of any moral caliber, even those, for instance, who might cavalierly step over a drunkard lying in the gutter. The political advocate for social justice need take no personal action in order to regard himself as virtuous. He need do nothing more than *vote* for the allegedly morally superior policy (funded by someone other than himself), that is, do nothing more than force other people to "do good."

It is difficult to respect the impulses behind what passes for moral superiority in the eyes of contemporary advocates of social justice. Indeed, such a political stance seems rather to typify what Irving Babbitt once dismissed as morality based on "sham vision," which indeed may partially explain its appeal.[115] Morality as traditionally conceived within Judeo-Christian civilization generally involves individual or *personal* effort, in the present case, a *personal* effort to help the homeless. Such effort generally involves sacrifice of *personal* resources, of one's own time and one's own money. Moreover, and most important, traditional morality presupposes moral action to be *voluntary* action. It makes no sense to either castigate action as bad or praise it as good if the agent has no choice in the matter; no rational person morally condemns or praises an individual for having blue eyes.[116] The appealing rhetoric of social

---

[115] Irving Babbitt, *Democracy and Leadership* (Indianapolis: Liberty Fund, 1979).

[116] As Thomas Aquinas said, ". . .[V]oluntary is what proceeds from the will. . . a man may be dragged by force, but it is contrary to the very notion of violence that he be thus dragged of his own will. . . if this were by compulsion, it would no longer be an act of will . . . nor have external acts any measure of morality, save in so far as they are voluntary. . . if we speak of the goodness which the external act derives from the will . . then the external act adds nothing to this goodness. . . The involuntary deserves neither punishment nor reward in the

justice and the altruistic social morality it advances cloaks a kind of moral blindness. Traditional morality cannot be realized by *forcing* other persons to do good, whether by pointing a gun or voting for politically imposed redistribution. The good, to be good, must be willingly pursued, and this requires freedom of choice. Governmental redistribution of wealth, like the point of a gun, eliminates such choice, forcing certain persons to transfer their resources to other persons under penalty of law, whether they will or not. Such policies violate not only freedom and justice but the fundamental moral injunction against theft. A law is not a suggestion, and forced "charity" is not charity.

---

accomplishment of good or evil deeds. . . ." Anton C. Pegis, ed., *Introduction to St. Thomas Aquinas* (New York: Modern Library, 1948), pp. 530, 542.

Acton, H.B. 2003. *The Illusion of the Epoch: Marxism-Leninism as a Philosophical Creed.* Indianapolis: Liberty Fund.

———. 1993. *The Morals of Markets and Related Essays.* 2nd. Indianapolis: Liberty Fund.

Aquinas, Thomas. 1988. *On Law, Morality, and Politics.* Edited by William P. Baumgarth and Richard J. Regan S.J. Indianapolis: Hackett Publishing Company.

Billington, James. 1980. *Fire in the Minds of Men: Origins of the Revolutionary Faith.* New York: Basic Books.

Boetke, Peter. 2012. *Living Economics.* Oakland: Independent Institute.

Boetke, Peter, Christopher Coyne, V.H. Storr, eds, 2017. *Interdisciplinary Studies of the Market Order: New Applications of Market Process Theory.* Lanham, MD: Rowman & Littlefield.

Capaldi Nicholas, Theodore Roosevelt Malloch. 2012. *America's Spiritual Capital.* South Bend, IN: St. Augustine's Press.

Cohn, Norman. 1970. *The Pursuit of the Millenium.* New York: Oxford University Press.

Crossman, Richard H., ed. 2001. *The God That Failed.* New York: Columbia University Press.

DeJouvenal, Bertrand. 1990. *The Ethics of Redistribution.* Indianapolis: Liberty Fund.

DiLorenzo, Thomas. 2016. *The Problem with Socialism.* Washington, DC: Regnery.

Ebeling, Richard. 2016. *Austrian Economics and Public Policy.* Future of Freedom Foundation.

Evans, M. Stanton. 1994. *The Theme is Freedom: Religion, Politics, and the American Tradition.* Washington, D.C.: Regnery Publishing, Inc.

Friedman, Milton. 1962. *Capitalism and Freedom.* Chicago: University of Chicago Press.

Hayek, F. A. 1978. *Law, Legislation and Liberty, Rules and Order.* Vol. 1. 3 vols. Chicago: University of Chicago Press.

_____. 2012. *Law, Legislation, and Liberty, The Mirage of Social Justice.* Vol. 2. 3 vols. Chicago: University of Chicago Press.

_____. 1981. *Law, Legislation, and Liberty, The Political Order of a Free People.* Vol. 3. 3 vols. Chicago: University of Chicago Press.

_____. 1996. *Individualism and Economic Order.* Chicago: University of Chicago Press.

_____. 1960. *The Constitution of Liberty.* Chicago: University of Chicago Press.

_____. 1979. *The Counterrevolution of Science: Studies on the Abuse of Reason.* Indianapolis: Liberty Fund.

_____. 1988. *The Fatal Conceit: the Errors of Socialism.* Edited by W. W. Bartley III. Chicago: University of Chicago Press.

_____. 2007. *The Road to Serfdom.* ed, Bruce Caldwell. Chicago: University of Chicago Press.

_____. 1978. "The Errors of Constructivism." In *New Studies in Philosophy, Politics, Economics, and the History of Ideas.* Chicago: University of Chicago Press.

_____. 1945. "The Use of Knowledge in Society." *American Economic Review* (American Economic Association) XXXV (4): 519-30.

Hazlitt, Henry. 1988. *Economics in One Lesson.* New York: Crown [reprint}.

_____. 1995. *Critics of Keynesian Ecoomics.* Auburn, AL: Ludwig von Mises Institute.

Hoffer, Eric. 1951. *The True Believer: Thoughts on the Nature of Mass Movements.* San Bernardino: Borgo Press.

Kirk, Russell. 2003. *The Roots of American Order.* Wilmington, DE: Intercollege Studies Institute.

Kirzner, Israel M. 2011. *Market Theory and the Price System.* Indianapolis: Liberty Fund.

_____. 2009. *The Economic Point of View.* Indianapolis: Liberty Fund.

Koenker, Ernest B. 1965. *Secular Salvations: The Rites and Symbols of Political Religions.* Philadelphia: Fortress Press.

Lubac, Henri de. 1995. *The Drama of Atheist Humanism.* San Francisco: Ignatius Press.

Mazlish, Bruce. 1976. *The Revolutionary Ascetic: Evolution of a Political Type.* New York: McGraw-Hill.

Menger, Carl. 1981. *Principles of Economics.* New York: New York University Press.

Mises, Ludwig von. 2010. *Human Action.* Auburn: Ludwig von Mises Institute.

_____. 2005 [1929]. *Liberalism.* Indianapolis: Liberty Fund.

_____. 1951. *Socialism.* New Haven: Yale University Press.

Novak, Michael and Adams, Paul. 2015. *Social Justice Isn't What You Think It Is.* New York: Encounter Books.

Opitz, Edmund. 1992. *Religion and Capitalism: Allies, Not Enemies.* Irvington-on-Hudson, NY: Foundation for Economic Education.

Orwell, George. 2010. *Politics and the English Language and Other Essays.* Oxford: Benediction Classics.

Raico, Ralph. 2012. *Classical Liberalism and the Austrian School.* Auburn, AL: Ludwig von Mises Institute.

_____. 1985. *Liberalism: In the Classical Tradition.* Irvington-on-Hudson: Foundation for Economic Education.

Roepke, Wilhelm. 2014. *A Humane Economy: The Social Framework of the Free Market.* Wilmington, DE: Intercollegiate Studies Institute.

Rosenberg, Nathan and Birdzell, L.E. 1987. *How the West Grew Rich.* New York: Basic Books.

Schumpeter, Joseph. 1954. *History of Economic Analysis.* New York: Oxford University Press.

Shaw, G. Bernard. 1889. *Fabian Essays in Socialism.* London: Fabian Society.

Siedentop, Larry. 2014. *Inventing the Individual: The Origins of Western Liberalism.* Cambridge, MA: The Belknap Press of Harvard University Press.

Sowell, Thomas. 1987. *A Conflict of Visions: Ideological Origins of Political Struggles.* New York: William Morrow & Co.

_____. 2014. *Basic Economics.* New York: Basic Books.

_____. 2011. *Economic Facts and Fallacies.* New York: Basic Books.

_____. 2016. *Wealth, Poverty, and Politics.* New York: Basic Books.

Talmon, Jacob L. 1960. *Political Messianism.* New York: Frederick A. Praeger.

———. 1952. *The Rise of Totalitarian Democracy.* Boston: Beacon Press.

Voegelin, Eric. 1986. *Political Religions.* Translated by T. J. DiNapoli and E.S. Easterly III. Edwin Mellen Press.

———. 1968. *Science, Politics, and Gnosticism.* Chicago: Henry Regnery Company.

Williams, Walter E. 2008. *Liberty versus the Tyranny of Socialism.* Stanford, CA: Hoover Institution Press.

———. 2015. *American Contempt for Liberty.* Stanford: Hoover Institution Press.

Made in the USA
Columbia, SC
30 August 2020